Dubious Battles

Dubious Battles
Aggression, Defeat,
and the International System

By
John Arquilla

A RAND Research Study

CRANE RUSSAK
A member of the Taylor & Francis Group
Washington • Philadelphia • London

USA	Publishing Office:	Taylor & Francis
		1101 Vermont Ave., Suite 200
		Washington, DC 20005-3521
		Tel: (202) 289-2174
		Fax: (202) 289-3665
	Distribution Center:	Taylor & Francis Inc.
		1900 Frost Road, Suite 101
		Bristol PA 19007-1598
		Tel: (215) 785-5800
		Fax: (215) 785-5515
UK		Taylor & Francis Ltd.
		4 John St.
		London WC1N 2ET
		Tel: 071 405 2237
		Fax: 071 831 2035

DUBIOUS BATTLES: Aggression, Defeat, and the International System

1 2 3 4 5 6 7 8 9 0   B R B R   9 8 7 6 5 4 3 2

RAND books are available on a wide variety of topics. To receive a list of RAND books, write or call Distribution Services, RAND, 1700 Main Street, P.O. Box 2138, Santa Monica, CA 90407-2138, (310) 393-0411, extension 6686.

This book was set in Times Roman by Hemisphere Publishing Corporation. The production supervisor was Peggy M. Rote. Cover design by Michelle Fleitz. Printing and binding by Braun-Brumfield, Inc.

A CIP catalog record for this book is available from the British Library.
♾ The paper in this publication meets the requirements of the ANSI Standard Z39.48-1984 (Permanence of Paper)

Library of Congress Cataloging-in-Publication Data

Arquilla, John.
   Dubious battles : aggression, defeat, and the international system
   / by John Arquilla.
     p. cm.
   "A Rand research study."
   Includes bibliographical references and index.
   1. War. I. Title.
U21.2.A73 1992
355.02—dc20   92-23146
                                                       CIP

ISBN 0-8448-1734-1 (case)
ISBN 0-8448-1736-8 (paper)

Contents

For my family

Preface

Why another study of war? There is already a voluminous literature that examines its causes, patterns of outbreak, waging, and impact on the international system. However, there has been little analysis of the penchant for those who will lose to begin wars. If Clausewitz is right about war being "a continuation of policy by other means," then isn't it troubling that, and worth explaining why, its outcomes are often characterized by the "discontinuation" of policies and, from time to time, of states themselves?

It is possible to develop some hypotheses from existing theories about why "losers" start wars. Perhaps the inevitable occurrence of "balancing behavior" causes wars that begin reasonably, for the aggressor, to expand in an unanticipated, and highly unpleasant, way. Another possibility is that rising powers are overeager, and that they start wars against declining powers just a bit too soon for their own good. Finally, war may just be an inherently very risky business. Victory or defeat may hinge on chance factors virtually beyond the control of either combatant.

This study examines these plausible explanations, and finds them wanting. Balances often do not arise. When they do, they are frequently the creation of the war initiator. The Soviet Union's behavior from 1938–1941 is a good example of this phenomenon. It allied *with* Hitler instead of against him in 1939, taking a chunk of Poland, and later the Baltics, as its reward. In 1941, it entered the war by virtue of being invaded by 3,000,000 troops of the *Wehrmacht*. As to cycles of rising and declining power, this study finds little evidence of losing wars begun by the impatient. With regard to chance, the "loser" phenomenon's noticeable patterns (it increases with the intensity and scope of war) suggest that something more than German Chancellor Bethmann-Hollweg's "iron dice" are rolling. How is one to proceed?

The insight that this study introduces is that all interstate wars are not "created equal." There are two fundamental types, which require differing analytic treatment. "Land wars," fought exclusively on and over land, are hypothesized to be won by superior military skill (over and against "strength," measured any number of ways). Since combat effectiveness is hard to assess prior to a war's outbreak, it should be unsurprising that "losers" start land wars. "Land-sea wars" have significant maritime dimensions, with command of the sea posited by this study as mattering more than either skill or strength. But, since sea power is hardly an imponderable, why do losers so often start land-sea wars?

At this point, it is argued that leaders of continental powers, from Louis XIV to Saddam Hussein, have at best an imperfect understanding of land-sea war. Also, they often have navies (if their nations are big enough) that espouse offensive doctrines in peacetime, only to switch precipitately to the defensive with the onset of war. Thus, the argument goes, the leaders of land powers are led to rely, to their detriment, on expert advice that is itself influenced by organizational pathologies. Interestingly, this leads to some reformulation of existing ideas about the offensive lock-step into which organizational influences are supposed to thrust professional militaries. Another modification to existing theories of military organizations is that their influence is hypothesized to persist, if not increase, rather than abate in crisis and war.

Both quantitative and case study methods are applied in the testing of the "dual" theory of war. Their use is complementary, with the statistics relating, generally, to the issue of how wars are won. The detailed cases examine why losing wars are begun. Though the cases come after statistical analysis, the point must be made that these "how and why" questions are inseparable. One can't identify a "loser" as having started a war unless one knows something about how wars are won or lost.

This study concludes by considering some implications of its findings for organizations, policy, and deterrence. While there is certainly reason to support the maintenance of robust naval capabilities for defensive purposes, it will also be noted that this type of force may encourage "loser" war initiation, or at least leave conventional deterrence weakened. The recent war over Kuwait saw sea power exercising its traditional capabilities to blockade, lift ground forces from around the world, and bombard with missiles, planes, and guns. At the same time, it must be observed that the aggressor in this case may have been emboldened by the distant nature of the retributive threat. Indeed, Saddam went so far as to state publicly, in response to Hosni Mubarak, that he was not "intimidated" by navies.

Many people at Stanford University have had profound influences on this study, none of which were more salutary than that of Scott Sagan. Stephen Krasner, Terry Moe, Alexander George, and Judith Goldstein all made significant contributions, for which the author is deeply grateful. Here at RAND, Jonathan Pollack, Paul Davis, Sybil Sosin, and Elise Kalfayan have added a number of incisive observations. At Taylor & Francis, Ralph Salmi has provided inspired editing. Finally, the author must thank the members of his family, both for emotional support and for their seemingly unending willingness to "hear more about sea power."

John Arquilla
Santa Monica, California

Of war men will ask its outcome, not its cause.

Seneca, from *Hercules Furens*

Chapter 1

Introduction

Woe to the vanquished. . . . Livy

Perception of the centrality of war to international affairs, and of its invidious-ness, has led to a monumental effort to uncover its causes. Explanatory theories abound, ranging in scope from notions of inevitable systemic-level conflict under conditions of anarchy to the nature of individual and small-group cogni-tive and decision-making processes.[1] One oft-voiced theory, which draws its inspiration from German soldier-philosopher Carl von Clausewitz's notion that war is simply a "continuation of policy by other means,"[2] contends that wars are begun by those for whom it holds the reasonable prospect of gain. Because the linkage between policy aims and actions is strong, initiating a war is com-monly characterized as a rational, deliberate act.[3]

If war initiation is the result of a calculated process, should it follow that those who start armed conflicts will generally prevail? Presumably, the decision-making calculus of prospective initiators includes an assessment of the probability of victory.[4] At first glance, this notion seems quite well supported. Of all interstate wars occurring since Waterloo, initiators have won two of every three.[5] Indeed, when analyzed from the perspective of outcome, wars seem so carefully calculated that one observer has concluded: "initiators of interstate wars have enjoyed a disproportionately high probability of winning."[6] Even preemptive war initiators, who had to make highly pressured decisions to strike first in anticipation of being attacked, have done well.[7]

Despite what appears to be good *prima facie* evidence that war has often served to "continue" state policy, a closer analysis of the outcomes of interstate wars may create some doubts. For the period 1815–1980, when wars of great versus minor powers are controlled for, and only "fair fights"[8] are considered, initiators win just barely more than half of the time. The wars of Great powers among themselves show even worse results for the initiators, who win just one

1

in three wars. Major wars, a category that this study will classify in terms of their intensity and duration, show an initiator success rate only slightly better than that found in great power wars. Most astonishing, however, is the uniform failure of initiators in global wars.[9] Table 1.1 summarizes.

Why are so many wars begun by the "loser"? This is the problem that will be examined in the following chapters. Because of the enormous consequences and costs of interstate wars, it should be seen as an important, hitherto neglected[10] "puzzle" whose solution is vital, especially in an era characterized by the presence of weapons of mass destruction. While it is to be hoped that nuclear weapons have had a "dampening" effect on the propensity of nations to go to war (or at least on the eruption of wars between nuclear powers), the sad record of interstate conflict in the Nuclear Age suggests that war is going to be around for some time yet.[11] There is even the dismal possibility to be considered that superpower strategic nuclear parity may remove some constraints (such as existed during the U.S. period of nuclear superiority, characterized by the doctrine of "massive retaliation") on the conventional use of force in pursuit of a state's policy objectives.[12]

THEORETICAL APPROACHES

Chance

Two broad theoretical approaches to this task may be undertaken. The first, and more obvious, is to go along with Clausewitz's characterization of war as existing in an almost infinitely chaotic environment in which chance reigns supreme. War becomes his "game of cards."[13] That "losers" often initiate should be unsurprising, as either side may prevail through luck, courage, and skill. If one were to accept this formulation, then there would be little purpose to efforts that sought to delineate generalizable patterns surrounding the initiation and out-

Table 1.1
Initiator Success in Interstate War, 1815–1980

Category of war	Number	Won	Lost	Success rate (%)
All	63	39	24	62
Great versus minor power	25	19	6	76
"Fair fights"*	38	20	18	52
Major wars	19	8	11	42
Great power wars	9	3	6	33
Global wars	5**	0	5	nil

*Includes Great versus Great and minor versus minor power wars.

**Source: Thompson, *On Global War*. Category goes back to 1494. Other Source: Correlates of War dataset (from ICPSR).

come of interstate war. One would also expect to see some sort of randomness in the results of war initiators. However, even a cursory examination of the outcomes of some categories of interstate war, such as one may perform in recounting the uniform failures of initiators of global wars, suggests that something more than chance is at work. If chance were indeed behind all, or most, outcomes, then one would expect to find at least *one* global war initiator emerging victorious.[14] The lack of randomness in global war outcomes, however, does not rule out *any* role for chance in war; it simply suggests that chance does not exert a determining influence on outcomes.

An important subvariant of the chance approach, articulated to some extent by Schelling, concerns the role of strategic interaction. It might be argued that the "loser" of a given war will be determined by the interaction of the opposing sides' strategic choices over the course of a war. In short, strategy matters, but only relative to the opposition's chosen strategies. A good example of this phenomenon may be observed in the children's game of "odds and evens." Both players (one "odd" and one "even") simultaneously display a hand with from no to five fingers showing. The total fingers showing from both players will be either odd or even, with victory awarded accordingly. It is not even necessary that the objectively "best" strategy be pursued, as Schelling might insist; and long-term effects might not be contemplated or foreseen, though they lead to favorable outcomes.

An example of how this theory fits real situations may be seen in the struggle over Norway at the outset of World War II. The Germans planned and executed a daring amphibious assault on territory deemed essential to the protection of their iron ore supply lines with Sweden. The British response was an equally bold counter invasion that failed to consider the devastating impact of land-based air power on inadequately protected naval forces. The outcome of the immediate campaign was the tactical defeat of the British at Narvik, and the German conquest of Norway. The unintended longer-term effect of this strategic interaction, however, was that the German surface navy had been mauled sufficiently to rule out any role for it in a cross-Channel invasion. Also, it never recovered to the point where it could effectively interdict the later Arctic convoys that provided vital aid to the Soviet Union at its darkest moments. Both of these effects had crucial impact on the further waging and outcome of the war, though neither had been foreseen—and neither resulted from an optimal strategic choice by the British. Indeed, it was the wise German choice to protect its supplies of a vital resource that, though immediately successful, contributed to an overall outcome highly inimical to German interests.[15]

Miscalculation

If chance factors do not reign, then some form of wrong thinking, faulty decision making, organizational biases, or misunderstanding of systemic verities must be causing these frequent initiator defeats. Perhaps wars are undertaken with certain assumptions, about who will or will not intervene to stem the tide of aggression, that turn out to be untrue. It is also possible that the relative power of a chosen foe, however measured, is underestimated, or that an aggressor's own capabilities are systematically overvalued.[16] After all, power is an extremely nebulous concept.

This study shall operate largely within the realm of the "miscalculation" framework,[17] suggesting, however, that war initiators often misunderstand the nature of the war they are embarking upon rather than the quantitative strength of prospective opponents. The "chance" approach will be viewed as a reasonable alternative explanation that requires careful examination and testing. Another important explanatory approach, that will also be considered, will deal with the possibility that "loser" war initiations may be explained by "strong state" aggressors that are defeated, ultimately, by the unforeseen rise of opposing coalitions. Miscalculation is hypothesized to arise not from a misunderstanding of the relative power of the initial combatants, but from a failure to realize that "balancers" would inevitably be drawn to aid the aggressor's enemies.[18]

SCOPE

Finally, it is important to note that this is not primarily a study of the underlying tensions that cause given wars, though these factors must not be neglected. Rather, it is, in general, limited to explaining why, when either external or self-created war-causing tensions have risen to near the flashpoint, nations, which frequently turn out to be the "losers," decide to start wars. Why does the choice to begin a war so often end up as a "discontinuation" of policy, or even of a given initiator? While related to the unfolding story of the causes of war, the explanation of "loser" initiation necessarily carves out an independent intellectual territory of its own.

Drawing from the key assumptions of expected utility theory, this study will focus on the decision to start a war, or risk one's eruption, as being a function of assessments of both the utility of (more simply put, the benefits that would accrue to) the initiator for the outcome, and the probability of achieving that outcome.[19] However, given that the positive utility for a victory in war is generally quite high, and that the negative utility for defeat is at least comparable, the "probability" aspect of the expected utility equation will be the subject upon which more attention is focused.

SOME KEY CONCEPTS

Interstate War

At this point, three crucially important concepts must be defined. The first is that of war itself. This study is broadly focused on the realm of interstate war, making it first requisite that "states" be present on each side of a given war. As there is general agreement that the modern interstate system began circa 1494,[20] primary references will be made to examples from this point forward. The analysis of global wars, which is designed to test the explanatory power of existing theories of the international system, will, since there are so few, begin with the Italian Wars (1494–1517) and continue through World War II. Further on, in Chapter 4, the universe of cases of interstate war from 1815 to 1980 will be subjected to quantitative analysis, in the effort to demonstrate what will be described as the "dual nature" of interstate war, and to delineate the causal paths to victory. By selecting the post-Napoleonic era as the starting point for statistical analysis, full measures may be taken of the impacts of the Industrial Revolution and the "rise of nationalism," which will underpin, respectively, the hypothesized technology- and resolve-related explanations of war outcomes.

The history of periods prior to 1494 may also provide insights into the enduring shape and functions of the modern interstate system. Therefore, previous eras will be plumbed frequently for relevant examples. Civil wars, insurrections, and revolutions fall outside the scope of this study, except to the extent that and at the point which they evolve into interstate wars. The French Revolution, for example, proved to be the spark that ignited a period of nearly a quarter-century of bitter Great power war. Just a few years earlier, the American Revolution had grown from strife within the British Empire to a Great Power war. The Vietnam War, it has also been argued, had its roots in what has been described as a civil war.[21]

To aid in the search for generalizable formulations in the realm of interstate wars, it is helpful to differentiate them by type. This study will suggest that a proper typology of wars should reflect aspects of what may be labeled "vertical" and "horizontal" differentiation. Vertical categories will sort out the types of wars among and between great and minor powers. Horizontal differentiation applies simply to the geographical extent of the conflict.

The first concept, though freshly labeled, is not a new one, as the wealth of existing terms for war types suggests. The "vertical" war typology, which this study will employ, consists of five categories. First, global wars are the severest, longest lasting, and widest in scope. To qualify as global, wars must, additionally, meet the criterion of having as "stakes" the leadership of the international system.[22] The second category is that of Great power wars, of which global wars comprise a subset. A war of this type is simply one in which a great power fights on each side. Wars with one or more great powers on one side and none on the other make up the third category.[23] In the fourth category, this study will suggest a new classification, for wars that surpass some threshold of duration and severity, in addition to or in lieu of great power participation. Therefore, wars that exceed six months in duration and have more than 50,000 battle deaths, or which have great powers on each side, will be labeled

"Major." All other wars will be lumped into the final category, "Minor Wars."[24]

Where "vertical differentiation" may seem simply a novel means for classifying well-understood phenomena, its "horizontal" counterpart strives to develop a new insight into the nature of war. Horizontal differentiation suggests that the physical scope of a given war or set of wars, if correctly typified, may help to achieve deeper understanding of causes, onset, and outcomes. The basic formulation is that, horizontally, there are just two types of wars: those fought only on and over land, and those that, additionally, include maritime aspects. Aerial warfare will be subsumed under each of these major types. Despite the unquestioned value of air weapons, their effective use is still limited, generally, to assisting in the prosecution of land, sea, and amphibious campaigns.[25] The dreams of Douhet and De Seversky for an air weapon that could win wars unaided[26] have never been realized, as the uniform failure of strategic bombing campaigns to compel surrender, from World War I to Vietnam, seems to indicate. Even the absolute air supremacy that the Allied forces enjoyed in the recent war with Iraq did not result in the latter's withdrawal from Kuwait. A ground offensive of massive proportions was still necessary to liberate Kuwait. Further, land and naval forces were vital to providing and maintaining secure bases from which the air offensive against Iraqi forces could be mounted.

The insight regarding the fundamentally dichotomous nature of war will be developed to suggest that there are differing causal paths to victory in each type, and that power may mean different things in different wars.[27] Indeed, this study will likely offer findings that may aid in the refinement and modification of traditional notions of power. Table 1.2 categorizes the types of wars.

War Initiation

The second key concept is that of war initiation. There is a considerable literature relating to the starting of wars; indeed, virtually every history of single wars seeks to "fix" the initiator. Since this study aims to solve the "puzzle" of loser initiation, it is absolutely crucial to identify correctly who started a given war. At the same time, it is equally important that the scope of the concept be carefully delineated. For the purposes of this study, the war initiator will be the side that started the actual fighting, or first seized either some of the homeland or valued territorial or property interests of another state or states. While the consensus of historians will be sought, it will be with regard to the facts as they apply to combat initiation and seizure of territory. Several datasets that include information on war initiation have been compiled previously, and they are all in virtually complete agreement.[28] While they will be relied on to some extent, their use will be tempered, in each case, by the historical facts that have been reported.[29]

Table 1.2
Typology of Interstate Wars, with Partial Compilation

Level	Land–Sea	Years	Land	Years
I. Global	Italian	(1494–1516)	None	
	Armada	(1588–1603)		
	Anglo-Dutch	(1652–1674)		
	Louis XIV	(1688–1713)		
	7 Years'/ American	(1756–1783)		
	Napoleon	(1792–1815)		
	German	(1914–1918)		
		(1939–1945)		
II. Great power*	Crimean	(1853–1856)	Franco-Prussian	(1870–1871)
			7 Weeks'	(1866)
III. Great versus minor power	Russo-Japanese	(1904–1905)	Franco-Spanish	(1823)
	Manchuria	(1931–1933)	Russo-Polish	(1919–1920)
	Sino-Japanese	(1937–1941)	Russo-Finnish	(1939–1940)
	Vietnam	(1965–1973)	Sino-Indian	(1962)
IV. Major**	Russo-Turkish	(1828–1829)	Lopez	(1864–1870)
			Chaco	(1932–1935)
	First Balkan	(1912–1913)	Nomohan	(1939)
V. Minor	Spanish-American	(1898–1899)	Palestine	(1948)
			Kashmir	(1965)
	B'ladesh	(1971)	Football	(1969)

*Category II includes all global wars.
**Category IV includes all global and great power wars.

War Outcomes

The final key concept that must be considered is that of the outcome of war. This study will assess war outcomes in a rather straightforward fashion, relying once again on the consensus of historians to identify simply the winning and losing sides in interstate war. No effort will be made to differentiate the scope of victory, from limited territorial gains to total conquest. Nor will the margin of victory, from hard-fought, narrowly won victories to total routs, be sorted out. When the historians cannot agree, the respective war aims of the combatants will be examined to determine which side achieved its ends. There are a few, and just a very few, wars in which neither of these methods will suffice to ferret out the winner. These rare cases ending in stalemate, of which the Korean War is one, fall outside the scope of this study, which seeks to explain only "losing" war initiations. The important point, though, is that the overwhelming majority of wars are fought to a conclusion characterized by recognizable winners and losers.[30]

In considering the outcomes of wars, one should also be sensitive to two other issues. The first is that one must guard against over-reliance on the course of military operations at the tactical and even strategic levels-of-analysis. It is the grand strategic-level outcome, in terms of the achievement of policy preferences, on which one should focus. The Anglo-Dutch Naval Wars of the seventeenth century provide a good example of bitter fighting of an ultimately indecisive tactical and operationally strategic nature. Modelski calls these wars a "draw."[31] However, when one considers the British grand strategic goal of blunting Dutch maritime power,[32] Britain may be seen as the winner of these wars. It was put, perhaps most succinctly, by Jacques Barzun, who commented on the favorable outcome of these wars for the British that "England took over Dutch trade and shipping, consolidating a large empire based on sea power."[33]

Another point of view is that an individual war is but one episode in a more protracted form of conflict, such as that between classes. Engels envisioned this type of conflict as growing between the capitalist and communist states. "Protracted conflict," allowing for defeats to be shrugged off in pursuit of ultimate goals, has been associated closely with communist expansionist efforts.[34] Even Clausewitz notes that defeat in one war is often viewed simply as a passing evil.[35] The so-called "Phoenix Factor," whereby "losers" recover and eventually prosper, which is elaborated in the work of Organski and Kugler,[36] suggests that Clausewitz may be right.[37] If these various formulations are correct, then it is possible that they contribute to the phenomenon of "loser" war initiation.

For the purposes of this study, however, it will be assumed that decisions to start wars weigh most heavily the immediate prospects for a favorable outcome in the impending conflict. This is not an assumption made to denigrate the importance of long-term effects, but simply to suggest that such extensive calculation is likely beyond the capabilities and desires of the decision makers of a state contemplating war initiation. It calls for too much suspension of disbelief to think that Nazi leaders, for example, were bolstered in their aggressive designs by the idea that even a total defeat could be rapidly recouped. In fact, Hitler's final orders to destroy the infrastructure of the Reich suggest that no view of recovery was then contemplated or seen on the horizon.

Finally, it is important to note that the solution to the puzzle of why the side that ultimately loses a war so often initiates it is, to some extent, intertwined with the issue of *how* defeat is inflicted. If the possibility of some recognizable pattern to initiator defeats is suggested by existing theories, or by the elaborations of them, which this study will endeavor to effect, then it may be possible to use the knowledge gained from a better understanding of war outcomes to assist measurably the study of decisions to initiate. However, the goal of this study remains primarily focused on explaining the decision of the ultimate loser to start a war. An additional benefit may be that new understanding of the causes of interstate war may be gained. Developing a deeper comprehension of war outcomes themselves, though important, is a secondary aim of this study. Yet, learning more about how wars are won or lost may enrich studies of interstate war's role and functions (or dysfunctions) in the international system, and in the foreign policies of its nation-state components.

PLAN OF THE STUDY—SPECIFIC THEORETICAL APPROACHES

How are wars won or lost? Why do "losers" begin them? These questions are, respectively, directed toward an understanding of "outcome" and "decision." In the effort to grapple with these concepts, this study will modify and elaborate on the broad "structural" theories, of which the classical "balance of power" is an example, which purport to explain the workings of the international system. While broad systemic theories may perform well in explaining "outcome," understanding and explaining "decision" will require the employment of more detailed theoretical tools. Analysis of the decision-making process will be guided, therefore, by the use of the key theories of group interaction, cognition, organizational influence, and bureaucratic politics.

The broad structural approach to understanding war outcomes will be employed first. Some modifications to existing theories will be made, based on the insight into the fundamental "duality" of war that will be developed. These modifications will be elaborated with a view toward generating hypotheses that may, in turn, serve to inform and direct further inquiry at the more "contextual" levels-of-analysis. Indeed, this study may be viewed, broadly, as pursuing a "phased" process. It suggests that the solution to the puzzle of why the initiators of wars so frequently turn out to lose must begin with some theorizing about how wars are actually lost. At this point, structural approaches should have their greatest benefit. But when the findings regarding why initiators lose are related to explanations of the decision to start war, the other levels-of-analysis must come to the fore. The final results will be obtained through what Graham Allison has referred to as a "blending" of the levels-of-analysis.[38]

The implication of the foregoing is that "structure" influences outcomes, while a variety of factors act upon the process of decision. It is appropriate, therefore, to consider briefly some of the specific issues and hypothesized answers that the explanatory theories to be employed will introduce.

Balance of Power and Power Transition

The key structural theories of balance of power and power transition must be considered first because, if they are correct, then the problem of loser initiation may turn out to be less puzzling than it first appeared. Balance of power theory suggests that any effort to achieve hegemony, a common behavior pattern in the anarchic international system, will be opposed in the form of an alliance of the weaker against the strivings of the strong. While fully elaborated theories such as realism or structuralism do not go so far as to predict directly the defeat of initiators, the immanence, or deeply rooted character, of balancing behavior in the system allows one to infer that initiator defeats should not be surprising.[39]

Power transition theories suggest that hegemony, rather than balance, is the natural state of affairs in the international system. Conflict arises when an existing hegemon's power inevitably wanes relative to some upcoming challenger. At this point, transitional theories offer divergent explanations for loser initiation. One point of view suggests that rising challengers are driven to initiate war too soon, in the hope of rapidly overtaking the incumbent hegemon. Since the material balance, however narrow, still favors the incumbent, the challenger loses. Another possible reason for loser initiation under conditions of power transition is the attempt of the incumbent to stave off the challenger via a preventive war. If the preventive effort is begun too late, the incumbent will face inevitable defeat, as the directional movement of relative power capabilities is viewed as irreversible. Both of these scenarios accept the notion that the outcomes of these transitional wars will be determined by the side that possesses a preponderance of material resources.[40]

Though the two major strands of structural theorizing are not generally complementary (balance of power sees stability when power levels near, while transitionism views this situation as fraught with conflict potential), both rely on power as the means by which their mechanisms are driven and regulated. The distribution of power will heavily determine when fighting occurs, who will side with whom, and who will win. The crucial, universally recognized importance of power has led to major efforts to delineate its seemingly multidimensional nature. Approaches vary, from the richly detailed, exhaustive listings of Morgenthau, to the mechanistic composite capabilities index of the Correlates of War Project. Still others have attempted to introduce notions of resolve, or motivation, as crucial to power measurement.[41]

While the statistical approaches to measuring power are parsimonious, they seem unable to grasp its essence. The richer-textured approaches make of power something so elastic as to be undefinable.[42] This study also recognizes the crucial importance of power. It will follow the parsimonious approach to understanding power, though without being statistical. It will draw, from the insight regarding the duality of war, the notion that command of the sea is a preeminent form of power that determines the outcomes of land–sea conflicts. In land wars, military "skill" will be hypothesized to outweigh in importance any of the more quantitative measures of "strength."

While these structural insights may go far toward explaining why initiators lose, this is only a necessary first step on the road to explaining why losers initiate. At this point, having elaborated and modified the existing structural approaches, this study will generate new hypotheses from them. Fundamentally, they will suggest that power generally has not been measured correctly by war initiators. Hypotheses generated on the basis of these new insights will then be aimed at and tested with regard to the decision-making processes of "losers" who have started wars.

At the sub-structural levels-of-analysis, a variety of questions will be asked. Is the naval preeminence of the defender unduly discounted when an attacker's high command is army-dominated? Do key decision makers of land powers reject the notion of maritime strength as a superior form of power? Do the naval leaders of primarily land powers behave in peace in an aggressively sanguine style that enhances their bureaucratic standing? Does their aggressiveness, which may encourage decisions to go to war, desert them in conflict, as one naval defeat could bring about organizational ruin? Is it generally assumed that victory will go to the "big battalions"? These are the kinds of hypotheses that will have to be generated in order for structural insights to be successfully utilized in focusing and informing investigations of the decision-making process.

THEORY TESTING

Because the object of this study is the understanding and explanation of phenomena that exhibit similar results, in this instance "losers'" war initiations, it is appropriate to utilize, in a general way, John Stuart Mill's Method of Agreement. This approach suggests that, when outcomes are similar, variables that are absent from some cases may be discarded, as the result may be achieved with or without their presence. Only those variables present in all cases may be considered to have causal impact on the object of scientific enquiry. Mill was careful to note the difficulty of using this approach in the context of social scientific endeavors that attempt to explain inevitably complex realities in simplified fashion.[43] With these cautions in mind, however, Mill's notions provide an excellent logical foundation for the investigation of loser initiations of interstate war. Indeed, Charles Ragin's recent work on comparative political analysis offers a ringing reendorsement of Mill's Method of Agreement.[44]

The universalistic theory that this study will advance is extremely simple, suggesting that all cases of loser initiation at the level of global war, and many wars at other levels, may be explained by pointing out that maritime supremacy, which affords control over movement and resources, is the crucial factor in determining a land–sea war's outcome. Further, war initiators that are continental powers systematically miscalculate the war-winning advantage of their maritime foes. In land wars, "skill" is hypothesized to be superior to "strength." While these formulations may be delineated in a most straightforward fashion, testing their validity and worth is quite another matter. They challenge long-held notions regarding the nature of power, what wins wars, and the manner in which the international system functions. Testing, therefore, must be "tough," and must deal adequately with existing alternative explanations for loser war initiation.

With this in mind, theory testing will be broken down into a two-step process. First, a quantitative analysis of the universe of cases of the different types of interstate warfare will be undertaken. Not only will the results of these tests suggest whether or not maritime supremacy and military skill are truly the key factors in determining the outcomes of the two fundamental types of war, but they will also allow for evaluation of some of the alternative explanations. The notion of the overarching importance of material capabilities, so crucial to both balance of power and transitional theories, may also be tested. Finally, successful statistical testing goes quite far in suggesting that chance is not the cause of war outcomes. This is only an indirect means by which to test chance. However, it may be argued that a chance theory of conflict outcomes purports to explain while making no pretenses about prediction. The "dual" theory of war outcomes, on the other hand, ought to be able both to explain and predict. In the Lakatosian sense of explaining more than the chance theory, and predicting where chance does not, the dual approach should thus supersede it.[45]

But the quantitative testing employed in this study should be understood as limited, generally, to the question of why initiators lose.[46] Thus, statistical-correlational analysis is a necessary but only preliminary part of this study, which must then use the derived insights to guide detailed case studies. Based on hypotheses to be generated from the "dual" theory, detailed case studies of the decision-making processes that led to the outbreak of two of the global wars will be performed. The insights and hypotheses derived will be used first to explain why Louis XIV thought he could win a war for European hegemony against the Grand Alliance (1688–1713). The detailed study will initially consider the impact, during the pre-war period, of key naval advisors on Louis's decision to go to war. Early on, their advice resulted in his approval of the building of a large battle fleet with which to challenge England. Later, once war began, these *same* advisors urged a relative neglect of the battle fleet, ceding control of the seas without a fight, in favor of pursuing a commerce-raiding strategy.[47]

The other detailed case study will consider the German naval leaders' impact on the Kaiser's decisions regarding war and peace prior to and during 1914. In particular, Admiral von Tirpitz's strong support of a battle fleet with which to obtain command of the sea may be seen very nearly to evaporate with the onset of war. Instead, an abrupt shift to submarine construction and a commerce raiding doctrine is espoused, again leaving the continental power's maritime foes in command of the sea.[48]

Both of these cases are clear examples of primarily land powers challenging maritime powers. Both are inherently important because of their powerful impacts on the shape of and quality of life within the international system at differing times. Both are well documented by historians, the German case in particular. With regard to the latter, there is a large literature that focuses on the civil–military relations of and the penchant for offensive doctrines in the German Army. This literature may be enriched by a study that considers the neglected realm of the naval aspects of these problems. The fact that the German Navy, which had clamored for decades for a substantial battle fleet, precipitately abandoned the offensive sea control doctrines that had been designed for its employment, suggests that offensive doctrines may not always be pursued by military organizations.

Once the testing of the relevant structural theories has been completed, it will be possible to assess the importance of the insight into war's duality in terms of its modifications to and elaborations of balance of power and transitional theories regarding the functioning of the international system. Its role in the reconceptualization of power will also be considered, as will the potential for its application to the defense and foreign policy questions that, due to the continued eruptions of interstate violence, retain such a prominent place on the agenda of the leaders and peoples of so many nations.

NOTES

1. Jack S. Levy, "The Causes of War: A Review of Theories and Evidence," in *Behavior, Society, and Nuclear War,* Philip E. Tetlock, J. L. Husbands, Robert Jervis, Paul C. Stern and Charles Tilly, eds. (New York: Oxford University Press, 1989), Vol. I, pp. 209–333 offers a comprehensive overview of the intellectual effort to come to grips with the causes of war.

2. Carl von Clausewitz, *On War,* ed. and trans. by Michael Howard and Peter Paret (Princeton: Princeton University Press, 1976), p. 87.

3. For Michael Howard, *The Causes of Wars* (Cambridge: Harvard University Press, 1983), p. 12: "However inchoate or disreputable the motives for war may be, its initiation is almost by definition a deliberate and carefully considered act. . . ." Bruce Bueno de Mesquita, *The War Trap* (New Haven: Yale University Press, 1981), p. 4 contends that war "occurs in a context of prior planning and preparation that can leave no doubt . . . war has been carefully calculated." Geoffrey Blainey, *The Causes of War* (New York: Free Press, 1973), p. 141, says, of war as "accidental or unintentional": "It is difficult . . . to find a war which on investigation fits this description."

4. Bueno de Mesquita, *The War Trap,* theorizes that decision makers contemplating war assess their "expected utility" in terms of how intensely they desire an outcome times their probability of success. The linkage of this "rational" process to victory is virtually axiomatic: "Generally, the side with the larger positive expected utility—and hence the greater incentive and pool of resources with which to keep on fighting—will win" (p. 92).

5. Source: the *Correlates of War* dataset (1982 update through the Inter-University Consortium for Political and Social Research). Appendix I to this study includes a listing of these wars, along with the coded data that form the core of the quantitative testing later employed.

6. Zeev Maoz, "Resolve, Capabilities, and the Outcomes of Interstate Disputes, 1816–1976," *Journal of Conflict Resolution,* vol. 27 (June 1983):195–229. Another clear effort to link the evidence gleaned from outcomes to notions of rational war initiation is found in Bueno de Mesquita, *The War Trap,* p. 19: "One clear indication of the rational planning that precedes war is that only about 10 percent of the wars fought since

the defeat of Napoleon at Waterloo have been quickly or decisively lost by the nation that attacked first."

7. Israel's victorious Six Day War (1967) is the only unambiguously clear case of preemptive war in the post-Napoleonic era. Other possible cases of preemption are examined in Chapter 4 in a discussion of dataset coding.

8. These would be conflicts limited to sets in which great powers were represented on each side, or were absent from both sides. The measure is a rough one in the case of minor power wars, as considerable disparities in capabilities and resources are more likely to occur in this category (Spain's two successful wars with much-weaker Morocco, 1859–1860 and 1909–1910, are good examples). However, the imbalances are much less than those that occur when minor powers are at war with great powers.

9. The global war "loser initiation" phenomenon is observed in passing in George Modelski, *Long Cycles in World Politics* (Seattle: University of Washington Press, 1987). The German historian Ludwig Dehio, in *The Precarious Balance* (New York: Alfred A. Knopf, 1962) considers the repeated defeats suffered by global war initiators the central question that must be answered in order to understand the workings of the international system. His answer suggests that successful defense of the global equilibrium hinges on the superior resources and coalitions (precarious "balances") usually controlled and directed by insular powers.

10. There is a vast but atheoretical literature which purports to explain how to win wars and, implicitly, addresses the causes of losing them as well. Every history written about a given war strives to address the issues of how it began and why one side or the other won. Yet there appears to be no study of the general phenomenon of "loser initiation." Ralph K. White, "Why Aggressors Lose," *Political Psychology*, vol. 11 (1990):227–42 observes the existence of the phenomenon, and attempts to explain how wars are lost. But, only by inferring from his suggestions about resolve and coalitions can one find a glimmer of guidance regarding why "losers" *start* wars. Zeev Maoz, "Power, Capabilities, and Paradoxical Conflict Outcomes," *World Politics*, vol. 41 (1989):239–66 identifies some very "surprising" results, but omits a discussion of why losing wars are begun.

11. The Stockholm International Peace Research Institute (SIPRI), which keeps watch over ongoing wars, reflects an annual average of 31 ongoing wars during the 1980s.

12. This last possibility was described very succinctly by Kenneth Waltz in *Man, the State and War* (New York: Columbia University Press, 1954), p. 236: "mutual fear of big weapons may produce, instead of peace, a spate of smaller wars."

13. Clausewitz, *On War*, p. 86. Thomas Schelling, *The Strategy of Conflict* (Cambridge: Harvard University Press, 1960), softens this formulation, but still views outcomes as functions of the interactions of chosen strategies. This latter notion suggests that any search for understanding of the influence of chance factors on war outcomes will necessarily lead one into the "black box" of strategic interaction. Nonetheless, even for Schelling, the existence of "threats that leave something to chance" suggests that strategic interaction itself is a complex phenomenon in which those possessing greater determination, or who enjoy better luck, may still prevail.

14. Admittedly, few global wars have been fought, making an examination of the outcomes of this class of conflict at best a weak test of "chance." In Chapter 4, 63 cases of interstate war will be analyzed, offering the opportunity for far more rigorous testing of the chance hypothesis.

15. Schelling, *The Strategy of Conflict,* p. 3, provides the inspiration for this notion. He states that outcomes result from the interplay of choices made by each side. As to the unforeseen long-term consequences of the Norwegian campaign, Winston Churchill, in *The Second World War,* Vol. 1, *The Gathering Storm* (Boston: Houghton Mifflin, 1948), p. 657, commented succinctly on Britain's defeat in the battle for Norway:

"From all this wreckage and confusion there emerged one fact of major importance potentially affecting the whole future of the war. In their desperate grapple with the British Navy, the Germans ruined their own. . . . The German Navy was no factor in the supreme issue of the invasion of Britain."

16. Kenneth E. Boulding's *Three Faces of Power* (Newbury Park, CA: Sage Publications, Inc., 1989) offers an exhaustive analysis of power, accepting its vital importance in understanding international affairs as well as the difficulty that exists in trying to capture the essence of its multidimensional nature. Hans Morgenthau, *Politics Among Nations* (New York: Alfred A. Knopf, 1948) makes the explicit effort to catalogue the multitude of components that make up national power. Richard Ned Lebow, *Between Peace and War: The Nature of International Crisis* (Baltimore: The Johns Hopkins University Press, 1981), p. 242, describes the tendency of key decision makers systematically to overestimate their own capabilities.

17. John George Stoessinger, in *Why Nations Go To War* (New York: St. Martin's Press, 5th ed., 1990), also observes the frequency of initiator defeat. He adopts the "miscalculation of power" framework, and finds the roots of error in the individual psychologies of the relevant decision makers in the cases he surveys. His approach will be considered among the alternative explanations for "loser" war initiation discussed in Chapter 5, especially in regard to his analysis of the onset of World War I.

18. This is the manner in which Kenneth Waltz's *Theory of International Politics* (New York: Random House, 1979), which predicts balancing behavior in the face of aggression, will be employed as a plausible "candidate" theory that purports to "explain" loser initiation.

19. See Bueno de Mesquita, *The War Trap,* Chapters 1 and 2. Very simply, his deductive theory suggests that decision makers actually do consider the probability of victory, as well as their utility for the outcome.

20. See Modelski, *Long Cycles in World Politics*; and Jack S. Levy, *War in the Modern Great Power System 1495–1975* (Lexington: University Press of Kentucky, 1983).

21. See George Herring, *America's Longest War* (New York: Alfred A. Knopf, 1986).

22. William R. Thompson, *On Global War: Historical Structural Approaches to World Politics* (Columbia: University of South Carolina Press, 1988), p. 5.

23. It has already been observed (see Table 1.1) that, when great v. minor power wars are controlled for, the phenomenon of "loser initiation" may be observed more distinctly.

24. Even though the clearest manifestation of the "loser" phenomenon occurs in global and great power wars, it persists, to significant degrees, in all types of war. Creation of this typology will assist in identifying factors that are working either all the time, or only under the conditions imposed by the different types of war.

25. This assertion applies to wars other than those that would include the use of strategic nuclear weapons.

26. As developed in Giulio Douhet, *The Command of the Air,* Ferrari translation

(New York: Coward-McCann, 1942); and Alexander P. De Seversky, *Victory Through Air Power* (New York: Simon and Schuster, 1942). Edward N. Luttwak, *Strategy: The Logic of War and Peace* (Cambridge: Harvard University Press, 1987), pp. 164–168, offers a thoughtful refutation of the notion that air power has an "autonomous" capability to achieve victory in war.

27. Hans Delbruck, *History of the Art of War Within the Framework of Political History*, 3 vols. (Westport, Connecticut: Greenwood Press, 1985 ed.) does reflect on some notion of war's duality, keying on wars as divided between those of "attrition" and those of "annihilation." It may well be that land-sea wars are primarily attritional, while most land wars are fought with sharp, decisive actions in mind. It may, therefore, be possible to refine some of Delbruck's formulations about the nature of these basic types of war.

28. This is likely because of their basic reliance on the dataset generated by the Correlates of War Project, a factor that requires cautious employment of the data. Therefore, all codings of interstate wars made by this study will rely primarily on the existing historical consensus. This will result in some changes from the COW coding, each of which will be noted.

29. A good example of a case in which the initiator will be redesignated is the Russo-Japanese War (1903–1905). Although it was Japan that declared war, Russia should be identified as the initiator. The first use of force consisted of the Russian invasion and occupation (with some 200,000 troops) of Manchuria and Korea, areas of vital interest to Japan. R. M. Connaughton's recent comprehensive, *The War of the Rising Sun and the Tumbling Bear* (London: Routledge, 1988) summarizes the modern scholarly consensus that the Russians were "first on the move," and that they accepted willingly (perhaps even eagerly) the possibility that their invasion might result in a forceful Japanese response. Appendix I to this study lists the two other recoded initiators which comprise the total variance from the COW Project's dataset (affecting the Crimean and Chaco Wars). In the former, Russian troops seized substantial Turkish holdings in the Balkans. In the latter, Bolivia conquered a third of Paraguay before it was opposed.

30. The COW project dataset reflects 64 interstate wars begun and ended during the Post-Napoleonic era, through 1980. Only two (Korea 1950–1953 and the Israeli-Egyptian War of Attrition) are coded as ambiguous in terms of outcome. This study agrees almost entirely with the COW project coding of outcomes, except that the War of Attrition will be recoded as an Israeli victory. Egyptian aims of achieving Israeli withdrawal from the Sinai were clearly frustrated. Only one change in outcome coding will be made among the decisively concluded wars: Vietnam will be designated the winner of its 1979 war with China. China's aim of effecting a Vietnamese withdrawal from Cambodia was not achieved.

31. Modelski, *Long Cycles in World Politics,* p. 81. The Anglo-Dutch Wars are not coded by the Correlates of War dataset, which goes only as far back as the dawn of the post-Napoleonic era; and only Levy designates them as "Great Power" wars.

32. Paul Kennedy, in *The Rise and Fall of British Naval Mastery* (London: The Ashfield Press, 1976), p. 48, cites General-At-Sea (Cromwell's choice of name for admiral) Monck's appraisal of the situation: "The Dutch have too much trade and the English are resolved to take it from them."

33. Jacques Barzun, *Introduction to Naval History* (New York: J.B. Lippincott Company, 1944), p. 47. A more recent affirmation of this point of view is provided by

Charles R. Boxer, *The Anglo-Dutch Wars of the 17th Century, 1652–1674* (London: H.M. Stationery Office, 1974).

34. See Friedrich Engels, *Anti-Duhring* (New York: International Publishers, Inc., 1939 ed.), the chapters on "force theory." Paul Strausz-Hupe, William R. Kintner, James E. Dougherty, and Alvin J. Cottrell, *Protracted Conflict: A Study of Communist Strategy* (New York: Harper & Row, 1963), offer a further elaboration of this notion that losing wars may be started as long as a view of ultimate victory is held.

35. Clausewitz, *On War,* Book I, Ch. I, Sec. 9, "The Result in War Is Never Absolute."

36. A.F.K. Organski and Jacek Kugler, *The War Ledger* (Chicago: University of Chicago Press, 1980), pp. 142–146.

37. Related to the notion of outcome as not always comprised of the sum of military engagements is the idea that thinking about war outcomes in terms of winning and losing is inappropriate. This point of view is championed by Berenice Carroll in "Victory and Defeat: The Mystique of Dominance," in *On the Endings of Wars,* Stuart Albert and Edward C. Luck, eds. (Port Washington, NY: National University Publishers, 1980). Her suggestion is that conventional notions of victory and defeat miss the important point that wars have very long-lasting effects that may not become clear until many decades after the cessation of hostilities.

38. See Graham T. Allison, *Essence of Decision: Explaining the Cuban Missile Crisis* (Boston: Little, Brown and Company, 1971), particularly pp. 258–263, for his conclusions regarding the ultimate complementarity of the various levels-of-analysis.

39. The seminal work in this area is Kenneth N. Waltz's *Theory of International Politics.* Stephen M. Walt's *The Origins of Alliances* (Ithaca: Cornell University Press, 1987) refines Waltz's power balancing notions, arguing that balancing occurs against "threat," primarily, and not against "power" as it has been variously conceived.

40. In addition to Organski and Kugler, *The War Ledger* and Modelski, *Long Cycles in World Politics* regarding transitions, Robert Gilpin's *War and Change in World Politics* (Cambridge: Cambridge University Press, 1981) should be considered a cornerstone of transitional theorizing. He is the only transitional theorist who holds preventive war by the incumbent hegemon to be the "first and most attractive response to a society's decline" (p. 191). Joshua Goldstein's *Long Cycles* (New Haven: Yale University Press, 1988) is an important recent addition to the body of work devoted to "transitional" theories. With regard to the winning of wars, Paul Kennedy, *The Rise and Fall of the Great Powers* (New York: Random House, 1987), advances and analyzes the notion that victory *is* a function of the possession of greater resources.

41. This approach was recently taken by James D. Morrow, "Social Choice and System Structure in World Politics," *World Politics,* vol. 40:75–97. Clausewitz, *On War,* p. 77, provides an earlier perspective on the importance of resolution, or "will," placing it on an equal level with material strength.

42. This dilemma is recognized, and left generally unresolved, in Richard L. Merritt and Dina A. Zinnes, "Validity of Power Indices," *International Interactions,* vol. 14, no. 2 (1988):141–151.

43. A particular problem, for the presence of which one must always be alert, is that of equifinality—the possibility that a given outcome may be derived via differing causal paths.

44. Charles C. Ragin, *The Comparative Method* (Berkeley: University of California Press, 1987).

45. On this point see I. Lakatos, "Falsification and the Methodology of Scientific Research Programs," in *Criticism and the Growth of Knowledge,* I. Lakatos and A. Musgrave, eds. (London: Cambridge University Press, 1970), pp. 91–196.

46. However, some effort will be made to draw inferences about loser initiation in an indirect fashion from existing statistical/correlational studies. For example, the work of Paul Huth, particularly *Extended Deterrence and the Prevention of War* (New Haven: Yale University Press, 1988), derives, from a statistical study of 58 cases, a purported set of conditions under which either peace is kept or war breaks out. His conclusions suggest, among other things, that theatre-level rather than overall material superiority maintains deterrence. Yet, when one notes that about half of his cases have deterrence being attempted by either the United States or Britain, one may contend that Huth is simply pointing out that aggressors do not really understand the war-winning potential of their maritime adversaries. This matter is discussed further in Chapter 6.

47. Geoffrey Symcox, *The Crisis of French Sea Power 1688–1697* (The Hague: Martinus Nijhoff, 1974), is the historical work that illuminates most clearly the French deliberations over sea power that were occurring at this time. Many original documents also exist, which should make it possible to test hypotheses drawn from organizational and bureaucratic political theories of decision-maker behavior.

48. Robert J. Art, *The Influence of Foreign Policy on Seapower* (Beverly Hills: Sage Publications, 1973), chronicles very specifically the rapid shift in German naval doctrine that occurred with the onset of World War I.

Chapter 2

Structural Explanations

Why do the nations rage? —Psalm 2

Understanding the phenomenon of war is vitally important to all endeavors that purport to explain the workings of the international system. For nation-states, the onset, duration, and, particularly, outcome of war largely determine their future influence or insignificance, prosperity or poverty, and even their survival in the system. Beyond war's immediate impact on the fortunes of individual states, it also significantly influences the overall structure of the international system itself. It should be observed that, while all warring states suffer the immediate consequences of defeat or savor the fruits of victory, system-wide effects are principally derived from the wars of and among the Great Powers. With this in mind, one should expect that those theories that strive to explain the nature and workings of the international system will have a certain degree of "bias" toward the conflict behavior of the Great Powers.[1]

Given that the aim of this study is the development of an explanation for acts of war initiation by the ultimate "loser," and that, proportionally, the most frequent loser initiations are found in the class of Great Power wars (global in particular), the realm of structural-level explanations appears to be an appropriate one in which to begin the search for answers. After all, global and other Great Power wars are highly visible, much scrutinized events; and comprehensive structural explanations should be able to grapple successfully with the phenomenon of loser initiation, at least in wars of these types.

The existing structural theories may be broken down into two broad categories, each centered around a composite military-economic concept of power. First, there are those that postulate the prevalence of power balancing behavior in an anarchic international system devoid of hegemonic control. Then there are theories in which the system is characterized by a certain degree of order provided by a "leader." The latter class of theories associates the breakdown of order and the onset of war with power "transitions." These occur as the leader's power inevitably declines while that of potential challengers grows, just as irreversibly. Table 2.1 depicts the major existing structural theories of the international system, and their progenitors.

Both of these major theoretical approaches must be carefully considered in this study of loser initiations. For even though (as will be shown), surprisingly, these structural theories do not directly address this issue in any sort of detail, important, falsifiable hypotheses may be generated from them regarding the "loser phenomenon." Interestingly, power is the "root of all war" in each of these theoretical "strands" of reasoning. Under notions of balancing, it is asymmetries of power that, in an anarchic international system permissive of the use of force, are likely to lead to war. Transitional thinking holds, on the other hand, that war is most likely when the potential combatants are nearly equal in power. The manner in which these theories contend (or do not) with "losers" will, at the least, enrich the current understanding of their scope and explanatory power.

From the results of the testing of these formulations, some indication may be gleaned as to whether or not these theories are sufficient to enable the explanation of war initiation by the loser. Indeed, the achievement of successful results from hypothesis testing of any of the key existing structural theories would suggest that the "loser phenomenon" might not really be so puzzling after all. If states generally do band together in the face of "growing power," or threat, giving them the wherewithal to withstand aggression, then there would appear to be little need to search for other explanations of "loser" war initiation. On the other hand, the failure of hypothesis testing to find positive findings of balancing would suggest that the current understanding of the workings of the international system afforded by these theories is imperfect, and that the theories themselves are in some need of "fixing."

In this chapter, the key structural theories will be outlined and some hypotheses will be generated from them. Then these hypotheses will be tested against

Table 2.1
Summary of Structural Theories

Balance of power		Transitional	
Theory	Proponent(s)	Theory	Proponent(s)
Realism	Thucydides, Hobbes, Morgenthau	Power transition	Organski, Kugler
Neo-realism	Waltz	Cycle of relative power	Doran
		Hegemonic change	Gilpin
		Long cycles	Modelski, Thompson, Goldstein

the universe of cases of global war. Because of their scope, duration, and intensity, and by definition their stakes of systemic control, global wars form a class of what Eckstein would call "most likely" cases.[2] If the hypotheses derived from structural theories work anywhere, they should work at the level of global conflict. The specific type of testing that will be employed will consist of "congruence analysis." All of the global wars will be examined in a narrowly focused fashion dictated by the various hypotheses. Results will be measured in terms of whether or not the hypothesized behavior is present. In the event that predicted actions are absent, it will be necessary to modify, elaborate, or, to some extent, reconstruct the existing structural approaches to understanding war in the international system. Because this study holds that outcomes are strongly related to "structure," as discussed in the previous chapter, an effort to "fine tune" existing theories of the international system is of paramount importance. Later, when the factors that influence "decision" are considered, structural insights are used to guide research at other levels-of-analysis.

BALANCE OF POWER THEORY

The assumptions about reality that underlie notions of the balance of power, and of what constitutes "balancing behavior," are really quite straightforward. First, the key units of analysis in the international system are thought to be nation-states, as opposed to individuals (in classical Liberalism) or classes (as in Marxism). Next, the system of nation-states is viewed as lacking a central authority that holds a legitimate monopoly on the use of force, rendering it "anarchic." Finally, it is assumed that nation-states will be vitally interested in their own survival. The theoretical insight that may be derived from these assumptions is that nation-states will engage in balancing behavior as they pursue their security in an anarchic world.

"Balancing" refers to the dynamics within a system that prevent the rise of any hegemonic leader, and may take two forms. First, a state may balance internally, by drawing on its own resources in pursuit of security. Or it may achieve a balance via external means, through alliances with other states. Of course, some combination of internal and external means is not only possible, but is the most frequently observed format for balancing in the international system. The most detailed explication of balancing is developed in the work of Kenneth Waltz; and it is from his insights that a key structural-level hypothesis regarding loser war initiation may be derived. He views war as "bound to occur" in a world "[w]ith many sovereign states, with no system of law enforceable among them," and "with each state judging its grievances according to the dictates of its own reason or desire."[3] Given that the structure of the international system itself creates a fertile environment for war, a plausible explanation for the dearth of hegemonic leaders throughout history may well be drawn from Waltz's later formulation that weaker states will band together against the strong.

It is crucial to note also that Waltz's theory holds that balancing is engaged in *prospectively*.[4] Therefore, the existence of *de facto* balances against aggressors is not sufficient to demonstrate that balancing behavior has been engaged in by weak or threatened states. To explain the rise of *de facto* balances in the absence of prospective alliance-forming behavior, to the extent to which this phenomenon occurs, it will be necessary to modify existing notions of who balances. It may be that aggressors, by their own acts, "create" the balances that ultimately oppose them.

While it is not explicit in Waltz's work that he believes external balancing will thwart all aspiring hegemons, his theory of structural realism does call for behavior on the part of threatened states that suggests that they will *try* to defeat any challenges to the systemic equilibrium. Therefore, according to this theory of balancing against power, one of the observations that sparked this study, that all initiators of global wars lose, should not be considered particularly puzzling. Alliances will form to oppose war initiators, which explains why they are defeated. As to why the "losers" initiate, the answer, per structural realism, would be that the original choices to start a war may have been quite rational in terms of the original power calculations done just prior to starting a war. However, the presence of balancing, when the systemic equilibrium is threatened, results in a shift in power that is as unfavorable as it is generally unforeseen by the war initiator.[5]

It is important to note that balance of power theory, though widely understood and generally considered as capturing some essential truths about the operation of the international system, has had and still has its share of thoughtful critics. While its supporters depict a universalistic theory whose roots may be glimpsed in the formulation of Thucydides that the Peloponnesian War was caused by a reaction to the "growing power of Athens," current detractors are looking at the same source materials and finding little support for arguing that Thucydides actually fit the description of structural realist.[6] David Hume also looked to antiquity in his search for enduring truths by which the international system is bounded, and found the interactions of the Greek city-states ambiguous with regard to balancing. What was clear to him from his reflections on the ancient world, however, was that no states engaged in external balancing against the rise of Rome.[7]

Despite the existence of opposing views, balance of power theory remains an important theoretical tool to be used in efforts to explain a complex political reality. If it is correct, then the frequency of loser war initiation that has been observed should not be surprising.[8] The hypothesis that may be drawn from balance of power theory that relates to loser initiation should thus be:

Hypothesis 1: States will band together prospectively in an effort to arrest the progress and deny the aims of those who threaten to disturb the systemic equilibrium and, therefore, the security of those who prefer the maintenance of the *status quo*.

While, in theory, balances should be possible in regional settings, the clear intent of structural realism is to address primarily issues of broader systemic-level interaction. Therefore, the hypothesis derived from this theory is deliberately biased toward Great Power wars; and it is in the universe of cases of one subset (global) of these wars that some empirical testing will be performed.

"TRANSITIONAL" THEORIES

While the basic tenets of the various transitional theories of the international system reflect a notion of the preeminence of power considerations in the ordering of relations among nations, there is some divergence from balance of power theory on the matter of "anarchy." Transitional theories do admit the lack of an enforceable international law; but they also suggest that the power of the leading state in the system is sufficient to provide for some type of governance. The leader furnishes certain "public goods" (e.g., freedom of the seas, trade openness) and maintains the system's existing politico-military *status quo*, implicitly underwriting international systemic functions (or regimes) with its own security guarantee.

All would be peaceful, except for the rude intrusion of the laws of systemic "gravity." Sooner or later, the power of the leader irreversibly wanes, either absolutely, or relative to the inevitable rise of a "challenger." One explanation of this process suggests that the incumbent hegemon suffers, eventually, from "overstretch." The costs of maintaining order in the international system are seen to mount steadily as benefits, relative to the gains that others with lower security expenditures enjoy, diminish. Inevitably, the incumbent grows more vulnerable to the rise of a new power whose fresh and underutilized capital is put to work creating strong new sinews of war. As their power levels near, war grows quite likely.[9]

Transitional theories are all in agreement that the period characterized by this type of flux is one of great peril. Three sequences of events may ensue. First, the declining leader may initiate a preventive war against the challenger, before the unfavorable trend has gone too far to be remedied by force.[10] Or, the challenger may start a war with the leader when it reasons that the balance is sufficiently in its favor. In these first two cases, a preventive war undertaken too late or a challenge made too soon would both lead to "loser initiations." The loser phenomenon would thus be a function of improper "timing." Finally, the leader may, with varying degrees of grace, bow to the inevitable and allow the new leader to ascend to power in recognition of its merits. While a single transitional period may be concluded in any one of these three ways, transitionists argue that the rising and falling phenomena are immutable.

One very important strand of transitional thinking has gone so far as to search out the cyclical regularities of power transitions. The theorists of "long cycles"[11] have argued that transitions occur after global wars, which come at the end of century-long periods of leader-produced peace. The declining leader is able to hold off the rising power of the challenger, which always starts the global war. However, the leader is exhausted in the process, and peacefully, seemingly gratefully, "hands off" the reins of power to a new leader. Britain's stand against Nazi Germany and later acquiescence to American hegemony affords an example of the workings of this kind of theory. Another variant of this type of theorizing is represented in Doran's formulations regarding the "cycle of relative power," which works quite similarly to long cycles, though without the same degree of temporal precision and regularity.[12]

There are a few key points about transitional approaches that are worth highlighting. First, the time of greatest peril to peace is that during which the respective power capabilities of leader and challenger near. Second, virtually all of the exponents of transitional approaches agree that power may be measured in terms of quantifiable factors (GNP, population, share of world trade, or steel production are the most popularly used indicators).[13] When war for control of the international system erupts, it is further assumed that the side that commands greater power resources will win (or "always win," according to Paul Kennedy).[14] This must be the case, the argument goes, because a war of great magnitude does not consist of what Clausewitz described as a "single, sharp blow."[15] Instead, these wars are grinding, attritional struggles, with both sides earning victories and suffering defeats. The final outcome is the result of cumulative gains made and losses incurred, added up on some "cosmic toteboard."

If the rise and decline of international systemic leaders is both irreversible and clearly measurable, and the path to victory in war so clear, why, then, do global wars ever occur? Why do their initiators lose? If change is irreversible, should not the challenger simply wait until its capabilities far outweigh the leader's? Should not leaders engage in preventive localized wars to discourage the rise of viable challengers? These are particularly thorny questions for the transitional theories. Some of them are answered by notions of peaceful submission of the old to the new leader, and of preventive war as the leader's "most attractive" option. But the failure of the challenger to win the leadership post for itself appears beyond the scope of simple rationales.

The transitionalist's answer to the puzzle of why losers initiate may be adduced from the notion that wars are won by "strength." Thus, it would have to be hypothesized that challengers initiate wars when the "cycle of relative power" is favorable to them. They lose because, even in the only-somewhat-ordered world of leaders, challengers, and transitions, balancing behavior against the strong persists.[16] Therefore, even perfectly rational war initiation decisions by challengers may lead to unforeseen and unwanted outcomes for the challenger. This is the manner in which both the classical transitional approach of Organski and Kugler,[17] and the long cycle variant of Modelski solve the "puzzle" of loser initiation. Thus, it may be seen that transitional theories are not entirely in conflict with notions of power balancing behavior.

The key hypotheses that may be drawn from transitional theories, and which must be tested along with the hypothesis drawn from balance of power theory, are:

Hypothesis 2: Incumbent hegemons may start preventive wars to arrest the rise of challengers (Gilpin).

Hypothesis 3: Challenges to declining leaders, often initially indirect, will be met with balancing behavior.

Hypothesis 4: Exhausted leaders will "hand off" peacefully to their successor once they have defeated a determined challenge.

Hypothesis 5: Wars are won by superior material strength.

It should be noted that hypotheses 1 (from balance of power theory) and 3 are substantially the same. Therefore, it will be necessary to test only four of the five hypotheses that have been generated by this review of the existing structural theories of conflict and change in the international system.

TESTING THE STRUCTURAL HYPOTHESES

As previously mentioned, if the structural theories are at all useful, they should have explanatory power in the realm of global wars. There is a general agreement that five wars (or series of wars) of this type, distinguished by their severity, duration, and scope of aims, have erupted during the last 500 years.[18] This study will also introduce the notion that, given the standards of classification currently in use, two other cases (i.e., Anglo-Dutch, 1652–1674, and Seven Years'/American Independence, 1756–1783) of protracted warfare should be considered "global."

These cases are "most likely" in that the hypotheses derived from structural theories of systemic conflict should certainly be working at this level of conflict. For example, balancing behavior is far more likely to be evident in the history of the struggle against Germany's drive for hegemony than it would be in a more limited conflict, such as any of the wars initiated by Bismarck. Table 2.2 lists the global wars that will be considered in this "plausibility probe" of the structural theories.

The major hypothesized activity that should be found in these cases is balancing behavior by the defender(s). It is important that balancing, for purposes of congruence testing, not be simply equated with the final "line-ups" of the contending nations. The fact that nation C ends up fighting alongside B against war initiator A does not, by itself, prove that C and B were engaging in balancing behavior against A. C might end up on the same side as B because A decided to attack it as well as B. Joining an ongoing war by being attacked will, therefore, not be considered balancing behavior. As discussed earlier in this chapter, it is thus possible to view the existence of balances that arose in the absence of balancing behavior. Just why the war initiator might "create" the coalition that it faces will be considered in the next chapter, when some modifications to this structural theory will be effected.[19]

Table 2.2
Listing of Global Wars Since 1494

War	Initiator(s)	Defender(s)	Winner(s)
1. Italian (1494–1516)	France, Spain, Portugal	Venice, Ottoman Empire	Venice
2. Armada (1588–1603)	Spain	Britain	Britain
3. Anglo-Dutch (1652–1674)	Britain, France	Holland	Britain
4. Louis XIV (1688–1713)	France	Grand Alliance	Grand Alliance
5. 7 Years'/ American (1756–1783)	France, United, States, Spain, Holland	Britain, Prussia	Britain, United States
6. Napoleon (1792–1815)	France	Coalitions	Coalitions
7. German (1914–1918) (1939–1945)	Germany, Austria-Hungary	Allies	Allies

Since the cases being observed are all wars that were actually fought, the transitional hypothesis regarding peaceful change can not be examined. The possibilities that these wars were begun either preemptively or preventively will be considered. The major effort, though, will be made in considering the validity of existing structural notions as to why so many of these initiators lost their bids for hegemony. In this regard, the testing that follows differs substantially in purpose from that which has previously been done by those propounding either balance of power or transitional theories. Their tests have been more focused on determining whether or not the given theory explains something about the structure of the system, rather than the mechanics of a given war's onset and outcome.[20]

Nonetheless, the findings developed below may shed further light on the overall explanatory power of the theories being examined. This study refines the testing of the balance of power by differentiating between anticipatory balances and those which arise only from an aggressor's act of war initiation. With regard to long cycles, the same cases that Modelski and Thompson use will be examined. But new emphasis will be placed on the significance of hegemonic successors directly attacking incumbents. According to long cycle theory, this should not be occurring. Thus, this study will analyze Spain's conquest of Portugal in 1580, and Britain's systematic assault on Dutch power between 1652–1674, adding substantially to the body of testing of transitional approaches. Even Kennedy's comprehensive analyses of the outcomes of the global wars of the last half-millennium will be recast, with emphasis placed on the material balance of forces during key intra-war periods, as opposed simply to aggregate totals for all war participants. For example, the balance during the years in which Britain stood alone against Napoleonic France will be examined, as well as during and after the French decisions to widen the war by invading, first Spain, then Russia. One may see, therefore, that even though this study makes demands on the structural theories that differ from those previously placed upon them, the findings developed may prove generally useful.

THE CASES

I. The Italian Wars (1494–1516)

Historical summary. By the latter part of the fifteenth century, both Spain and France were well on the way to modern nationhood. The Spaniards would, in 1492, expel the Moors from Iberia, after a struggle of some six centuries duration. The French, just a short time earlier, were finally able to substantially rid their territory of British interlopers, also after some centuries of intermittent warfare. Both nations were forged by the blast of patriotic wars; and when no threats to domestic security remained, they began to look outward. The Spaniards followed a "two-track" policy of exploration of new territories and conquest of old ones. The French were far more concentrated on immediate territorial expansion rather than exploration, perhaps because, not being peninsular like the Spaniards, they still had ample opportunities for growth among their adjacent neighbors.

Eventually, these "warrior states" butted up against each other in Italy, at the time a riotous crazy-quilt patchwork of city-states primarily engaged in internecine strife caused by their various efforts to dominate trade with the Orient. The so-called "Italian Wars" were thus generally characterized by the competition of two Great Powers over the territory and trade controlled by the Italians. The outcome of these wars was the *de facto* partition of Italy into "spheres of influence." All of Italy, except for Venice, came under the control of either Spain or France.

The global aspect of this period's conflict is provided by the Portuguese, who were vying with the Spanish for control of newly discovered territories. After some generally mild, indecisive fighting (prior to the French and Spanish invasions of Italy), the Treaty of Tordesillas was agreed upon; and the New World was divided into spheres, just as effectively and more peacefully than Italy would be. The only other "global" operations consisted of the Portuguese attempt to break Muslim naval power in the Indian Ocean. The perceived general success of this latter endeavor has led the long "cyclists," Modelski and Thompson, to label Portugal the first global hegemon of the modern interstate system.[21] They are joined by Mowat, Dehio, and Toynbee in considering the Italian Wars the first global conflict.[22]

Hypothesis testing. The most important question to ask is whether or not external balancing behavior is evident in these conflicts. Were the weak combining to defend against the strong? Second, could any of the war initiations be characterized as "preventive?" The sorry record indicates that Machiavelli's "exhortation" to the Italians to unite against foreign oppressors was ignored. The Italian city-states never combined to resist either Spain or France. The only time several of them did align was during the War of the Cambrian League. However, this alliance consisted of a grand coalition, which included France, Spain, Austria, and the "bandwagoning" Italian city-states, whose aims were the defeat and dismemberment of Venice. Thus, the behavior of both great and minor powers may be seen, in the climactic events of the Italian Wars, to run absolutely counter to the predicted behavior that is hypothesized by structural theories. For Venice, though in substantial control of world trade, which gives these wars their global cast, was a tiny principality whose interests were almost entirely commercial.

The outcome of the war against Venice was absolutely unexpected. Though its *condottiere*-led mercenary army was thoroughly routed in the opening days of fighting, Venice itself remained resolute, unconquered, and, more importantly, unconquerable. Eventually, the two major coalition partners, France and Spain, fell out, and peace almost immediately ensued. Venice enjoyed terms of the *status quo ante bellum*. Charles Habsburg was frustrated in his design for hegemony, and had to face the growing enmity of France. The other Italian city-states that had joined the campaign of the great powers against Venice were rewarded for their allegiance with the loss of their liberty. They were divided up between France and Spain, while Venice remained the only independent Italian principality, enjoying a gilded sunset that would last another 300 years.[23]

There is little evidence to support the notion that Portugal had become the leading global power. While it did predominate the trade route around Africa, its function was more that of *entrepreneur* than imperial power. Also, it had no monopoly of trade with the Orient as Venice retained control over all routes coming through the Levant. Spain enjoyed far richer returns from the portion allotted it in the generally well-observed Treaty of Tordesillas, as the wealthy Aztec and Incan prizes fell into its sphere of influence. Claims of Portugal's global power are further vitiated by observing its swift conquest by and absorption into Spain later on in the sixteenth century. Even the extent of its victories over Muslim naval power in the Indian Ocean has been questioned, with the observation made that Ottoman holdings and commercial enterprises were little affected by Portuguese military and naval operations.[24]

The hypothesized notion of preventive war is also without much support in this case. In fact, there is simply no evidence to suggest that the types of power transitions that are supposed to lead to global war (the decline of the leader interacting with the rise of the challenger) were occurring. Instead, the great powers were all rising together, and all at quite similar rates if not in like ways.[25] Even Venice was still expanding at a rapid rate, both in commercial and naval terms. It would reach its zenith over half a century after the Cambrian War, furnishing the most powerful contingent of the multinational Christian fleet, which would blunt Muslim naval power in the Mediterranean at the Battle of Lepanto.[26]

In summary, this case of global war does not support the notion that active and inevitably unforeseen balancing behavior will be engaged in to thwart hegemonic aspirations. Instead, bandwagoning is quite evident. Nonetheless, Habsburg expansionism was blunted by the lonely resolution of Venice. Indeed, the triumph of the maritime republic against such long odds suggests the possibility that it might well be what Eckstein has called a "crucial case."[27] Therefore, the foregoing events will be reexamined in a new light later on, after the exposition of original theoretical insights, which will constitute the heart of the next chapter.

For now, the phenomenon of loser initiation in this case stands out starkly, and remains puzzling. France and Spain, as well as their hangers-on, attacked Venice in an effort to plunder its wealth, and to gain control of trade with the East. They failed completely. Portugal attacked Ottoman holdings on the littoral of the Indian Ocean, in its attempt to control the other world trade route (around Africa) to the East. Muslim power withstood the Portuguese assault, and Portugal itself would soon after suffer a disastrous defeat in its attempt to conquer Morocco. Reeling from this unexpected defeat, it would immediately thereafter be absorbed by Spain.

With regard to the structural hypothesis that victory in war goes to the materially stronger side, this global conflict provides much disconfirming evidence. At the outbreak of the War of the League of Cambrai, the attacking coalition outnumbered Venice in population by a ratio of 15:1.[28] France and Spain controlled just over a quarter of global naval power assets, while Venice had none.[29] However, if one counts Venice's galleys as on a par with French and Spanish warships (which Modelski and Thompson do not), the city-state's navy outnumbered its combined opposition by 65 to 38.[30] Thus, it may be necessary to modify the concept of "power."

Finally, one cannot even find evidence that the hapless Italian city-states engaged in balancing against either France or Spain. Indeed, those that resisted either great power did so without the benefit of alliances with the other, with all going down swiftly to defeat. The city-states that aligned with France and Spain joined up only when the conquest of Venice was the object. When France and Spain failed in this enterprise, they turned ravenously upon their diminutive supporters, annexing them.

II. The War of the Armada (1586–1603)

Historical summary. Despite its rebuff in the Italian Wars, the Habsburg drive for hegemony remained serious and growing. In the decades after the ending of the first global war, Spain consolidated its holdings in Italy and completed its conquests in the New World. It even added the Philippines to its growing imperial holdings. It played an important role in the naval rebuff of Muslim power at Lepanto, and annexed Portugal and all of its colonial holdings. On the continent, Austria was Habsburg-ruled, and control was exerted over an archipelago of principalities running in a long, broken crescent from Burgundy to the Low Countries.

France, riven internally by Catholic–Protestant strife, was quiescent, with only England acting in defiance (not very openly) of Spanish hegemonic aims. Spain first launched a diplomatic "charm offensive" against England, culminating in Philip II's marriage proposal to Elizabeth. Turned down, Philip resorted to more coercive measures, leading to the seizure of English ships and cargo and the incarceration of their seamen. English policy remained, for a time, as unprovocative as it was unyielding. However, Elizabeth, after one particularly vexing series of Spanish actions seizing English ships, cargo, and seamen, did sanction what turned out to be a wildly successful riposte through privateers led by Drake. Philip's response was to begin the "Enterprise of England" whose aim was the total conquest of the stubborn islanders, escalating the low-intensity conflict he had begun to the level of global war.[31]

No nation came to England's aid in its time of trial, though the Dutch rebels fighting for independence from Spain were pursuing a common end with their Protestant coreligionists. Even so, Britain's attempt to ally with the Dutch rebels, embodied in the expeditionary force of the Earl of Leicester, foundered almost immediately. The British and Dutch simply could not get along, failing even to agree upon a unified command structure. The British went home, awaiting Philip's next move.

The details of the defeat of the Armada in 1588 are well known and have been exhaustively chronicled from many perspectives; but this should in no way diminish the luster from an exceptionally surprising outcome in which the world's strongest power was humbled and turned down the path toward ruin. The war dragged on for nearly two decades after the defeat of the Armada in 1588, past the deaths of Philip and Elizabeth, resulting in English victory and Dutch independence.[32]

Hypothesis testing. It has already been noted that England was not joined in its fight by any nation. It may also be observed that Spain's war effort was in no way preventive, based on fears of growing English power. Rather, the war was fought to remove the last obstacle to growing Spanish hegemony, both in Europe and around the world. Indeed, the relative balance of material resources, which is so crucial to war outcomes according to transitional theories, was heavily in favor of Spain. While it is impossible to be precise about economics in the sixteenth and seventeenth centuries, it is hard to disagree with Dehio's assertion that Spain's vast continental and overseas holdings[33] made it by far the wealthiest nation on earth.[34]

In terms of the other material measures of strength, Spain's population was roughly double that of Britain; and its standing army was some five times greater in size than Elizabeth's. Spain possessed nearly half of all global sea-power assets, while Britain had under a quarter.[35] This figure is likely to be misleading, though, as Modelski and Thompson count only "government-owned" ships in their dataset. While this is not a problem in more modern times, it does fail to recognize the substantial naval assets privately provided to the British fleet by the likes of Frobisher, Hawkins, and Drake. Indeed, the 130-ship Armada,[36] which Spain sent off to win control of the Channel to allow the Duke of Parma's forces to invade Britain, was opposed by at least a numerically equivalent force. While Britain had only 20 government-owned ships of war, an additional 123 had been hired by Elizabeth for this campaign.[37] This case suggests that Modelski and Thompson are right to emphasize naval strength as a key measure of national power, though their standard of "government ownership" should be relaxed to reflect accurately the naval balance between these antagonists. It also implies that a reconceptualization of traditional quantitative measures of power should find a prominent place for naval strength.

III. The Anglo-Dutch Wars (1652–1674)

Historical summary. With the blunting of Spain's power, it was inevitable that England and Holland would be driven toward conflict with each other due to their respective "growing powers." While loosely united in their willingness to engage in depredations against the still-intact Spanish overseas empire, they clashed frequently during the first five decades of the seventeenth century over the control of trade. Despite the tremendous domestic political turmoil that hardened the rule and ruined the health of Oliver Cromwell, this redoubtable "Protector" fixed upon one firm British foreign policy objective: the destruction of the military and economic global power capabilities of the Dutch.[38] In a series of three primarily naval wars, this objective was achieved. Also, the Third Anglo-Dutch Naval War was characterized by the French joining with the English, as the former attempted to gain in terms of continental territory the counterpart of the latter's winnings in trade and colonial booty. While England gained almost all that it had hoped for, France earned only partial territorial satisfaction and the total Dutch enmity, which sparked the later formation of the Grand Alliance that thwarted Louis XIV's designs for continental hegemony.

Hypothesis testing. Britain's initiation of a war to destroy Dutch naval power and control of trade[39] suggests that long cycle theory has not contemplated the possibility that the duel for global leadership may be quite direct, and need not involve all of the great powers at one time. If one accepts the long cyclists' notion that the Dutch were global leaders in 1650, then the direct challenge by England, and its success, runs strongly counter to this theory's prediction. Structural realism is also quite unhelpful in this case, as the French entry into the war on the side of the English looks quite a bit like a naked "power grab," and most unlike balancing.

When Britain launched its third war against the Dutch in 1672, France joined in with gusto. Its fleet fought the Dutch in the Mediterranean, while its army invaded through Flanders. It was only in 1674, when the Dutch bought peace with Britain by making concessions that recognized British maritime predominance, that some small relief was gained. War with France dragged on until 1678, with France's land invasion stopped by the Dutch willingness to flood large sections of their own country.

In summary, the Anglo-Dutch Wars were certainly global in terms of aims and consequences. They also appear to fall well outside the realm of explanation of either the "balancing" or the "transitioning" schools of structural thought. In particular, the formulation that, in long cycles, successor hegemons do not attack incumbents is challenged by this case. With regard to notions of balancing behavior, French bandwagoning in the third war against the Dutch, who had been seriously weakened in their first two wars with Britain, strikes a very discordant note.

With regard to the hypothesis that superior material strength wins wars, this case is ambiguous. The Dutch were certainly a greater economic power than Britain in 1652 (this is why, according to Kennedy, the latter began the struggle). However, British naval strength was equal to the Dutch from the outset and, in the third war, the addition of France tilted the overall balance heavily against the United Provinces. Even in this last phase, though, the value of material strength must be viewed with some question, as the Dutch were able to negotiate peace (at a price) with the British, while withstanding the French invasion attempt.

IV. The Global War of Louis XIV (1688–1713)

Historical summary. With the defeat of the Spanish drive for continental European hegemony, a power vacuum arose in the international system, into which France attempted to move. The long reign of Louis XIV (1643–1715) was thus one characterized by continuing French expansionism. In the early decades of Louis' reign, France was largely confined to continental power politics. However, a systematic naval building program was begun by the early 1660s, under the able leadership of Colbert, Louis' brilliant Minister of Marine, which gave France a much broader "reach." When Louis joined Britain in attacking the Dutch in 1672, France's land operations were well complemented by a navy that harassed Dutch interests around the world, and decisively defeated Dutch naval power in the Mediterranean. By the late 1680s, the stage was set for Louis' global war, which he initiated by his declaration of war on Britain and the United Provinces in 1688. His aims throughout this global war were to conquer the Dutch, blunt British sea power, consolidate his holdings east of the Rhine, and exert control over the thrones of Austria and Spain.

France's key antagonist, and the political *zeitgeist* of this age, was William III, leader of the United Provinces and, from 1688, the invited king of an England nostalgic for some form of Protestant monarchy in the wake of Cromwell's grim "Protectorship." It was William who kept together the "Grand Alliance" that frustrated Louis' aims. In the end, after more than 20 years of war, France stood exhausted, with only marginal territorial and political gains. Clearly, its drive for hegemony was defeated. The Dutch suffered heavily as well, in terms of blood and treasure. Only Britain emerged an obvious winner from the generation of global war that climaxed the reign of the Sun King.

Hypothesis testing. Did balancing behavior lead to the thwarting of Louis' drive for hegemony? Clearly, the German states that comprised the League of Augsburg balanced when they banded together prior to Louis' invasion in the summer of 1688. The League's successor, the Grand Alliance, would find France facing a formidable coalition, which would include Austria, the Dutch, Spain, and Britain. However, when one examines the manner in which this coalition came together, it is clear that, save for Austria and the smaller German states, no one entered the fray until attacked by Louis. Neither Holland nor Britain came to the aid of the German states when they were invaded. Spain stayed out of the fighting until France attacked. Indeed, it was Louis who exerted the greatest degree of control over the make-up of his enemies in this war.[40]

With regard to preventive motivations for war, there were simply no rising powers challenging France. Additionally, France possessed, in the summer of 1688, both the largest army and navy in Europe. Only by attacking a number of unaligned states (which Louis did) could France create a force concentration of enemies large enough to imperil its own security. The only preventive motivation that did weigh on Louis' mind was the problem of Austria, which had recently inflicted a severe defeat on the Ottoman Empire. This would soon free up substantial forces for the defense of the Palatinate. But this is hardly the kind of preventive war motivation that Gilpin's theory of hegemonic change has in mind.[41]

In terms of structural thinking about the importance of material strength, Louis' global war saw France opposed, from the time Holland and Britain entered the fray, by states whose aggregated economic strength was far greater its own.[42] France's manpower pool, though, remained larger than that of its foes throughout the war, even though its population dropped from 20,000,000 at the outset to 17,500,000 by its end.[43]

V. The 7 Years'/American Wars (1756–1783)

Historical summary. The rebuff to France's continental ambitions suffered during the wars of Louis XIV in no way brought an end to its striving. Indeed, French geopolitical aims took on a more explicitly global perspective after the demise of Louis, while still retaining expansionist desires on the European

continent. The Caribbean, North America, and India all became important areas for French economic, military, and political operations, within the context
of a growing global rivalry with Britain. The fusion of these continental and
global aims may be seen in French behavior during the Seven Years' War
(1756-1763).

Though considered too brief, by some "transitional" scholars, this war was
quite global in scope. Aside from major operations on the continent, pitting
Prussia against France, Austria, and Russia, its global operations saw France
and Spain attacking British interests all over the world.[44] Britain allied itself
with Prussia, providing it with financial subsidies, some Hanoverian troops,
and harassing operations along the French coast. The results of field operations
in Europe were relatively inconclusive, with Prussia making some limited gains
(Silesia) and France making none. Abroad, however, the coalition that sought
the defeat of Britain was itself routed. France lost its place in North America as
well as in India, blows from which it never, in a global sense, recovered.
Britain gained, almost entirely at France's expense, a world empire buttressed
by vast new tracts of territory in North America and on the Asian subconti-
nent.[45]

The next phase of the global conflict came when France entered the American War for Independence (1776-1783) on the side of the rebels. France was
joined in its efforts by Spain and Holland, who were nursing grudges of varying
vintages against the British. While the efforts of these allies helped the American colonies to win their freedom, the attempt to dismember the other parts of
the nascent global British Empire ended in disastrous rebuffs for all three. For
France, the failure to recapture any of its former holdings was accompanied by
the need to shoulder the enormous financial burdens that resulted from the war.
Some historians have even argued that the roots of the French Revolution may
be directly traced to the financial crisis that was caused by their aid to the
Americans.[46]

Hypothesis testing. Does the Seven Years'/American Revolutionary conflict
qualify as a preventive war, begun by a hegemon striving to arrest its decline?
The problem with answering this question is that it is hard to identify the
initiator of this war clearly. Both France and Britain had substantial holdings in
North America, which each sought to expand. The French were trying to link
Canada with the Mississippi valley, while the British colonists were pushing
west from the eastern seaboard. They encountered each other and fought over
the Ohio River valley. The war, begun in the wilderness, spread to the plains of
Europe and on to India. A good analogy for its start is that of two drivers on
perpendicular courses trying to make it through an intersection before the other.
A terrible collision ensued, from which Britain emerged far the better. This war
was not preventive, in Gilpin's sense.[47] Its second phase, from 1776-1783, was
retributive rather than preventive. France and Spain declared war on Britain,
subsequent to the American rebels' victory at Saratoga, hoping to recoup losses

from the first phase of this global war. Holland decided to forgo a declaration of war, entering the fray by preying on British commerce.

As to balancing, both France and Britain wound up in alliances. France's was much larger, with Spain, Austria, and Russia enlisted. Britain's ally, Prussia, was small but led by the most skillful field general of the day, Frederick the Great. Prussia was also bent on expansion in Central Europe, an area in which both Russia and Austria had designs. Far from balancing against growing power or threat, it appears that the sides were largely determined by national self-interest in gains.[48] This is even truer of the second phase of the war, in which Britain stood alone against a "bandwagoning" coalition.

In terms of material strength, France's coalition (the losing side) was considerably greater throughout this global war. At the outset, the aggregate populations and standing forces of the French coalition were 68,500,000 and 860,000, respectively. For Britain and Prussia, the comparable figures are 16,500,000 and 395,000.[49] The relevant ratios are 4.2:1 for population and 2.2:1 for standing armies. In ships-of-the-line, this era's key measure of naval strength, Britain was still outnumbered, by 133:117, a ratio of 1.1:1. This worsened at the outset of the second phase of the war to 175:104 (or 1.7:1 against Britain).[50] While GNP figures are hard to compare for this time period, a difficulty that persists to a lesser degree to this day, it is possible to measure the nations' shares of world output. At the outset of this war, the French coalition controlled 11.9%, the British 4.8%.[51] Thus, it can be seen that the winner of this war, who made great gains in the first phase and held onto almost all of them in the second, was the materially weaker side throughout.

VI. The French Revolutionary/Napoleonic Wars (1792–1815)

Historical summary. Whatever its causes, the French Revolution had the practical effect of returning France to a primarily continental foreign policy, much like that of Louis XIV. Though couched in terms congenial to the new nationalistic cause, France's aims were once again for territorial expansion to the point at which it could finally be "secure." Its invasion of the Austrian Netherlands in 1792 was immediately opposed by a coalition that followed a policy of containment, at least after hopes of overthrow had dimmed. With the rise of Napoleon as military leader, France was able to beat off its foes, hold some of its gains, and arrive at a favorable ceasefire in the form of the Treaty of Amiens (1801).

Limited gains were not enough for France, however. The nervous peace was broken by French incursions in Italy, and by a smooth, rapid takeover of Switzerland. Britain stepped in at this point to try to arrest French progress. Its attempt to resurrect a coalition against France was largely unsuccessful, and it fought alone for over two years. When Austria finally joined Britain, it was rapidly demolished by Napoleon. Prussia, which was determined at this point to avoid entangling alliances, found itself in France's way despite its neutrality.

After its crushing defeat at Jena, it was absorbed into the growing French Empire.

After some desultory fighting between France and Russia in Eastern Europe, these parties agreed to a peace characterized by Russian acquiescence to the new European order. While Britain fought on alone, Spain actively joined the French cause. Indeed, Spain first joined with France in 1797, casting a greedy eye upon Gibraltar and other British outposts in the Mediterranean. The French instituted a Continental "system" designed to exclude British goods from Europe. While unpopular even from the start, the system was backed by the Treaty of Armed Neutrality, in which several nations, among them the conquered or coopted, had, years earlier, agreed to unite in their opposition to British naval depredations. Britain found itself compelled to fight League naval forces, most notably the Danes. Russia's active entry into the war against Britain was narrowly averted by the assassination of that Napoleonic admirer, the young Tsar Peter. At the height of Britain's lonely struggle, in 1812, even the United States declared war on Britain. If its maritime grievances were the proximate cause of American aggression, they were almost immediately overshadowed by the urge to conquer Canada.

Ultimately, though, Napoleon had problems enforcing compliance with his "Continental System" at either end of Europe. Portugal and Russia "defected," to some degree, by trading with Britain, prompting France to invade first Iberia and, later, Russia. Each of these war-widening efforts forced new allies onto the British side, and the French campaigns associated with each endeavor both failed catastrophically. The ebbing French Empire was then (1813) beset by the rise of other conquered states that were being liberated, most notably Prussia and Austria. The end was near. Napoleon abdicated in 1814, to return the next year for a brief, unsuccessful encore, after which peace reigned under the auspices of the newly formed Concert of Europe.

Hypothesis testing. During the wars of the Napoleonic Era, there is some evidence that balancing behavior was practiced from time to time by a few of the relevant nations. The enduring, recurring alliance of Britain and Austria formed the heart of the behavior which may be characterized as "balancing." Outside of these actors, however, there was little consistent evidence of balancing. Prussia tried to go its own way and was overrun by Napoleon. Spain was openly allied with France for the first half of these wars, switching sides only after the Napoleonic usurpation of the Spanish throne. Russia made an early peace with Napoleon, returning to the British fold by virtue of being invaded by Napoleon in 1812.[52]

There is little evidence that French motivations for starting wars in the Napoleonic Era were "preventive," in Gilpin's sense, since nearly bankrupt France was hardly the leading power of the day fearing the rise of challengers. There is a moderate case to be made, though, that preemptive pressures existed in 1792. There was considerable evidence that an effort to restore the Bourbons was underway. However, France's invasion of the Low Countries responded to no particular threat, suggesting instead that France may have "gone to war in a mood of ideological fervour."[53] As to the wars that Napoleon began after 1801, they were not preemptive. He broke the Treaty of Amiens by enlarging his holdings in Italy and conquering Switzerland. Then he invaded Central Europe, Iberia, and Russia, ever expanding the scope of the war of his Empire. None of these actions were taken because of the fear of impending attack.

The ultimate defeat of the French in this conflict cannot be explained by balancing behavior either. Among the continental states, only Austria consistently behaved as a balancer, joining coalitions before being attacked. Austria was the only state to respond favorably to Britain's call to arms when Napoleon renewed the war by breaking the Treaty of Amiens. Prussia, though part of the first effort to restore the Bourbons in the early 1790s, tried to stay out of Napoleon's way. Its isolationism resulted in its being conquered in 1806. Prussia again rejoined the fray only after Napoleon's defeat in Russia. The Russians briefly joined with Austria and Britain (1806), but soon concluded a separate peace with Napoleon (1807), joining in the Continental System. Indeed, Russia even used its considerable military might to coerce Finland and Sweden into honoring the embargo on trade with Britain. Russia rejoined the fight against Napoleon only when 500,000 soldiers of the *Grande Armee* began their march on Moscow in the summer of 1812.

Finally, it should be noted that France was not without allies during this global war. Spain, still looking to humiliate the British, was an early and active participant on France's side. Indeed, it remained involved as a combatant until after Trafalgar in 1805. Relations with Napoleon deteriorated in the next few years, and a pro-French *coup d'etat* in 1806–1807 was soon followed by French occupation, and the installation of one of Napoleon's brothers as the new king. In addition to Spain, a League of Armed Neutrality was formed to fight the British blockade. The Netherlands, Denmark, Sweden, and Russia were all key players in this alliance, which necessitated sharp preventive measures by the British (as in the Royal Navy's attack on the Danish fleet at Copenhagen in 1807) to maintain a favorable naval balance. The Poles, though lacking a formal nation, were ardent supporters of the French emperor, providing him with forces up until the Russian campaign. Finally, there was the United States, which, at the height of Napoleon's power, declared war on Britain, trying unsuccessfully to wrest Canada away from it. The balancing record against Napoleon was indeed spotty.

With regard to the hypothesis that material superiority wins wars, this is a most fascinating case. In the first part of this global conflict (1792–1801), France held off significantly superior forces. Between 1803–1812, it failed, despite amassing larger armies and more economic assets, to defeat its one consistent enemy, Britain, whose only resource was its superior navy. Only at the end, from 1813–1815, was France overwhelmed by vastly superior numbers.

In terms of manpower, France began with a 180,000-man army, which was opposed by the First Coalition's 530,000 troops, a ratio of nearly 3:1 against France. However, the *levee en masse* soon made up for France's numerical deficiencies. Over the course of the war, France would mobilize over 3,000,000 troops. Britain would mobilize only 300,000. However, after the Russian campaign of 1812, Napoleon's remaining forces would be outnumbered by 1,270,000 to 600,000, a ratio of better than 2:1.[54] The key points here are that France escaped defeat when inferior in terms of manpower, failed to win during the 10 years in which it enjoyed superiority (1803–1812), and was significantly outnumbered in the final phase of the war.

France's share of world economic output in the early years of this conflict amounted to 4.2%, opposed to the 13.5% controlled by the First Coalition.[55] During the Imperial period, when one adds the value of Napoleon's conquests to France's output, it can be seen that Britain's 4.3% was facing a "Continental System" in control of 13.4% of world economic output. As with manpower, the issue raised here is why greater economic strength failed to defeat France in the beginning, or work in France's favor during the middle years of this long conflict.

Finally, an examination of the naval balance points out that, numerically at least, France's sea power was quite comparable to Britain's. When Spanish ships were added to France's in the war's first phase, a rough parity in gross numbers was in evidence. In the year before Trafalgar, Spain and France possessed 126 ships-of-the-line to Britain's 122. After Trafalgar, the balance moved steadily against France. Britain built more ships, destroyed the Danish fleet, and gained some naval components when Spain began its fight against French occupation. By 1812, the naval balance against France had grown to 154:101.[56]

VII. The Germans (1914–1918, and 1939–1945)

Historical summary. If one can picture the procession of aspiring hegemons as beginning on the western edge of the European littoral, with Portugal in the early sixteenth century, and moving ever eastward, through Spain and France, over the next three centuries, it should not be difficult to guess that the Germans would be next. Despite the resounding failures of each previous challenge, they remained undaunted. Once the political and limited military operations needed to unify the modern German state had been effected, largely under the guidance of Bismarck, the Wilhelmian drive for *weltmacht* began. Germany industrialized with a vengeance during this period, sought and obtained foreign colonies, and embarked upon a vigorous military and naval expansion to provide the "tip of the spear" of their power capabilities.

It did not take long for other nations to become concerned about the "growing power" of Germany. France, recently defeated (1871) by the Germans in the Franco-Prussian War, sought a defensive alliance with Russia (formalized in

1894) to offset the enhanced threat posed by its militarist neighbor. Britain kept a weather eye on the growth of the German fleet, launching its own building program to offset German naval gains. Germany, in turn, allied with Austria, in a move that classically depicts the effects of the "security dilemma."[57] Each actor's efforts to provide better for its own defense were seen as threats by onlooking states that, in turn, built up their own militaries and sought more allies. This endless cycle of amassing military wherewithal turned Europe, in the early 1900s, into a vast armed camp.

When a political crisis developed in the Balkans, the Germans, in the form of the Kaiser's famous "blank check" offer to the Austrians, affirmed that they were ready for, if not desirous of, a major war. That is just what they got. Save for the United States, which entered the war on the side of the Allies in 1917, all of the major participants were members of one or the other of the existing alliances.[58] The Germans lost this conflict, it is commonly argued, because of the preponderance of material capabilities that their foes amassed against them.[59]

However, the Great War turned out to be merely the first round in the German drive for global mastery, and many observers of the time were aware that the Treaty of Versailles was more truce than final reckoning. Indeed, its harsh provisions served to harden German resolve to recover from the indignity of defeat, and helped to pave the way for the rise of fascism in the person of Hitler. The recovery was spectacular, if initially uneven; and, by the mid-1930s, Germany was economically out-producing France and England combined, in some sectors. The return to prosperity was accompanied by the renewal of an aggressive foreign policy, aimed first at the recovery of continental territories lost in the Great War, and then at the newly created Central European nations that were located near the heart of the Kaiser's beloved *Mitteleuropa*.

German "nibbling" at these territories was initially successful without starting a new war with Britain and France. But these Great War victors did, finally, over the matter of Danzig, opt to oppose German expansionism with force. The war that the Germans initiated over Danzig was one that they may not have thought would escalate to the global level, but this risk was certainly one that they were willing to undertake.[60]

Initial operations were wildly successful, with Poland conquered in one month (September 1939), and France knocked out of the war, and partially occupied, in a campaign of some six weeks' duration during the spring of 1940. The earlier invasion of Norway, along with the incidental conquests of Denmark and the Low Countries, rounded out a picture of virtually unbroken success. By the summer of 1940, only Britain stood defiant against the Germans. Like its hegemonic predecessors, Germany could do little at this point, beyond employing its newly acquired capability to engage in aerial bombing, to force Britain to capitulate, due to the latter's control of the English Channel. Also, like its predecessors, Germany cast about for ways to "conquer the sea by conquering the land."

In the year after the fall of France, Germany conquered the Balkans and sent a military contingent to Africa to retrieve the faltering Italian position there. It was immediately quite successful, recovering Libya and threatening Egypt to the point at which Marshal Wavell began to plan for the evacuation of his troops from this British colony. In June 1941, Germany invaded Russia. The Germans hoped by this maneuver to free themselves from any threat on their landward rear, enabling them time to prepare for the final reckoning with Britain.

The *blitzkrieg* against the Soviet Union initially exhibited the usual signs of success. However, dickering over whether or not to divert German armor to support a large encirclement operation in the Ukraine, resulting ultimately in the diversion, delayed the drive on Moscow until the onset of winter. Though the Ukraine was lost, Moscow was saved. As the German advance was grinding to a frozen halt within sight of the Kremlin towers, though, Germany added a new enemy by declaring war on the United States. While this declaration may have solidified the German alliance with Japan, and simply formalized the recognition of the existing hostile relationship of the two powers, it did result in very significant negative near-term effects.[61]

Almost immediately, and in quite significant amounts, American shipments of war *materiel* were increased to both British and Russian forces.[62] Within a year of Germany's declaration of war, the United States invaded North Africa, helping to trap nearly 300,000 Axis troops in Tunisia. Invasions of Sicily, Italy, and France followed, sealing the fate of Germany's challenge for *weltmacht*. In the end, some 15 million troops were converging on the Reich from all sides. Day and night aerial bombing went on virtually unopposed during the waning months of the war; and Germany's U-boats were reduced to ineffectiveness. Certainly, of all the challengers for global power, Germany suffered the greatest consequences in defeat, as it was completely occupied and partitioned.

Hypothesis testing. Again, since this global war was begun by the challenger, the hypothesis regarding preventive war by the incumbent hegemon cannot be validated. That said, the war may have had some preventive "flavor," in that Germany may well have seen 1914 as the best time for a war that was likely to be inevitable. This is debatable. Less problematic is the notion that a power transition was going on. In 1860, Germany's level of industrialization was one fourth of Britain's. By 1913, it had surpassed British production.[63] Clearly, a major shift was going on and, as the challenger neared the old leader, tensions did rise.[64]

There appears to be a good *prima facie* case to be made in favor of the notion that balancing was going on in the effort to thwart the German challenge. The original alliance between France and Russia (1894), entered into because both were, separately, weaker than Germany, is cited by Waltz as evidence of balancing.[65] After the Great War, France allied with both Britain and Poland, as well as with Czechoslovakia. During World War II, Germany found itself up against an overwhelming group of foes, in which the United States and the

USSR were added to the list of Germany's enemies. These events not only tend to confirm that a restraining balance arose, but that, as transitional theories hypothesize, the gross material superiority of the Allies caused the defeat of Germany.

When one examines the diplomatic history of the period, however, much behavior exists that cannot simply be characterized as balancing. The elaborate alliance structure that attended each contending side in the Great War can not be reckoned as confirming the presence of balancing against the stronger, unless both sides felt that they were the weaker. France and Britain's abandonment of Czechoslovakia, and their failure to align with the USSR during the late 1930s, also tend to disconfirm balancing. In fact, the USSR signed a formal treaty with Germany, invading Poland from the East and occupying the Baltic countries. The ultimate presence of the Soviet Union and the United States on the Allied side ensued because of either German invasion or declaration of war. Therefore, though *de facto* balances resulted, they did so in the absence of balancing behavior.[66] The key point is that, in order to "balance," a nation must *choose*, free of the duress of being under attack itself, to join an ally.

As to the importance of material capabilities, it cannot be doubted that the Germans faced an insurmountable balance against them from the times that the United States joined the Allies during the first phase of this global war in 1917, and from Hitler's invasion of Russia and declaration of war on the United States in 1941. However, the truly puzzling period is the year from June 1940 to June 1941. How is it that Britain was able to stand alone when so many had fallen so swiftly? Certainly, notions of victory as caused by material superiority suffer from this counter-example. In the year between the fall of France and Hitler's attack on the Soviet Union, Germany's material superiority should have enabled it to conquer Britain. Admittedly, Hitler gave himself only a year to achieve this aim before bringing others into the war, whereas Napoleon had material advantage for nearly a decade before he attacked Russia. But it was Hitler's choice to expand the war when he did, no doubt because there was no way for him to gain command of the sea approaches to Britain, and because the failure of his air campaign was already quite evident.

In terms of statistics, during the first phase of the global war (1914–1918), both military and economic measures of strength favored the Allies. Where Germany and Austria-Hungary would mobilize nearly 12,000,000 troops over the course of the war, Britain, France, and Russia would field nearly 31,000,000. The United States would add 4,000,000, and Italy nearly 6,000,000.[67] In terms of total industrial potential, using an index with Britain in 1900 as the basis (scored at "100"), France, Britain, and Russia amassed a combined rating of 261.1 to Germany and Austria-Hungary's 178.4. The addition of Italy (in 1915) and the United States (in 1917) changed this figure to 581.7.[68]

In the second and last phase of the global war (1939–1945), as in the first, Germany and its allies would be outmobilized by a ratio of more than 3:1.

Economically, however, Germany's share of world production capabilities, at 14.4%, initially equalled Britain and France's combined. If one assumes that Germany could add even half of France's assets to its own, its figure would grow to 16.%, while Britain's was at 10%.[69] However, the USSR, which was attacked in June 1941, brought one sixth of world production potential to Britain's aid, while Germany's declaration of war on the United States put an additional 50% of world production in opposition to the Axis. By contrast, alliance with Japan added only 3.5%.[70] The massive industrial potential of the Allies translated into an overwhelming production edge in key weapons. In planes, for example, the Allies produced 634,000 from 1939–1945 (500,000 from 1942 on) to the Axis production figure of 207,000.[71]

As far as the numerical naval balance is concerned, in 1914 the Germans had 22 Dreadnoughts, two thirds of Britain's total. In 1939, Germany's navy would have one third the strength of Britain's.[72] However, when fleet concentration capabilities are considered, later in this study, it will be demonstrated that the actual balance was far closer to parity.

In summary, though, these statistical measures all show that the Germans were simply up against very long numerical odds in the latter stages of each phase of their drive for global power. The most intriguing question that arises from this analysis, though, must continue to be "Why did the Germans, 'gratuitously,' in Taylor's words, bring the USSR and the US into the war by, respectively, invasion and declaration?" That they did not align against Hitler before these events raises serious questions about the validity of traditional notions of balancing behavior.

ASSESSMENT OF THE CASES

The two major "strands" of structural-level thought differ markedly in their characterizations of the international system, with realism finding stability when the most powerful states near each other in capabilities, and transitional approaches viewing such a time as one fraught with the risk of war. From one perspective, parity suggests that deterrence should hold, from the other that it should encourage efforts either to fight preventively (if one is the *status quo* power) or prospectively (if challenging the *status quo*). However, both schools of thought do concur that, despite the fundamentally anarchic nature of the system, order may be achieved. For realism, this order is preserved, or reestablished when disturbed, by the "balancing" behavior of states, which thwarts the efforts of those who would disturb the natural equilibrium. States act somewhat like antibodies, fighting a harmful virus. For transitionalism, order is provided by leaders who either prevent new challenges or build coalitions to overcome them. This latter form of behavior is what links both of the structural-level schools of thought.

"Balancing" or "coalitioning" is the key behavior that the structural theories predict; and it is this kind of state action that has been primarily tested for in the foregoing analysis of global wars. Other hypotheses, regarding preventive war and the importance of material capabilities, were also tested. Favorable results of this testing would have explained both the reasons for initiator failure and why losers initiate wars. The hypothesized explanation for loser initiation is really quite simple, under structural theory. It suggests that actual war-initiating decisions may be quite rational, based on a state's interests and relative capabilities. Unfortunately, when these rational decisions are being made by states that threaten the systemic balance, opposing forces are ineluctably drawn together, which ensure the initiator's defeat. Thus, an initiator's contemplated "limited war" inevitably grows into a much larger conflict in which the balance of forces weighs heavily against the initiator. The fact that initiators succeed in over three quarters of non-Great Power wars, while almost all global war initiators lose, suggests that something like this phenomenon may be going on.

However, when one examines the results of hypothesis testing of this "most likely" set of cases, there is little support to be found for notions of balancing behavior (see Table 2.3 for a summary of the findings). While unfavorable balances do occur (as in the wars against France and Germany), they arise in the absence of balancing behavior. Rather, states found themselves aligned against the French, and later the Germans, because of having been attacked by them. This suggests that existing notions of balancing behavior must be either discarded or reformulated. Perhaps it will be possible to rehabilitate some notion of balancing by suggesting that it is the war initiator who creates the opposing balances. This idea will be considered in the next chapter as a possible modification to existing structural theory.

Aside from balancing, notions of preventive war, the existence of transitions

Table 2.3
Analysis of Global Wars

War	External Balancing	Power Transition	"Strength" Wins	"Loser" Initiates
Italian	Little	No	No	Yes
Armada	Little	No	No	Yes
Anglo-Dutch	None	Yes	Yes	No
Louis XIV	Significant	No	Yes	Yes
7 Years'/ American	Little	No	No	Yes/mixed
Napoleonic	Moderate	No	Unclear*	Yes
World Wars	Moderate	Yes	Unclear*	Yes

*These wars are characterized by the initial triumph of the materially weaker side, which then enjoys material superiority for a significant period (measured in years) of time. Unable to convert material advantage into victory, the balance shifts (even if in the absence of balancing behavior) to the point at which the ultimately victorious side enjoys a highly favorable quantitative balance of forces and resources.

at the outset of wars, and the inevitable triumph of material capabilities have all suffered in this analysis of global wars. In particular, the theory of long cycles appears to suffer the most. The regular upheavals, followed by hegemon-led periods of tranquility, just do not seem to be occurring. Also, the existence of direct attacks on leaders (Spain's conquest of Portugal, and Britain's deliberate destruction of Dutch maritime power) runs absolutely counter to key tenets of long cycle theory.

In the next chapter, ways of reformulating and rehabilitating key formulations of transitionalism will be considered. Though long cycle theory has been criticized in this examination of global wars, its focus on naval power will be seen as quite important. When one notes that the superior naval power won every global war, the value of this sort of capability appears self-evident. Thus, long cycle theory may have pinpointed the key facet of power needed to control the global system.

SUMMARY AND CONCLUSION

The theorizing and hypothesis testing that has formed the core of this chapter has resulted in the finding that the existing structural-level theories, and their hypothesized balancing or transitioning behavior, do not adequately address the matter of why losers start wars, even in the "most likely" category of global wars. Notions of why initiators lose, largely congregated around belief in the efficacy of material superiority, have also been seriously challenged. The puzzle remaining unsolved, some preliminary efforts were made to suggest modifications to the existing structural-level theories that might allow their continued use in the endeavor to understand the vexing phenomenon of loser initiation. Specifically, a new notion of balances arising, in the absence of balancing behavior, will have to be explored. Also, one of the key transitional theories, that of long cycles, appears to have properly focused on the maritime dimension of power. This may prove to be the foundation for a new and more parsimonious view of relative power and its impact on the outcome of systemic conflict. In the next chapter, these structural modifications will be developed, as will be the potential for their use in serving to guide the investigation as it moves to the organizational and bureaucratic levels-of-analysis.

NOTES

1. Jack S. Levy, "The Causes of War: A Review of Theories and Evidence," in *Behavior, Society, and Nuclear War,* Philip E. Tetlock, J. L. Husbands, Robert Jervis, Paul C. Stern and Charles Tilly, eds. (New York: Oxford University Press, 1989), p. 215, notes that the Great Power bias is "clear" from any review of the significant works on the international system.

2. Harry Eckstein, "Case Study and Theory in Political Science," in *Handbook of Political Science,* vol. V, *Strategies of Inquiry* (Reading, MA: Addison-Wesley, 1975), p. 118.

3. Kenneth N. Waltz, *Man, the State and War* (New York: Columbia University Press, 1954), p. 159.

4. Waltz, *Theory of International Politics* (New York: Random House, 1979), p. 127, makes the points that "states . . . flock to the weaker side; for it is the stronger side that threatens them. On the weaker side, they are both more appreciated and safer, provided, of course, that the coalition they join achieves enough defensive or deterrent strength to dissuade adversaries from attacking." Levy's comprehensive survey, "The Causes of War: A Review of Theories and Evidence," p. 230, notes that balance of power theorists generally describe balancing this way: "External balancing refers primarily to the formation of alliances as a blocking coalition against a prospective aggressor. . . . "

5. Why don't aggressors foresee the formation of opposing balances? This is an additional puzzle which will have to be considered *if* the analysis which proceeds in this chapter confirms that balancing is actually going on. Waltz, *Theory of International Politics,* pp. 160–163, and 170–176 suggests that uncertainty about potential external balancing may be greater under conditions of multi- rather than bipolarity. Since the system was multipolar until the end of the World War II, it might be argued that, until the rise of U.S./USSR bipolarity, miscalculation was likely to occur because of the many possible alliance configurations and the inherent uncertainties of relying on the whims of potential allies or opponents.

6. See, for example, Daniel Garst, "Thucydides and Neorealism," *International Studies Quarterly,* vol. 33, no. 1 (March 1989): pp. 3–28. Garst argues that the threat posed by Athens, as reported by Thucydides, was not primarily to the balance of power, but rather to the "institutions, rules and conventions" which governed inter-city-state behavior. The "growing power" of Athens to alter the nature of Greek politics was, according to Garst, the proximate cause of the Spartan willingness to go to war. But Garst may actually be pointing out that the drive of Athens to control "institutions, rules and conventions" was nothing less than a "global" (for the time) ambition which would have eradicated any sort of systemic equilibrium.

7. David Hume, "Of the Balance of Power" (1752), in *Theory and Practice of the Balance of Power,* Moorhead Wright, ed. (London: J.M. Dent & Sons, 1975). Hume is more concerned with Rome's early wars of conquest, neglecting its relationship with Carthage. However, when one notes that Carthage was an existing great power that *initiated* the first two of its three wars with a then-very-provincial Roman republic, his omission seems justified. Indeed, it was Carthage which found allies in its aggressive designs upon Rome. When the tables turned in the final Punic War, Carthage, the victim now of Roman aggression, fought and lost without the benefit of allies. See Brian Caven, *The Punic Wars* (New York: St. Martin's Press, 1980).

8. Indeed, a recent refinement of balance of power theory, Stephen M. Walt's *The Origins of Alliances* (Ithaca: Cornell University Press, 1987), implies that the defeat of aggressors should almost be expected. This is so because balancing, according to Walt, will occur in the face of *threat,* even if the potential aggressor's actual power is inferior to that of the intended victim.

9. Paul Kennedy's *The Rise and Fall of the Great Powers* (New York: Random

House, 1987) champions this point of view, in its survey of the Great Power wars fought between 1500 and the present.

10. Robert Gilpin, *War and Change in World Politics* (Cambridge: Cambridge University Press, 1981), p. 191 refers to preventive war as the declining hegemon's "first and most attractive response."

11. Key works in this area include: George Modelski, *Long Cycles in WorldPolitics,* and *Exploring Long Cycles* (Boulder: Lynne Rienner, 1987); and Joshua Goldstein, *Long Cycles* (New Haven: Yale University Press, 1988).

12. Charles F. Doran, *The Politics of Assimilation* (Baltimore: The Johns Hopkins University Press, 1971); and Doran and Wes Parsons, "War and the Cycle of Relative Power," *American Political Science Review,* vol. 74 (December 1980):947–965.

13. George Modelski and William R. Thompson, in *Seapower and Global Politics, 1494-1993* (Seattle: University of Washington Press, 1988), suggest that a global "leader" is present any time that one nation commands more than 50% of global seapower assets (which vary over time, from galleons to ships-of-the-line during the Age of Sail, to dreadnoughts and aircraft carriers in the twentieth century). Though not developed separately from other military and economic indices of power, naval strength, by implication, appears, from their perspective, to be a preeminent indicator of national strength.

14. Paul Kennedy, "The First World War and the International System," in *Military Strategy and the Origins of the First World War,* Steven Miller, ed. (Princeton: Princeton University Press, 1985), p. 38. In *The Rise and Fall of the Great Powers,* Kennedy refines his theory of victory as "caused" by material superiority (see the "On the Winning of Wars" sections of each chapter).

15. Clausewitz, *On War,* pp. 79–80.

16. George Modelski, *Long Cycles in World Politics,* p. 223, argues explicitly that global leaders possess more of the "inner stability" and "external openness" needed to forge and maintain coalitions than do challengers.

17. As propounded in A. F. K. Organski and Jacek Kugler, *The War Ledger* (Chicago: University of Chicago Press, 1980).

18. See Modelski, *Long Cycles in World Politics*; William R. Thompson, *On Global War* (Columbia, SC: University of South Carolina Press, 1988); and Jack S. Levy, "Theories of General War," *World Politics,* vol. 37: 344–374, which provides an excellent overview of the scholarly endeavor to catalogue the cases of global war.

19. An explanation of the initiator acting as creator of opposing coalitions would be a very substantial modification to balance of power theory. It might also facilitate the solving of some of the great puzzles posed about the eventual opposing "line-ups" which emerge in global wars. A. J. P. Taylor, *The Origins of the Second World War* (New York: Atheneum, 1961), p. 278, closes with this tantalizing observation about coalition creation: "The British people resolved to defy Hitler, though they lacked the strength to undo his work. He himself came to their aid. . . . He gratuitously destroyed the source of his success. In 1941 he attacked Soviet Russia and declared war on the United States, two World Powers who asked only to be left alone."

20. Existing tests vary widely in their composition, from Waltz's informal analysis of the balance of power notion in *Theory of International Politics* to Modelski and Thompson's highly structured examination of naval strength as an indicator of long cycles in *Seapower in Global Politics, 1494-1993*. Kennedy, in *The Rise and Fall of the Great Powers,* uses comprehensive economic and military data in his effort to delineate

transitional phases. He also tests for the importance of "strength," using these same measures, in the winning of wars.

21. See Modelski and Thompson, *Seapower in Global Politics, 1494–1993,* pp. 151–185.

22. R. B. Mowat, *A History of European Diplomacy* (London: Edward Arnold, 1928); Ludwig Dehio, *The Precarious Balance* (New York: Alfred A. Knopf, 1961); and Arnold Toynbee, *A Study of History* (London: Oxford University Press, 1954), Vol. 9, pp. 234–260.

23. Ludwig Dehio, *The Precarious Balance,* pp. 36–40, found the triumph of Venice amazing, given the odds, in terms of simple manpower, of some 15 to 1. John Julius Norwich, *A History of Venice* (New York: Alfred A. Knopf, 1982), pp. 395–430, provides a more extended and insightful explanation of Venice's ability to withstand the lethal embrace of the Cambrian League.

24. Andrew C. Hess, "The Evolution of the Ottoman Seaborne Empire in the Age of the Oceanic Discoveries," *American Historical Review,* vol. 75 (1970):1892–1919, argues that, not only did the Portuguese fail to defeat the Ottomans, but Muslim naval power grew during this period, providing security and commercial stability for this part of their empire.

25. Toynbee, *A Study of History,* Vol. 9, pp. 234–260, provides this analysis.

26. See William L. Rodgers, *Naval Warfare Under Oars* (Annapolis: Naval Institute Press, [1940] 1967), pp. 143–240, for a comprehensive analysis of Venice's strength and major contribution to the Christian fleet.

27. Eckstein, "Case Study and Theory in Political Science," pp. 113–123.

28. Dehio, *The Precarious Balance,* pp. 28–42, reflects the following population figures: Holy Roman Empire, 9,000,000; Spain, 7,000,000; France, 14,000,000; Venice, 2,000,000. Venice's army was similarly outnumbered at the war's outset, according to Dehio. Its complete destruction in the war's opening campaign gave the attacking coalition an insuperable advantage on land.

29. George Modelski and William R. Thompson, *Seapower in Global Politics, 1494–1993* (Seattle: University of Washington Press, 1988), p. 114.

30. Ibid., p. 62, and pp. 318–320. Similarly, Portugal's 93 warships are credited with comprising roughly two thirds of global naval power at the outset of this war, with the Ottoman Empire having none. Yet, if the Muslim navy of 260 war galleys is counted against the Portuguese fleet, it should be unsurprising that the Empire withstood Portuguese aggression so well.

31. However one wishes to determine the starting point of the war, it is clear that Spain began it. By fair means and foul, Spain had been bullying Britain for decades before the Armada set sail. When a diplomatic marriage failed to bring the British into the Habsburg fold, a policy of maritime harassment was begun. It culminated in the events surrounding Spain's "plea," in 1585, for Britain to sell foodstuffs to its hard-pressed viceroyalties in the New World (the crisis had been precipitated by a drought in Spain). Britain responded wholeheartedly. When the relief fleet arrived, its goods were accepted. However, the only recompense the British received was the confiscation of their ships and the imprisonment of their crews. Drake's raid was a response to this act, signalling Britain's continued defiance. Philip's declaration of war was soon followed by the gathering of the Armada. Garrett Mattingly, *The Armada* (Boston: Houghton Mifflin, 1959), provides a comprehensive discussion of these events.

32. A recent study of these events is provided in Peter Padfield, *Armada* (Annapolis: Naval Institute Press, 1988). Alexander McKee, *From Merciless Invaders: An Eyewit-*

ness Account of the Armada (New York: W.W. Norton, 1963), has compiled much of the original diplomatic and military correspondence from both sides into a compelling narrative.

33. Which, by the mid-sixteenth century, included the enormous wealth of the conquered Aztec and Incan empires, portions of which were shipped in annual *flotas*.

34. Kennedy, *The Rise and Fall of the Great Powers*, p. 43, cites the many holdings of Spain (including dominion over one-fourth of Europe's total population, as well as over the vast majority of the New World, and near-monopolistic control of gold and silver production). Spain was "blessed with riches." Kennedy also (pp. 44–55) chronicles the costs of Spain's wars with France and against the Ottoman Empire, contending that Spain's protection of Western Europe from Islam was at the root of its imperial "overstretch," in that other European nations were able to "free ride" on Spain's efforts.

35. Modelski and Thompson, *Seapower in Global Politics, 1494–1993*, p. 116.

36. See Mattingly, *The Armada*, p. 424, for a discussion of Spanish naval strength.

37. See Padfield, *Armada*, pp. 62–65, for a discussion of this matter which includes a reckoning that, in heavier (12lb. and up) naval guns, the British advantage was 385:267.

38. Cromwell's General-at-Sea, Monck, gave this laconic assessment of the situation: "The Dutch have too much trade and the English are resolved to take it from them." Cited in Paul Kennedy, *The Rise and Fall of British Naval Mastery* (London: The Ashfield Press, 1976), p. 48.

39. Though the spark that set the war off was Monck's decision to fire upon Dutch Admiral Tromp for failing to "dip" his colors in salute, the incident was clearly an excuse for aggression. Kennedy, *The Rise and Fall of British Naval Mastery*, p. 48, points out that the British were spoiling for a fight, being "deeply jealous of the Dutch superiority in the fields of shipping, Oriental trade, control of Baltic commerce, fisheries, and general credit and finance. . . . "

Charles Boxer, *The Anglo-Dutch Wars of the 17th Century* (London: H.M. Stationery Office, 1974), a most comprehensive study of these conflicts, strongly confirms the above assessment of the wars' origins.

40. Prince Michael of Greece, *Louis XIV: The Other Side of the Sun* (New York: Harper & Row, 1983), pays considerable attention throughout to Louis' propensity for gaining new opponents by virtue of having attacked them. Olivier Bernier, *Louis XIV: A Royal Life* (New York: Doubleday, 1987), is also in agreement on this point.

41. Gilpin, *War and Change in World Politics*, p. 191, sees preventive war as the "most attractive option" for an incumbent hegemon faced by the rise of a challenger.

42. D.W. Jones, *War and Economy in the Age of William III* (New York: Basil Blackwell, 1988), chronicles the material balance against France, contending that it was the determining factor in Louis's defeat.

43. See Quincy Wright, *A Study of War*, Vol. I (Chicago: University of Chicago Press, 1951 ed.), pp. 658–660.

44. Both Levy, "Theories of General War," and Mowat, *A History of European Diplomacy*, view this as a global war. Kennedy, *The Rise and Fall of British Naval Mastery*, p. 98, contends that "the Seven Years War can lay a far stronger claim to the title of the first *world* war than many others before or since, because sustained and significant fighting took place in three continents and because the two chief combatants attached a great deal of significance to their colonial campaigns."

45. Kennedy, *The Rise and Fall of British Naval Mastery,* p. 97, calls this British triumph "the most decisive victory in her history as a nation-state."

46. Kennedy, *The Rise and Fall of the Great Powers,* p. 121, points out that, during the American Revolutionary War, France's military spending exceeded the expenditures in its three previous wars combined. This placed an intolerable strain on the "old regime," which it was unable to alleviate.

47. Richard Smoke, *War: Controlling Escalation* (Cambridge: Harvard University Press, 1977), provides an excellent narrative of the onset of this war. H. Butterfield, *The Reconstruction of an Historical Episode: The History of the Enquiry into the Origins of the Seven Years' War* (Glasgow: Jackson, Son, & Co., 1951), is the most comprehensive analysis of the various efforts made to understand why this war began. Patrice Louis-Rene Higonnet, "The Origins of the Seven Years' War," *Journal of Modern History,* vol. 40 (1968):57-90 is another important analytic effort. All confirm the great difficulty that exists in trying to pinpoint the initiator of this war.

48. Self-interest in expansion is a theme that surfaces throughout Karl W. Schweizer, *England, Prussia, and the Seven Years' War* (Lewiston: E. Mellen Press, 1989). Patrick F. Doran, *Andrew Mitchell and Anglo-Prussian Diplomatic Relations During the Seven Years' War* (New York: Garland Books, 1986), offers additional insights, particularly into the British abandonment of Prussia after the former's conquest of Quebec had been completed.

49. See Kennedy, *The Rise and Fall of the Great Powers,* p. 99. Also, B.R. Mitchell, *European Historical Statistics, 1750-1970* (New York: Columbia University Press, 1976).

50. See Modelski and Thompson, *Seapower in Global Politics, 1494-1993,* pp. 69-70. Later in this study, a means for adjusting Modelski and Thompson's "raw" figures, based on the concentration capability of each nation's fleet, will be developed. This will modify the ratios developed from the gross numbers somewhat.

51. Kennedy, *The Rise and Fall of the Great Powers,* p. 149.

52. It has to be noted, though, that Russia's illicit trade brought Napoleon's wrath down upon it. Will and Ariel Durant, *The Story of Civilization,* Vol. XI, *The Age of Napoleon* (New York: Simon and Schuster, 1975), p. 693, puts it succinctly: "The direct cause of the Franco-Russian war of 1812 was Russia's refusal to continue the Continental blockade declared by Napoleon's Berlin decree of November 21, 1806." Whatever Russia's sympathies, it complied with the Decree for several years, and only allied with Britain after having been invaded.

53. Michael Howard, *The Causes of Wars* (London: Temple Smith, 1983), p. 15.

54. Sources: Wright, *A Study of War,* pp. 656-658; and Kennedy, *The Rise and Fall of the Great Powers,* p. 99.

55. Kennedy, *The Rise and Fall of the Great Powers,* p. 149. As a reference point, it should be noted that Europe as a whole controlled just over a quarter of world economic output in 1800.

56. Modelski and Thompson, *Seapower in Global Politics, 1494-1993,* pp. 70-71, list the gross numbers, but do not make allowances for ship and crew quality, or fleet concentration capability. These latter issues are discussed in this study's following chapters, with specific comments on the French navy of the Napoleonic period made in Chapter 5.

57. See Robert Jervis, "Cooperation Under the Security Dilemma," *World Politics,* vol. 30 (1978):167-214 for an analysis of this phenomenon.

58. As to the British, there was little doubt about which side they would take *if* they entered the war. With regard to the global "cast" which British entry gave the war, Brian Bond, in *War and Society in Europe, 1870–1970* (Leicester: Leicester University Press, 1984), p. 95, has noted: "Germany did not plan for a general war in August 1914 but she welcomed it when the opportunity occurred."

59. Paul Kennedy, "The First World War and the International System," provides a detailed analysis of the economic disadvantages of the German-led coalition.

60. Williamson Murray, *The Change in the European Balance of Power, 1938–1939: The Path to Ruin* (Princeton: Princeton University Press, 1984), p. 326, puts the issue succinctly: "When he embarked on his Polish adventure, Hitler apparently believed it unlikely that the West would intervene. Should they do so, the fuhrer was not particularly concerned."

61. See Gerhard L. Weinberg, "Germany's Declaration of War on the United States: A New Look," in Weinberg, *World in the Balance: Behind the Scenes of World War II* (Hanover, NH: University Press of New England, 1981), pp. 75–95.

62. *The Times Atlas of the Second World War,* John Keegan, ed. (New York: Harper and Row, 1989), pp. 98–99, provides precise listings of the massive amounts of tanks, planes, and artillery that were sent to British and Soviet forces. Despite its late entry into the war, U.S. tank production totalled over 85,000, the majority of which were sent, in 1942–1943, to British and Soviet forces. Total German war production, 1939–1945, reached only 66,000 tanks.

63. See Kennedy, *The Rise and Fall of the Great Powers,* pp. 149, 258.

64. Paul Kennedy, *The Rise of the Anglo-German Antagonism, 1860–1914* (London: George Allen & Unwin, 1980), chronicles the many causes of these rising tensions, focusing in particular on Germany's ever more aggressive foreign policies and naval building program.

65. Waltz, *Theory of International Politics,* pp. 166–167.

66. See the discussion, earlier in this chapter, of the "prospective" aspect of the theory of balancing, against either "power" or "threat."

67. The overall odds were thus in excess of 3:1. Manpower data source: G. Barraclough, ed., *The Times Atlas of World History* (London: The Times, 1978), p. 252.

68. See Kennedy, *The Rise and Fall of the Great Powers,* p. 201. The index figures are relative rather than absolute, making them ideal for comparing the productive capabilities of the contending sides.

69. Ibid., p. 332. These are necessarily rough figures, but they give some idea of the relative powers of the combatants.

70. Ibid., p. 332.

71. Ibid., p. 354.

72. Modelski and Thompson, *Seapower in Global Politics, 1494–1993,* p. 78.

Chapter 3

Modifications to Existing Theories

Who commands the sea commands all. —Themistocles

In this chapter, the previously considered structural approaches to explaining the onset and outcome of interstate war will be modified by introducing and developing a new insight into its character. War will be described as having a dual nature, with given conflicts categorized as either "land" or "land–sea." Each will be hypothesized to have a distinctive causal path to victory. Once the key variables that lead to victory are clearly delineated, they will be employed in an effort to improve the explanation of those decisions to initiate war that have gone awry. Hypotheses will be developed that focus, at both the structural and decision-making levels-of-analysis, on the systematic failure of continental powers successfully to pursue their aims when opposed by a sea power. The proposed explanation for these "loser" war initiations will consider the possibility that the leaders of continental powers, and their advisors, simply did not understand what was needed to win a land–sea war. Also, the potential for organizational and bureaucratic pathologies to contribute to poor decisional outputs will be analyzed, as will their interaction with the chief political executive's imperfect understanding of maritime affairs.

The means by which the hypotheses generated should be tested will be developed as a two-step process. First, in order to demonstrate that there *are* divergent paths to victory in the differing types of war, statistical study of interstate wars of both kinds will be formulated.[1] If this testing achieves positive results, it will then be possible to move on to detailed analyses of a few of those decisions to begin wars that ended in defeat. The key point is that the detailed studies will be focused by the variables identified as significant in this "modifying" chapter.

ON THE DUALITY OF WAR

In the introduction to this study, a suggested typology of wars has been delineated and organized as a matrix. Along the vertical axis, wars are categorized, quite traditionally, according to their aims and intensity, in five types varying from "global" to "minor" (see Table 1.1). The horizontal axis, however, argues for only a division between land and land–sea wars. This distinction is based quite simply on the geographic scope of conflict. "Land" wars, unsurprisingly, are those fought almost entirely absent naval operations, save for those of an incidental nature. Bismarck's wars of unification, the Franco-Prussian War (1870–1871), the Chaco War (1932–1935) between Bolivia and Paraguay, and the various Arab-Israeli wars provide good examples of land wars. "Land–sea" wars, on the other hand, are composed of a mix of land and naval operations. Global wars, by definition, must be land–sea wars, as 70% of the world is covered by seas that separate most of the continents. Virtually all Great Power wars are also of this type.

Throughout history, there have been a multitude of efforts to differentiate wars vertically. There has been little or no attempt at "horizontal differentiation." The closest that one can come in earlier works is Hans Delbruck's formulation about duality. His contention was that wars are either of "annihilation" or of "attrition." The former are characterized by furious offensives designed to achieve swift victory, with the wars of Napoleon being arch-typical. The latter consist of a gradual "wearing down" of one side relative to the other, apotheosized in the strategy employed by Pericles during the early phase of the Peloponnesian War. But these are, rather than fundamental varieties of war itself, alternate strategies to be employed, when appropriate, in pursuit of victory. According to Delbruck, it is those waging the war who impose their wills on its course. Geographic scope does not alter the very nature of the war being fought.[2]

Clausewitz offers little assistance with regard to typologies of war. Careful reading of his treatise suggests that he would likely oppose the creation of a typology. For him, each war is composed of a multitude of unique facets, cloaked in myriad guises. War is, inherently, a "chameleon." Its practitioners are enjoined by Clausewitz to develop their abilities to engage in "critical analysis," a discipline that will foster clear thinking and decisiveness amid the inevitable "fog of war."[3] This study counters with the notion that, if war is a chameleon, it is limited to two basic "tints"; and that the analytic and decisional inputs needed to direct successful efforts in the two kinds of war are likely to differ.

The only reference to war's duality that, however implicitly, actually deals with the land–sea dichotomy, comes from King Archidamus of Sparta. Thucydides reports him as urging caution on the part of the ephorate, and credits him with a speech that outlines the basic issue which would determine the outcome of a war with Athens. His key question is whether or not the benefit of superior Spartan strength on land could outweigh the advantages brought to the Athenians because of their command of the sea. He expresses a clear understanding that

Sparta, the preeminent continental power, was contemplating entry into a land–sea war against a dominant sea power, and that this factor had to be added to the Spartan decision-making calculus. Victory could not be won simply by the marching and skillful fighting of Spartan hoplites, and Archidamus knew it.[4]

In more recent times, the British geographer Halford Mackinder showed a remarkable sensitivity to the enduring struggle between land and sea powers that has characterized Western history, from the thalassocracy of Athens to the Pax Britannica. While he refrained from delineating a theory of war based on this observation, his work provides a solid intellectual foundation from which hypotheses regarding war's duality may be deduced.[5] Mahan, the great American apostle of sea power, was developing his theories of maritime predominance at roughly the same time that Mackinder's "heartland" theory was being expounded. While Mahan was also aware of the continental versus sea power theme of history, he explicitly eschewed any effort to dichotomize war. Indeed, he went to the opposite extreme. Where Clausewitz and Jomini do not even consider the maritime aspects of warfare, Mahan, a self-professed disciple of Jomini, urged that the best understanding of war could be achieved if one simply thought of the oceans and seas as deserts upon which navies comprised a force capable of moving with some rapidity.[6]

Even though there has been an almost universal lack of recognition of the dual nature of war, which arises from the separation of the earth into land and sea, there has always been a lively interest in and awareness of the importance of those attributes required to succeed, separately, in war on land and at sea. Generalship on land has received a far greater degree of attention,[7] but predominance at sea has also been appreciated. From the formulation of Themistocles that "who commands the sea commands all," to Bacon's sixteenth-century essay that very nearly equates national greatness with sea power,[8] there has been a keen awareness of the importance of maritime preeminence. Mahan was quite convinced of the importance of sea power, so much so that his latter-day critics have suggested that he went a bit too far, "exalting" rather than just explaining its influence.[9]

While Mahan is considered the foremost apostle of sea power, it is interesting to observe that he links naval strength to the winning of wars in a very limited way. Despite the inspiration he drew from pondering the countermaneuver aspects of naval supremacy so evident in the Second Punic War, Mahan's historical study of the "age of fighting sail" concentrates almost exclusively on fleet tactics and economic warfare. In the latter case, he falls in neatly with the "strength" theory of victory, arguing that sea power allows the accumulation of greater resources for attritional fighting. Consequently, his monumental study of the naval aspects of the Napoleonic wars[10] spends hundreds of pages describing the economic effects of the British blockade, but just a few paragraphs on the Peninsular Campaign. Because of this emphasis, the ability to draw hypotheses from Mahan's work, regarding the impact of sea power upon victory in land–sea war, should be viewed as somewhat limited. The preceding chapter of this study has suggested that material superiority is not the overarching cause of victory in war. Therefore, it is crucial to delineate the many ways in which command of the sea influences war outcomes.

Based on the notions developed by those who have thought, in an operational way, about war on land, war at sea, and the interaction of land and naval forces, it should be possible to deduce hypothesized causal paths to victory in the two kinds of war. Once testable hypotheses have been generated regarding the paths to victory and defeat, they may be utilized to structure the effort to understand why those who lose so often start wars. This latter endeavor will require the employment of individual and group levels-of-analysis. However, it is the structural insight into war's duality that will serve to focus the investigation of the decision-making process. With this in mind, an additional set of testable hypotheses regarding decisions to go to war will also have to be generated.

ON THE CAUSAL PATHS TO VICTORY

Land Wars

The best way to reflect upon how land wars are won and lost is to sort the vast literature on war and strategy into two major categories: those that favor "skill" and those that argue the case for "strength" as leading to victory. The former includes all approaches that enshrine generalship and troop quality as the crucial factors in war; the latter pertains to those that see victory as going to the "big battalions." Which is right? In the matter of land war, this study suggests that, in a certain sense, both are.

The key to this particular puzzle may be found in Clausewitz's reflections on the Battle of Borodino. He notes that, when the proficiency of troops is equivalent, their numbers will determine the outcome of the struggle.[11] The important point is that the relationship between skill and strength is interactive. A side whose forces are much more effective than their foes may well defeat superior numbers. The greater their relative skill, the greater the unfavorable odds at which they may fight with some reasonable chance for success. A good example of triumph against heavy numerical odds is provided by the 1948 Israeli War for Independence, where the Arab foes of nascent Israel outnumbered it, just in terms of population, by some 33:1,[12] and still lost the war. That there are limits to what even the most effective troops can achieve is evident when one considers the failure of Finland to overcome odds of more than 58:1 in the Winter war of 1940 against Stalin's recently purged Red Army.[13] It is also true, though, that as skill levels near, the importance of the numerical balance should grow.

The relationship between skill's and strength's impacts on victory is not simply arithmetic or linear. Troops who are twice as effective as their foes may actually be able to prevail in a war against numerical odds well in excess of two to one. While this notion may be consistent with the classical formulations about victory catalogued by Alger, it runs directly counter to formal models of attrition in war. F. W. Lanchester's famous "squared" equation posits instead that, though the interaction of skill and strength does occur, greater numbers matter far more than combat effectiveness.[14] Even sophisticated modern alternatives to Lanchester theory eschew any attempt to emphasize the primacy of skill.[15]

This study hypothesizes the general supremacy of skill over strength in land wars. It will provide, for the first time, a quantifiable argument in favor of those whose efforts represent the "quality-over-quantity" approach to understanding war, which Alger has so well compiled, over and against the findings of the operations analysts who emphasize strength. It will also be argued that, in theory, there exists some degree of superior effectiveness that virtually overrides numerical or strength considerations.

The key hypotheses regarding victory in land war that this study develops, suggest, in line with Clausewitz's comments about the Battle of Borodino, that skill will generally outweigh strength, though strength does grow in importance as skill levels near. A well-led army of superior troops ought simply to be able to achieve its objectives through some combination of maneuver and attrition at favorable exchange rates. Its objectives are always reachable by these means, at least in land wars. This notion is completely consistent with the "skill" school of thinking about war, which, as Alger notes, has virtually dominated the intellectual "quest for victory."[16]

If this hypothesis is true, then it should not be surprising that a significant number of initiators of land wars lose. While gauges of strength in land war are relatively well known in the pre-war period, the combat effectiveness of the relevant forces, and the skill of their leadership are imponderables. How many political leaders, contemplating starting a war, are likely to be told by their military commanders that their forces are not adequate to achieve their goals? One line of argument has suggested that *all* militaries tend to overstate their capabilities.[17] If this is true, then the frequency of loser initiations should come as little surprise.

This theorizing about the primacy of skill purports to "solve" at least the land war part of the puzzle of loser war initiation, and will be thoroughly tested in the following chapter. Therefore, the remainder of this study, including the detailed cases, will focus primarily on the onset and outcome of land–sea wars, upon which the skill-strength interaction will be hypothesized to have little impact. The implications of the "imponderability" of military skill measurement *prior* to a war's outbreak will be considered in the concluding chapter of this study.

Land–Sea Wars

Should the causal path to victory in land–sea wars be the same as in land wars? Logically, the answer must be a conditional no, for several reasons. First, the nature of command of the sea creates a strategic environment that upsets all conventional notions of how victory is pursued. Superior numbers or strength may mean very little if they cannot be applied against a foe who controls movement over the sea. Conquerors such as Napoleon and Hitler, commanding the finest armies of their eras, could only gaze out across the Channel at Britain, their finely honed tools of force useless.

Another reason that sea control upsets the traditional calculus of victory in war is that it subjects both superior numbers and quality of troops to a "force divisor" effect. While a land power may not invade, it is subject to invasion. Therefore, its armies must be dispersed to protect whatever points may be vulnerable to amphibious assault. Superior numbers and combat effectiveness are degraded by the need for defensive strategic dispersion of forces. This need to "spread out" violates the cardinal principle of concentration, and allows a numerically inferior sea power to mass against locally weaker forces, and to fight successfully against better troops whose maneuver capabilities have been restricted by the need for static defense. The strategic dilemma of the Napoleonic Empire, with its long, exposed coasts, provides a good example of these problems. Indeed, Napoleon himself put it best when he noted: "With 30,000 men in transports in the Downs, the English can paralyze 300,000 of my army, and that will reduce us to the rank of a second-class Power!"[18] Spain, due to its peninsular nature, made French forces deployed there particularly susceptible to the "divisor" effect of sea power. Thus, a French occupation army that reached, at one point, 370,000[19] found itself engaged and ultimately beaten in detail by a British expeditionary force of roughly one tenth its size.[20]

Yet another effect of sea power is its ability to concentrate massive fire support at points of invasion, which are selected by the invader, maximizing the effects of concentration and surprise on dispersed, statically placed defenders. Where the defender is subjected to a "divisor effect," the forces of the sea power benefit also from a "force multiplier" due to the added firepower, mobility, and surprise factors that accrue to those in possession of command of the sea. The best examples of these effects are provided by the many Allied amphibious campaigns of World War II. The ability of six infantry and three airborne divisions to effect a lodgement in a France occupied by some 60 German divisions in the D-Day campaign was very much the product of the abovementioned multiplier-divisor factor. When the German forces in Norway, some 12 divisions, and the Balkans (more than 10) are included, this important effect of sea power grows even clearer.

Some final aspects of sea command are related, broadly, to communications. The first is that the side in control of the sea retains access to its distant trade connections, while at the same time severing those of its continental foe. Economic blockade is a major tool of sea power, slowly draining the strength of the land power. A compelling example of economic blockade is the British naval cordon that did such grievous harm to the German war effort during World War I. The other aspect of blockade, more directly military, is that supplies and communications with distant outposts may be cut by sea power. Then, even inferior forces may be concentrated to effect the conquests, one by one, of these outposts. The long British wars with Spain and France provide innumerable examples of how, as Bernard Brodie put it, "England, always a small country with weak armies, gained at the expense of the great military powers opposing her an empire containing some of the most desirable regions of the earth."[21] The French losses in North America and India during the Seven Years' War are prime examples of this principle at work. Even Napoleon fell prey to this when his Egyptian expedition was cut off and forced, after his solitary escape, to capitulate.[22] The more modern examples of the island-hopping campaigns in the World War II Pacific theater provide equally good examples of the disruption of supply lines, followed by concentration against isolated outposts.

To summarize, in land–sea wars, command of the sea should logically be considered the necessary condition for the achievement of victory. This is not to say that the sea power's land forces may be infinitely small in numbers or of excessively poor quality. But it does mean that neither numerical nor qualitative superiority is needed to defeat a continental foe. The key points regarding command of the sea are that it:

1. acts as a divisor of the land power's forces;
2. multiplies the sea power's forces;
3. controls distant economic resources and military communications;
4. enhances effectiveness via surprise and concentration; and
5. grants freedom from invasion while threatening to invade.

When the above factors are taken into consideration, a reexamination of the global wars delineated in Chapter 2 (see Table 2.2) brings out the point that the winning side has always had at least equal (in the Armada case) or greater naval strength (in all the other cases), as adjusted for fleet concentration capability. Where theories of balancing, transitioning, skill, strength, and even luck fail, a simple test of the naval balance works. Table 3.1 reflects the proportion of systemic sea power assets in the possession of both the challengers to and defenders of the *status quo*.

The foregoing analyis of sea power suggests theoretical reasons why land powers ought to be losing wars against sea powers, and points out that this indeed is what is happening. This is a correlative observation that will be subjected to more rigorous testing over a given universe of cases in the next chapter. While this theorizing may explain why war initiators lose, there is limited insight that may be derived at the systemic level-of-analysis to explain why land powers *start* these wars. It might be argued that the respective natures of land and sea power differ so greatly that it is impossible to say, *ante bellum*, which side will come out the victor. However, the axiomatic understanding of the superiority of sea power, which is so evident from the dawn of recorded history,[23] argues against this notion.

Table 3.1
Proportional Sea Power in Global Wars

| War | Naval strength | | | | Initiator-defender Ratio | |
| | Initiator | | Defender | | | |
	Raw	Adjusted	Raw	Adjusted	Raw	Adjusted
Italian	Spain, France		Venice			
	.19	.095	.49	.49	.39:1	.19:1
Armada	Spain		Britain			
	.46	.23	.23	.23	2:1	1:1
Anglo-Dutch*	Britain		Holland			
	.41	.41	.41	.205	1:1	2:1
Louis XIV	France		Britain			
	.362	.181	.567	.189	.64:1	.96:1
7 Years'/	France		Britain			
American	.24	.12	.419	.14	.66:1	.86:1
Napoleon	France		Coalitions			
	.219	.11	.332	.166	.66:1	.66:1
World War I	Central Powers		Allies			
	.256	.256	.554	.266	.46:1	.96:1
World War II	Axis		Allies			
	.093	.093	.389	.194	.24:1	.48:1

*Only global war won by the initiator.
Source for raw data: Modelski and Thompson, *Seapower in Global Politics.* Adjusted figures are based on geostrategic constraints requiring the frequent division or impairing the theater movement of the naval forces of a given war participant (coding choices are discussed in detail in Chapter 4). Divisors used are:

Spain, 2	England, 1 (until after the Anglo-Dutch Wars)
Holland, 2	3 (through the Napoleonic Wars)
Russia, 3	2 (thereafter)
France, 2	Germany, 1

An alternative explanation is that the leaders of land powers have an *imperfect* understanding of the manner in which sea power functions. While they may accept the need to provide a credible naval challenge, their thinking regarding the winning of wars may be mired in "land" strategy. Their views of the potential foe's combat effectiveness and numbers of land forces may dominate, rather than concerns about economic blockade, or the more invidious aspects of the divisor effect. If this hypothesis is true, one should expect to find that land powers do start wars, and even expand them, given that their decision-making calculus discounts, to some extent, the war-winning advantage held by the sea power. The irony of the situation is that, with each successful land conquest, the continental power grows ever more vulnerable to the effects of sea power, as it adds an increasing number of countries that it has attacked to the opposition. Napoleon and Hitler provide excellent examples of this phenomenon, creating large opposing coalitions by their aggressions, and becoming increasingly susceptible to sea power as their continental domains expanded. They followed logical land war strategies. Unfortunately, for them, they were fighting land–sea wars.

The foregoing hypothesis provides the foundation for a new understanding of the balance of power. Where the previous chapter's analysis of global wars found only weak evidence that states flock together to resist the aggression of the strong, *de facto* balances were observed despite the absence of balancing behavior. Perhaps a clearer understanding of international relations may be developed by thinking of balances as direct creations of the aggressor. In particular, land powers will keep expanding, based on their assessment of chances for victory in land wars, with their various opponents united by virtue of having been attacked. That they ultimately fail is due to their inability to achieve command of the sea, a realm that is hardly the province of balance. Indeed, traditional notions of the balance of power should be revised to reflect its limitation to "land power." Where Britain has, from time to time, acted to preserve this latter form of balance, it has always vigorously pursued an "imbalance of power" at sea.[24] The fact of British naval mastery vitiates classical balance of power theory, for, as the Duc de Choiseul sagely observed, there is neither balancing behavior nor balance at sea.

There is some empirical evidence that suggests that land powers are not adequately assessing the consequences of fighting with sea powers. In Huth and Russett's statistical-correlational studies of extended deterrence, it has been found that deterrence failures are often related to the local balance of forces rather than the overall assessments of relative capabilities.[25] If one looks carefully at the 54 cases from 1900–1984, which form the core of their argument, it becomes apparent that either the United States or Britain is making the deterrent effort nearly half of the time. Not only does this create a statistical bias that might cloud an effort to generalize about deterrence, but it also suggests very strongly that aggressors may be unmoved by the latent threats characteristic of sea power.[26]

This insight regarding land powers' diminished capacities for appreciating the strength of sea power may also be used to focus investigations at the organizational and bureaucratic political levels-of-analysis. Only here will conclusive answers to the puzzle of why "losers" initiate be found. Key questions will be raised about what counsel leaders of land powers receive from their naval advisors who, presumably, have an enhanced understanding of and sensitivity to maritime affairs. The problems that the navies of land powers, as "junior" services, have in coping with dominant army factions must also be considered. Finally, hypotheses regarding organizational influences on the formation of naval doctrine will need to be developed.

INDIVIDUALS, ORGANIZATIONS,
AND BUREAUCRATIC POLITICS

How does the decision-making process of a land power operate? Why does its policy output ever include the initiation of a "losing" war against a sea power? To answer this question, it will be necessary to identify correctly the key sets of policymaking actors, and the manner in which they interrelate. Specifically, the political chief executive and the relevant organizations must be examined, as well as their bureaucratic interactions. Existing theories of the behavior of these actors, and of their interplay in peace, crisis and war, will be reexamined in this effort to discern how they might reach the point of agreeing upon the initiation of a losing war.

The Executive

Theoretical explanations of the key decision-maker's thought processes encompass a wide spectrum of analysis. On the one side, there are those who hold that the executive will behave in a "purely" rational manner. Relevant facts will be correctly analyzed, and the appropriate amount of time will always be spent to arrive at the objectively "best" solution to a given problem.[27] A modification of the notion of pure rationality suggests that, instead, exigencies may constrain the amount of time that the executive may have, or the costs that he may expend in pursuit of the best answer to a given problem. This notion of "bounded" rationality holds that pure, "classical rationality is an idealization."[28] Finally, another school of thought argues that various forms of psychological and cognitive pathologies vitiate a decision-maker's ability to perform in either a pure or boundedly rational manner.[29] This last notion suggests that the executive may evaluate inputs on the basis of what he either "wants" (motivated bias) or "expects" (cognitive bias) to see.[30]

For purposes of explaining the decisions of continental powers to start "losing" wars, this study agrees with Keohane's view of pure rationality as an "idealization." It is assumed, therefore, that political chief executives are "boundedly" rational, subject to constraints imposed by time and cost. While Jervis's various formulations regarding cognition are not explicitly adopted, this study introduces the notion that the leader of the land power has an "imperfect" understanding of the impact of sea power on wars which have significant maritime aspects. This assumption is consistent with Jervis's findings regarding learning, which contend that "the chance of misperception is increased by events that one actor experiences but that others with whom he interacts know of only indirectly."[31] Thus, the chief executives of land and sea powers have, respectively, indirect and direct experiences of naval mastery, conditions ripe for misperception.

Another factor, which might add to the likelihood that the land power's chief executive will have an imperfect understanding of maritime matters, is that the facets of sea power tend to vary in importance and effectiveness over time. This may create a situation in which the continental leader mis-rates a particular aspect of sea power. For example, amphibious operations may not work well in the major conflict of one era (such as at Gallipoli in World War I), but become quite potent in the next (invasions from the sea were a vital part of Allied success both in Europe and the Pacific during World War II). Therefore, in the detailed case studies, which are developed in Chapter 5, this phenomenon will be considered and searched for as a possible source of misperception.

Military Organizations

While organizational theory was introduced, in a scientific way, nearly half a century ago,[32] it is only more recently that intensive efforts have been made to relate it to militaries. Specifically, organizational theory has been used to demonstrate that militaries will be reluctant to change weapons systems or doctrines, and that their planning processes will be rigid, as well as heavily inclined toward the offensive. Much of the work done in this area has employed case studies of the armies of the various European powers as they tottered on the brink of war in 1914.[33] Another important study looked at organizational influences upon the doctrines of air forces as well as armies, and moved beyond World War I to examine the interwar period (1920–1940) in France, Britain, and Germany.[34]

All of these studies agree that militaries, if left to their own devices, will tend to develop offensive doctrines. Such doctrines require larger forces than do defensive ones, hence larger military budgets are necessary. They allow military commanders greater autonomy "in the field," as offensive fighting is more likely to take place outside the homeland, further away from prying civilian political intervention. Finally, offensive doctrines are held to provide a certain intellectual and emotional satisfaction for the professional soldier. The possession of clear plans for achieving victory by seizing the military initiative is far more attractive, it is theorized, than the adoption of reactive, static defensive plans, which are inherently more related to the simple avoidance of defeat.

In addition to theorizing about the organizational pathologies of professional militaries, Posen's important work hypothesizes that there are limits to the scope of organizational influence. His study of France, Britain, and Germany during the interwar years develops the finding that, while militaries have relatively free doctrinal reign during peacetime, as crisis and war near, civilian intervention will overcome organizational impedimenta.[35] In this way, organizational rigidity is lessened, reducing the tendency of military doctrine, when largely determined by organizational influences, to be weakly integrated with the foreign policy of the state that it serves.

Curiously, none of these studies of military organizational behavior deals directly with naval affairs. Are navies doctrinally rigid? Will they generally tend toward offensive doctrines? Will naval leaders be overcome by civilian intervention in doctrinal matters in crisis and war? For the purposes of this study, these are the questions that must be answered. It cannot simply be assumed that the findings of recent works on armies and air forces are applicable to navies. Therefore, it is necessary to return for guidance to the original, and some later, general studies of organizations.

At best, it seems, the portrayal of military organizations as averse to change is only a partially accurate depiction. Certainly, routines and standard operating procedures are prevalent in all organizations, not least in those of a military nature. But a richer understanding of the nature of organizations, and the individuals of whom they are composed, should suggest that change, even of a sudden sort, is predictable. The foundation of an organization's ability to change is described succinctly by Herbert Simon: "The individual who is loyal to an organization will support opportunistic changes in its objectives that are calculated to promote its survival and growth."[36] In other words, if it is good *for the organization*, change will be supported. Can change, even if supported, be effected by organizations? Another classic work, that of Cyert and March, develops the theory that both successful and unsuccessful organizations have great capability for change. The former have "slack" resources, created by previous successes, which are put to work in support of innovation. The latter must innovate, or face extinction.[37]

Why is it, then, that the European armies examined by Snyder and Van Evera failed to innovate in the years leading up to World War I, and the fighting that ensued consisted largely of massed infantry assaults on entrenched defenders employing machine guns from behind barbed wire? The answer is that continued offensive doctrine gave the militaries of these powers the best chance for expansion and autonomous action. There was no reason for immediate change, because the existence of heavy casualties simply pointed up the need for more troops. Indeed, Britain went from voluntarism to conscription for the first time in its history because of these perceived needs. The survival of the militaries was enhanced because of the need for more troops. That they could be trained *en masse*, and put "into the line" relatively quickly pointed up the fact that heavy casualties were not organizationally "life threatening." These European armies may have had the ability, therefore, but not the incentive to change.

If the naval organizations of continental powers, like other military organizations, are considered to be capable of innovation, one must next ask if they have an incentive to change. Here the answer is "yes," if Simon's dictum regarding organizational survival is accepted. Contrary to fighting on land, where replacements are relatively plentiful, and may be supplied in short order, naval vessels take a long time to be replaced. Very simply, the loss of a substantial part of a fleet cannot likely be replaced during a war. This is one reason why naval mastery is either gained or confirmed so often by major single battles (from Actium to Midway).

Thus, the navy of a continental power, smaller than that of the current naval hegemon, should, from an organizational perspective, insure its survival by avoiding the potential for destruction.[38] In terms of organizational theory, then, the navy of a continental power, one of the key objects of examination in this study, should espouse an offensive sea control doctrine during peacetime, shifting to the defensive in war.[39] That these shifts are unanticipated beforehand, by either naval or political leaders, is one of the reasons, this study hypothesizes, for "loser" war initiation. The shift from offense to defense will be abrupt because naval leaders will lobby, in peacetime, for large fleets which will give them the chance to achieve naval mastery. Only when war sets in will they be driven, by their instinct for "organizational survival," to shift to the defensive. The political leader, having no similar behavioral imperative, will be taken completely aback by this development.

It is at this point, in crisis and on the brink of war, that Posen hypothesizes the successful intervention of political authority into the affairs of professional military organizations. Given that military organizations are subordinate to political authority, or at least ought to be, the hypothesized ability of civilians to compel change in the military seems reasonable. Yet, it seems equally reasonable to hypothesize that crisis and war are the very times during which professional military opinions will be carefully assessed, if not always heeded. Graham Allison's classic study of the Cuban Missile Crisis makes this point;[40] and this study of "loser" war initiation assumes that organizational influences do not dissipate with the onset of crisis and war.

Bureaucratic Politics

Having considered the theoretical roles of the executive and the relevant organizational actors in the decision-making process, one must still endeavor to understand the manner in which interaction takes place. The executive will interact with these organizations (among which are the various military services), and they, in turn, interact with each other. The decisional output that is reached will, according to the theory of bureaucratic politics, be some function of these interactions.[41] Though the general findings regarding executive-bureaucratic relations suggest that the executive's options are frequently quite circumscribed,[42] the view that executives may overcome bureaucratic preferences has also been articulated.[43]

In addition to executive-bureaucratic interactions, inter-bureaucratic relations must also be considered. Generally, they are thought to consist of much "pulling and hauling," with the more powerful actor wresting concessions from the weaker. Again, Allison provides the paradigmatic vision of this type of behavior.[44] Krasner's view of the ultimate supremacy of the executive serves again to suggest that, whatever the nature and extent of bureaucratic machinations, their exertions may be quieted at the executive's insistence.

For the purposes of this study's concern with "loser" war initiation, theories of bureaucratic politics are quite useful. They may assist in explaining the behavior of the navies (and armies) of continental powers, both as they prepare for and wage war. The classical notion of bureaucratic "pulling and hauling" is, therefore, explicitly adopted. It will be hypothesized that the armies and navies of continental powers are engaged in a bureaucratic rivalry. However, though they act as theory suggests, this study adopts Krasner's position that the executive retains the ability to overcome bureaucratic preferences. This study diverges, however, from Bueno de Mesquita's idea that bureaucratic influences might matter in peacetime, but are brushed away by the executive in crisis and wartime. Instead, it suggests that the executive, who always has the capability to override, will be more inclined to do so in peacetime, and less so disposed in war.

In summary, it is accepted that bureaucracies "pull and haul," but that, despite their exertions, the executive retains the power to determine the decisional output. Finally, though, the executive is more likely to intervene in peace than in war. This last point runs counter to Posen's thinking regarding civil intervention, and is supported by Allison's "Model III" explanation of the Cuban Missile Crisis.

The implications for the military and foreign policies of continental powers striving for global mastery are significant. The notion of the preeminence of the executive suggests that the bureaucratically more powerful army may not prevail over navy calls for a buildup. Army/navy "pulling and hauling" also guarantees a considerable amount of interservice rivalry, even to the point of discouraging combined operations planning. The executive's imperfect understanding of land–sea war, and his reluctance to sweep aside bureaucratic preferences during war, suggest that he will be relatively insensitive to the failure to engage in combined planning, and will be reluctant to override bureaucratic choices on military doctrine during war.

SUMMARY

Previous efforts to explicate war have classified it, from global conflict to border clash, on the basis of the policy aims of the participants. This study theorizes, additionally, that understanding the dual nature of war affords improved chances for achieving a high level of integration between strategy and policy. War is not Clausewitz's "chameleon," nor are all wars created equal. Those fought only on land differ strikingly from those with significant maritime aspects. But, within the two major kinds of war, the causal paths to victory are the same.

Land wars are hypothesized to be won by superior combat effectiveness, which includes better generalship and troop quality. The interaction between quantitative and qualitative strength, at which Clausewitz hints in his discussion of the Battle of Borodino, does exist, but not in a linear way. Instead, superior skill offers a far more significant advantage to its possessor than do greater numbers. Paraguay's victory in the Chaco War, and Israel's many triumphs against consistently long odds, are good examples of the preeminence of combat effectiveness over quantitative considerations in land war. This notion strongly challenges the approaches of formal theories of combat, which hold that numbers are more important than quality, suggesting that it should be unsurprising that the "loser" of a given land war so often turns out to have started it. The inability to know beforehand which side will achieve greater "skill" in war makes the problem generally intractable. The only subset of land wars that might be prevented would be that which is characterized by the war initiations of those who believe that they can compensate for their known inferior combat effectiveness with quantitative superiority.

By recognizing land–sea wars as the other distinctive type of conflict, it is possible both to overturn conventional notions regarding the interaction of skill and strength, and to explain the all-too-frequent decisions of "losers" to initiate. Command of the sea generates a multiplier-divisor effect that diminishes the land power's strength at the same time that it enhances the maritime power's. The land power cannot invade, though it is subject to invasion. Its forces must be strategically dispersed while its maritime enemy's are concentrated. Its distant bases, communications, and maritime trade are all subject to rapid attrition, and no reciprocal threat may be made. The greater the territory of its conquests, the weaker it becomes. Neither greater strength nor skill can overcome an opponent who commands at sea. The path to victory in land war leads, if blindly followed in land–sea war, to disaster.

According to this theory, continental powers start land–sea wars for two primary reasons. First, key decision makers have an awareness but also an imperfect understanding of the importance of sea control. This alone lessens their inhibitions regarding fighting against a maritime power, especially when the land power's armies are well-led troops of high quality. But there is another powerful impetus toward war that is provided by the assurances given by the naval authorities of land powers, to their leaders, that there is indeed a reasonable chance of wresting sea control from the incumbent. This chance exists because the continental power's navy has, for organizational reasons, exerted pressure for the construction of a battle fleet with which to achieve naval mastery. However, with the onset of war, the same organizational imperatives that led to the creation of a potent naval force during peacetime and an offensive sea control doctrine to accompany it, cause a shift to efforts aimed at protecting the hard-won fleet. A defensive doctrine will suddenly emerge, and the *guerre de course* or the *kleinkrieg* will take the place of the declaratory offensive sea control doctrine. This strategic shift from a doctrine aimed at command of the sea virtually eliminates the continental power's chances for winning a land–sea war.

Interservice rivalry may not have a powerful impact on the war initiation decision-making process, but it will surface in ways inimical to the interests of the state. War plans will fail to coordinate the actions of the land and sea services, and each will fight for precious budgetary resources. The armies of land powers are senior services, to counteract whose influence navies must make ever more sweeping claims of effectiveness. New missions have to be defined, even in peacetime, to put the growing fleet to work. The protection of sea lanes and trade, and the acquisition of colonies are espoused. Foreign policy develops a more global shading, which development cannot help but catch the attention and inspire the concern of the maritime power.

The hypotheses generated in this chapter fall into two categories: those that explain how initiators lose wars, and those which address the puzzle of why "losers" start them in the first place. A summary listing is as follows:

I. On Winning (or Losing) Wars
  Hypothesis 1: Skill generally overcomes strength in land war.
  Hypothesis 2: Maritime strength predominates the outcomes of land–sea wars.
  Hypothesis 3: Armies and navies of land powers fail to cooperate.

II. Why "Losers" Start Wars
  Hypothesis 4: Leaders of land powers do not fully understand sea power.
  Hypothesis 5: Navies of continental powers develop offensive doctrines.
  Hypothesis 6: Their leaders base decisions for war on these doctrines.
  Hypothesis 7: Organizational influences do not fade with the onset of war.
  Hypothesis 8: These influences cause switching to defensive doctrines.

The Category I hypotheses are somewhat independent, though numbers 1 and 2 would both have to be true in order to confirm the notion of war's duality. The Category II hypotheses are interrelated, and within them are embedded elements of Category I. Thus, a continental leader whose understanding of sea power is flawed may believe that he can win a war with the superior "skill" of his army. The organizational influences that drive naval doctrine to the defensive remove the chance to achieve the one objective, command of the sea, whose attainment could lead to victory.

TESTING

The causal paths to victory in war may be confirmed via quantitative testing, while the path to "loser" initiation can only be delineated in detailed case studies. Therefore, in the next chapter, the universe of cases of interstate war from 1815 to 1980 will be examined in a statistical-correlational study. In addition to testing the theory developed in this chapter, alternate explanations, which explore the possibility that wars are won by superior technology or through greater relative resolve, will be examined. The time period selected takes into consideration the effects of both the Industrial Revolution and the nationalism that profoundly influenced the power potential of states in the wake of the Napoleonic Wars. These events bear, respectively, on technology- and resolve-oriented alternative explanations of war outcomes, which will be more fully explicated in the following chapter. By halting case selection at 1980, at least some of the historical "dust" raised by more recent events will be allowed further time for settling.

Only detailed case studies will be able to determine the validity of the Category II hypotheses. The global wars of Louis XIV and Kaiser Wilhelm will be examined in their maritime origins and aspects. These cases were chosen for several reasons. First, they represent different nations, both great land powers, challenging a maritime power. The ruler of each was quite sensitive to naval affairs, making these "tough tests" of Hypothesis 4. Each nation also had engaged in a generation-long buildup of naval power before going to war, achieving either marginal superiority or rough parity with its enemy (see Table 3.1). Each had explicit and well developed offensive naval doctrines. For these reasons, these are "least-likely" cases for the navies of continental powers to go on the defensive once war had begun. The balances at sea in each instance were such that a precipitate shift from their declaratory offensive doctrines should have been highly unlikely. In the French case, there was really no history of prior doctrines other than fleet fighting for the purpose of achieving positive sea control. Organizationally, it should have been difficult, therefore, to break new doctrinal ground. In the German case, on the other hand, their leaders had the benefit of viewing the consistent failure of commerce raiding from Louis XIV's day to the recently ended American Civil War.

The selection of these cases also offers an opportunity to prove E.H. Carr's observation that a new theory may cause a reappraisal of history.[45] The naval debacles visited upon the continental powers in each of these cases have been extensively chronicled. In Louis's case, the fatal doctrinal shift is blamed on financial concerns. France simply couldn't afford to keep up a battle fleet any longer.[46] In the German case, the shift to commerce raiding has been previously explained in terms of the technological potential opened up by submarines.[47] It seems clear that the theory developed in this chapter is in considerable conflict with these notions, providing an opportunity for important historical reappraisals to be effected.

Finally, it should be noted from the outset that doctrinal shifts, from strategically offensive notions of sea control won by battlefleets, to the defensive *guerre de course* and *kleinkrieg* strategies, occur across the cases of global wars. Charles and Philip Habsburg, as well as Napoleon and Hitler, all approved the building of large battle fleets. Each of their navies espoused offensive doctrines of sea control as won by decisive battle. Yet the naval aspects of their global wars were characterized by uniform switching to attrition-oriented commerce raiding early in each conflict.

Quantitative testing of the universe of post-Napoleonic cases will be considered first, for if the duality of war and the preeminence of sea power are not confirmed, then there is little purpose in trying to identify aberrant behavior in the naval bureaucracies of continental powers as the source of "losing" war initiations.

NOTES

1. The dataset in Appendix I will provide the raw materials for the aspect of testing. Note that it delineates also the initiator of each conflict.

2. See Hans Delbruck, *History of the Art of War Within the Framework of Political History,* 3 vols., trans. by Walter Renfroe (Westport, CT: Greenwood Press, 1975). Throughout his survey, Delbruck characterizes the two modes of warfighting, by either "annihilation" or "exhaustion," as choices within the control of political leadership. Russell Weigley, *The American Way of War* (New York: Macmillan Publishing, 1973), adopts a similar notion of duality, with wars of "maneuver" or "attrition" being the options facing warmakers.

3. See Carl von Clausewitz, *On War* (Princeton: Princeton University Press, 1976), ed. and trans. by Michael Howard and Peter Paret. Book One, in particular, deals at length with these themes.

4. For Archidamus's cautionary speech, see Thucydides, *History of the Peloponnesian War,* 1.80-85. Historians generally neglected the implications of this speech, contending that the Spartans discounted the value of sea power. See P. A. Brunt, "Spartan Policy and Strategy in the Archidamian War," *Phoenix,* vol. 19 (1965):255–80. However, with Thomas Kelly's "Thucydides and Spartan Strategy in the Archidamian War," *American Historical Review,* vol. 87 (1982):25–54 the tide of opinion turned, and the Spartans are now seen as having been keenly aware of the differing requirements of land and sea warfare. While Donald Kagan, *The Fall of the Athenian Empire* (Ithaca: Cornell University Press, 1987), p. 418, concurs that the Spartans were sensitive to maritime concerns, he also ventures the opinion that the Periclean attritional strategy could not have led to victory, due to the Athenians' possession of insufficient resources for fighting a very long war.

5. Mackinder's *Britain and the British Seas* (Oxford: Clarendon Press, 1902); and "The Geographical Pivot of History," *Geographical Journal,* vol. 23 (1904):421–37 formed the foundation of his heartland/rimland theory of global power.

6. A. T. Mahan, *The Influence of Sea Power Upon History 1660–1783* (Boston: Little, Brown and Company, 1894), pp. 20–21.

7. John I. Alger, *The Quest for Victory: The History of the Principles of War* (Westport, CT: Greenwood Press, 1982), provides an exhaustive catalogue of previous strategic thought. Its sixty-eight appendixes, which summarize the various endeavors to understand war throughout history, consist of only one that makes explicit reference to maritime affairs.

8. Francis Bacon, "Of the True Greatness of Kingdoms." In *The Essays of Francis Bacon,* Mary Augusta Scott, ed. (New York: Charles Scribner's Sons, 1908), pp. 132–146. Bacon contends that "this much is certain, that he that commands the sea is at great liberty, and may take as much and as little of the war as he will. Whereas those that be strongest by land are many times nevertheless in great straits" (p. 144).

9. See Philip Crowl, "Mahan," in *Makers of Modern Strategy,* Peter Paret, ed. (Princeton: Princeton University Press, 1986).

10. Alfred Thayer Mahan, *The Influence of Sea Power Upon the French Revolution and Empire, 1789–1812*, 2 vols. (Boston: Little, Brown and Company, 1898).

11. Clausewitz, *On War*, p. 282.

12. If the ratio is figured on the basis of opposing field armies, the Arab advantage grows to 39:1.

13. These ratios are intended for illustrative purposes, and are based on the populations of the various combatants at the outset of these wars. Source: The Correlates of War dataset, made available through the Interuniversity Consortium for Political and Social Research.

14. Which is why his equation "squares" the value of numbers, relegating skill to a much less significant role. See his *Aircraft in Warfare* (London: Constable and Co., 1916). In this work, Lanchester argues that there may have been a time, prior to the Industrial Revolution, when skill and strength coexisted under conditions of equal importance (thus his "linear" law). But he posited that skill *never* outweighed quantitative strength. The continuing fascination with Lanchester exhibited by operations analysts is catalogued and critically examined by John W. R. Lepingwell, "The Laws of Combat? Lanchester Reexamined," *International Security*, vol. 12 (Summer 1987):89–133.

15. See Joshua M. Epstein, *The Calculus of Conventional War: Dynamic Analysis without Lanchester Theory* (Washington, DC: Brookings Institution, 1985). The major difference in this approach is the emphasis on favorable changes in attrition rates for the side that retreats. Given the myriad disasters which have accompanied many, if not most, retreats throughout history, Epstein's assumption seems far more speculative than Lanchester's.

16. See Alger, *The Quest for Victory*, Appendixes. The ideas of more than sixty different proponents of the "principles of war" are listed, with almost every one favoring "skill" over "strength."

17. Richard Ned Lebow, *Between Peace and War* (Baltimore: Johns Hopkins University Press, 1981), p. 242.

18. Cited in Bernard Brodie, *A Guide to Naval Strategy* (Princeton: Princeton University Press, 1944), pp. 172–173.

19. Paul Kennedy, *The Rise and Fall of British Naval Mastery* (London: The Ashfield Press, 1976), p. 135.

20. It should be noted that British forces, under the command of Wellington, were greatly aided, strategically, by Spanish partisans. However, guerrilla operations were extremely dependent for supplies on the Royal Navy's ability to land them virtually anywhere along the Spanish coast. The sea became, in effect, a sanctuary for partisan war materials and munitions. It is unfortunate that Mahan chose not to analyze the influence of naval supremacy on this campaign, especially since Sir Charles Oman's classic *A History of the Peninsular War* (London: H.M. Stationery Office, 1903) also omits much discussion of this topic. Elizabeth Longford, *Wellington: The Years of the Sword* (New York: Harper & Row, 1969), however, gives full credit to the Royal Navy and the Spanish partisans in her discussion of the Peninsular War.

21. Brodie, *A Guide to Naval Strategy*, p. 172.

22. Sea power also played an important role defeating Napoleon's invasion of Russia in 1812. E. B. Potter, ed., *Sea Power—A Naval History* (Englewood Cliffs, NJ: Prentice-Hall, Inc., 1960), pp. 181–182, analyzes the campaign thus: "Only by water, the sea and the rivers, could the Grand Army obtain the needed quantities of provisions and supplies. Now the consequences of . . . failure [to open the Baltic] lay starkly

revealed. Some two million pairs of boots for his barefoot army were stored at Napoleon's principal base of Danzig. There they stayed, for . . . British patrol ships blocked all coastal communication to the rivers."

23. Even fanciful Herodotus saw clearly that, regardless of Persian numbers, the Greeks could hurl back their invasion by winning command of the Aegean Sea. After Salamis, the Persian threat to Greece virtually evaporated, and their control over the Mediterranean's eastern littoral became tenuous.

24. The Duc de Choiseul, observing the international scene during the 18th Century put it thus: "the English, while pretending to protect the balance on land which no-one threatens, are entirely destroying the balance at sea which no-one defends." Cited in Michael Sheehan, "The Place of the Balancer in Balance of Power Theory," *Review of International Studies,* vol. 15 (1989):123–134, p. 127.

25. This point was first made in Paul Huth and Bruce Russett, "What Makes Deterrence Work? Cases from 1900 to 1980," *World Politics,* vol. 36 (1984):496–526. Their subsequent "Deterrence Failure and Crisis Escalation," *International Studies Quarterly,* vol. 32 (1988):29–45, and Huth's *Extended Deterrence and the Prevention of War* (New Haven: Yale University Press, 1988) confirm this point. Though their methodology has been criticized, as in Richard Ned Lebow and Janice Gross Stein, "Deterrence: The Elusive Dependent Variable," *World Politics,* vol. 42 (1990):336–369, their formulation regarding the local balance of forces has not been directly attacked.

26. Since the primary defenders, the United States and Britain, are democracies as well as maritime powers, it is also possible that aggressors may be counting upon this type of political structure to make military intervention more difficult to effect.

27. Thomas C. Schelling, *The Strategy of Conflict* (Cambridge: Harvard University Press, 1960); and Bruce Bueno de Mesquita, *The War Trap* (New Haven: Yale University Press, 1981), particularly pp. 29–33, are classic examples of the use which may be made of the assumption of pure rationality.

28. Robert O. Keohane, *After Hegemony* (Princeton: Princeton University Press, 1984), p. 110. See Chapters 6 and 7 for extended discussions of the pure and bounded models of rationality in the context of international relations. Herbert A. Simon, *Models of Bounded Rationality,* 2 vols. (Cambridge: MIT Press, 1982), provides an overview of behavioral perspectives on thought. Graham Allison, *Essence of Decision* (Boston: Little, Brown & Company, 1971); and Glenn Snyder and Paul Diesing, *Conflict Among Nations: Bargaining, Decision Making, and System Structure in International Crises* (Princeton: Princeton University Press, 1977), both suggest that the behavioral approach to the bounded rationality of individuals in general is particularly applicable to political leaders.

29. See Robert Jervis's pathblazing *Perception and Misperception in International Politics* (Princeton: Princeton University Press, 1976).

30. Lebow, *Between Peace and War,* utilizes this approach.

31. Jervis, *Perception and Misperception in International Politics,* p. 244.

32. With Herbert A. Simon's classic *Administrative Behavior* (New York: Macmillan Press, 1945).

33. Jack Snyder, *The Ideology of the Offensive: Military Decision Making and the Disasters of 1914* (Ithaca: Cornell University Press, 1984), and "Civil-Military Relations and the Cult of the Offensive, 1914 and 1984," *International Security,* vol. 9 (1984):108–146; Stephen Van Evera, "The Cult of the Offensive and the Origins of the First World War," *International Security* vol. 9 (1984):58–107; and Jack S. Levy, "Or-

ganizational Routines and the Causes of War," *International Studies Quarterly,* vol. 30 (1986):193–222 are seminal works.

34. Barry R. Posen, *The Sources of Military Doctrine* (Ithaca: Cornell University Press, 1984).

35. Ibid., pp. 239–241, for a discussion of Posen's findings on this point.

36. Simon, *Administrative Behavior,* p. 118.

37. Richard M. Cyert and James G. March, *A Behavioral Theory of the Firm* (Englewood Cliffs: Prentice-Hall, Inc., 1963), especially pp. 278–279 for their conclusion that both successful and failing organizations have great ability to innovate. Gordon L. Lippitt, *Organizational Renewal* (New York: Appleton-Century-Crofts, 1969); Cyril Sofer, *Organizations in Theory and Practice* (New York: Basic Books, 1972), Chapter 16; and James Q. Wilson, *Bureaucracy* (New York: Basic Books, 1989), especially Chapter 12, which deals explicitly with innovation (including in militaries), all support the point that organizations have both the will and the capability to achieve change.

38. Mahan referred to this situation, throughout his works, as the need for the secondary naval power to maintain a "fleet in being." Its loss could not be risked, and its continued existence, even in port, would impose some constraints on the naval mastery of the leading maritime power.

39. In the context of this study, "defensive" naval doctrines will be any which fail to call for the achievement of command of the sea. Thus, fleet-in-being, cruiser (light skirmishing, or *kleinkrieg*), and commerce raiding (the classic *guerre de course*) approaches to naval warfare are all considered defensive.

40. Graham T. Allison, *Essence of Decision: Explaining the Cuban Missile Crisis* (Boston: Little, Brown and Company, 1971), especially chapters 3 and 4. Allison recognizes that crisis is a logical time for civilian intervention. This makes the case he examines a "tough test" of organizational and bureaucratic theories, which they pass.

41. Allison, *Essence of Decision,* again, offers a comprehensive view of the web of bureaucratic interests and influences which encompass the executive. See Chapter 5. Richard E. Neustadt, *Presidential Power* (New York: John Wiley & Sons, 1960), suggests that these influences are very powerful. Indeed, the President can only overcome bureaucratic opposition by his "power to persuade."

42. In addition to Allison and Neustadt, this point of view is consistent with the work of: Wilson, *Bureaucracy*; David Nachmias and David Rosenbloom, *Bureaucratic Government USA* (New York: St. Martin's Press, 1980); Harold Seidman and Robert Gilmour, *Politics, Position, and Power,* 4th ed. (New York: Oxford University Press, 1986); and Jack Knott and Gary J. Miller, *Reforming Bureaucracy: The Politics of Institutional Choice* (Englewood Cliffs: Prentice-Hall, Inc., 1987).

43. Stephen D. Krasner, "Are Bureaucracies Important" (Or Allison Wonderland) *Foreign Policy,* vol. 7 (1972):159–179 is representative of this position. Bruce Bueno de Mesquita, *The War Trap* (New Haven: Yale University Press, 1981), takes a similar position, suggesting that, though bureaucratic influences may be important during peacetime, they tend to be minimized when the issue at hand is the decision of whether or not to go to war (p. 16).

44. Morton Halperin, *Bureaucratic Politics and Foreign Policy* (Washington, D.C.: The Brookings Institution, 1974), pp. 41–51, addresses specifically the issue of interservice rivalries within the model of bureaucratic politics, finding that notions of relative institutional power hold sway in the military realm as well as in the civilian bureaucracy.

45. See E. H. Carr, *What is History?* (New York: Random House, 1961), p. 10.

46. Geoffrey Symcox, *The Crisis of French Sea Power* (The Hague: Martinus Nijhoff, 1974), the leading work on this problem, reaches this conclusion inductively after exhaustive analysis of French finances.

47. Robert J. Art, *The Influence of Foreign Policy on Seapower: New Weapons and Weltpolitik in Wilhelminian Germany* (Beverly Hills, CA: Sage Publications, 1973), provides the most incisive portrayal of this line of thinking.

Chapter 4

On Winning (or Losing) Wars

Big armies don't win; good ones do. —Maurice de Saxe

In order to explain why "losers" start wars, it is necessary first to identify those conditions that lead to victory or defeat. Only then might it be possible to claim that a "loser" had started a war because of his ignorance of the means by which wars are won or lost. Once the causal path to victory has been delineated, an analysis of the decision-making process of the war initiator may be more fruitfully undertaken. The insight regarding war's dual nature developed in this study has been used to theorize that, in land–sea wars, sea power will overcome superior skill and strength. In land wars, skill and strength interact, though skill is relatively more important.

If these hypotheses are true, then at least a part of the puzzle of loser initiation, in land wars, will be solved. For, unlike the *numerical* military balance, the degree of military skill which is likely to be exhibited in war by a combatant cannot be known with certainty before a war. Therefore, initiator defeat in land war is not susceptible to much prediction. This finding, if borne out and generally accepted, could tend to shore up support for peaceful solutions to crises, as the inherently high risks of starting a land war would be exposed. As to the unsolved half of the puzzle, land–sea wars, confirmation of the primacy of sea power would at least serve to focus the investigation on the initiator's decision-making process. For example, why would any state begin a land–sea war if it thought that it could not wrest control of the sea from the maritime power with which it intended to fight?[1] If the leaders of aggressor states do not understand the duality of war, can they be rational? Or is their understanding of sea power imperfect? Do both their navies and armies have strong institutional reasons for suggesting, respectively, that the maritime power may be overcome at sea, or that its reach does not extend to the land? The investigation of questions of this sort in detailed case studies will be encouraged by a finding which confirms the importance of sea power.

This chapter tests the hypothesized causal paths to victory. The universe of cases of decisively concluded interstate war from 1815 to 1980[2] were analyzed by means of logistic regression, a process designed to explain the variance in dichotomous dependent variables.[3] The logistic function describes an "S" curve in which all dependent variable values fall between 0 (defeat) and 1 (victory). Figure 4.1 depicts it graphically.

This method of analysis avoided the problem, which would have arisen were linear regression to be employed, of generating dependent variable values that fall outside the 0 (lose) to 1 (win) range. In other words, the scope of the dependent variable was limited to victory or defeat, conveniently represented by "1" and "0." Use of linear regression would, in effect, have tried to fit a straight line to a phenomenon better depicted by an "S-curve." It is also, according to recent comparisons of the two methods, a better means of modeling the outcomes of various forms of interaction in the realm of international relations.[4] Basically, the idea that Gary King advances is that certain phenomena either occur, or do not arise, in the affairs of states; but they do not happen "partially." Deterrence either works or fails, and wars are begun or peace continues. In neither of these cases can it be said that a given event (crisis or war) happened "just a little." King suggests that, until some critical threshold is crossed, an event will simply not happen. Beyond that point, it does. Therefore, he contends, the "S-curve" of the logistic function is ideally suited to such events as wars and crises.

The period selected for examination is one characterized by significant technological change, and also by the spread of nationalism. Each of these factors relates closely to alternative theories of the causal path to victory that will have to be tested. The first hypothesizes that the technologically superior side will generally win. The many wars won in the nineteenth century by small European forces against China provide good examples of this theory. The importance of nationalism is that it may suggest that the outcome of war hinges on social choices made by the combatants. Greater relative motivation, according to this

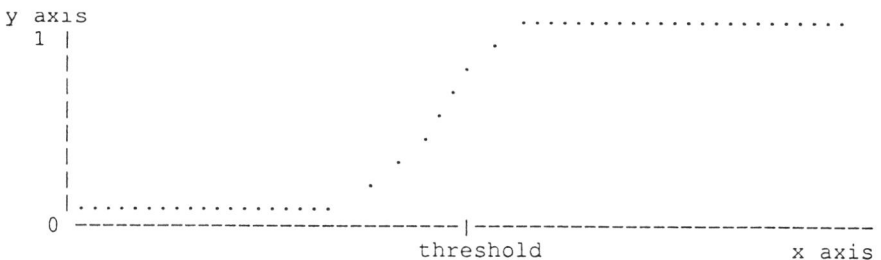

Figure 4.1 The logistic function.

idea, ought to be able to overcome superior skill, strength, and technology. The triumphs of Mexico in its war of liberation against France (1862–1867) and of North Vietnam against steadfast American opposition to its effort to conquer South Vietnam (1965–1973) offer plausible examples of the importance of resolve.

Skill and strength must not be forgotten either. In land wars, quantitative strength will be tested against skill, as the notion that victory goes to the "big battalions" must be seriously considered.[5] In land–sea wars, it is the interaction of skill and strength that must be considered, as well as the other abovementioned theories of technology and resolve,[6] in lieu of sea power, as viable alternate theories.

OPERATIONALIZATION

The Dependent Variable

In this study, wars are characterized as either "won" or "lost." The extent of victories won or defeats suffered, and the margins by which they were achieved, are not considered. Coding decisions were made on the basis of the consensus of historians with regard to any individual conflict. A further check for accuracy was provided by comparing the war aims of the contending sides, and determining whose aims were met and whose were denied.[7] Fortunately, the overwhelming majority of cases were clear-cut. The only coding change made from the Correlates of War dataset, with regard to outcome, was to identify Vietnam as the winner of its brief war with China in 1979.[8]

While the majority of the wars surveyed in this study were dyadic,[9] a sizeable minority were coalitional. It should be noted, therefore, that the coding of all variables refers, in aggregate where appropriate, to "sides" rather than to individual participants. This is a more logical formulation than one that might try to sort out winners and losers on an individual national basis. It would be very hard to contend that Russia won World War I, or that Poland emerged victorious in World War II. Thus, the coding of each war's dependent variable is dichotomous, with a "1" for the winning side and a "0" for the losing side.

Some Guidelines

The independent variables were also configured in a fashion that is sensitive to the need for random observation and single line-entries. The independent variables for one side convey information about the other by being expressed as ratios of the opposing side. For example, if the winning side's population, one of the quantitative measures of strength, was double that of the loser's, an entry of 2.00 was made. This entry reflects the population of the stronger side relative to the weaker. Conversely, if the losing side's perspective had been adopted in this case, the variable would have been coded .5, indicating that the loser's population was half that of the winner. The same principle was applied to as many of the variables as possible.

Where ratio representations are not feasible, a polychotomous approach to operationalization was employed. For example, the alternative explanation that wars are won by greater relative resolve is hard to depict in terms of ratios. Can it be plausibly demonstrated that side A is 2.66 times as resolved to win as side B? Hardly. Therefore, a variable of this sort will be formulated in qualititative terms. For any given variable, a "2" will be coded when the side from whose perspective the observation is made possesses the attribute in question, while the other side does not. A "1" will be entered if neither side has it, and a "0" if the obverse side possesses what its counterpart lacks. The logic that under-pins the polychotomous variables utilized in this study holds that superiority in a given quality (say resolve) leads to victory. If the perspective of the side deficient in this quality is chosen for the observation, the coding must still be able to reflect, with equal statistical power, the hypothesized effects of the given quality. With this in mind, the 2-1-0 polychotomous coding is quite functional. It captures the notion that the causal impact of superiority over parity, measured by the distance from 2 to 1, is the same as the negative impact of inferiority as opposed to parity, indicated by the equivalent distance from 1 to 0. Estimators should, therefore, remain unbiased when polychotomous variables are em-ployed.

The mix of qualitative and quantitative variables in some of the models to be tested will cause them to be of the analysis-of-covariance type. A further test of the validity of the models will be effected, after the initial evaluation, by con-verting them to an all-qualitative format (known as analysis-of-variance).[10] The results of the testing of both types of models should be highly similar. Another means of rechecking the validity of results will be to reverse the perspective of each observation, coding variables from the loser's point of view where the initial tests had shown the winner's perspective, and vice versa. Again, this is a form of doublechecking that should, ideally, achieve virtually identical test results.

The Independent Variables

Sea Power

In wars with maritime aspects, this study hypothesizes that sea power is the crucial factor in achieving victory. Naval strength ought to be able to overcome material disadvantages as well as opposing land (including air in the twentieth century) forces of superior quality led by better generals. To incorporate this concept into a single line entry per observation, conveying full information regarding both sides, presents certain difficulties. With regard to quantitative measures, the data become quite sparse outside the realm of the great powers.

There is also the problem, in the leading dataset, of understatement caused by the lack of recognition of privateers.[11] These problems are mitigated, however, by the fact that the set of Great Powers comprises virtually all who have wielded sea power. The problem of privateer measurement is minimal for the quantitative aspect of this study, which begins after Waterloo, given that the Age of Sail, and of privateering, came to an end not long after the Napoleonic Wars.

The dataset compiled by Modelski and Thompson reflects the percentage of global naval assets that a given power possessed at a specific time. The quantitative measure of sea power employed by this study is derived by composing a ratio based on the relative naval assets of each side. For example, the relative maritime strength in the Crimean War, viewed from the perspective of the Allies, was approximately 4:1, coded as 4.00. If the Russian perspective were randomly chosen for the line entry, the coding would be .25.[12] Ratios are computed based on the shares of naval power a state possessed at the time it entered the war. Computing the relative strengths at the end of the war would run the risk of endogeneity, saying, in effect, that a side won "by winning."[13]

An important assumption for quantitative coding is that all states possess some degree of ability to exert pressure at sea, even if only with coastal artillery. Therefore, all national participants are credited with a 1% share of total naval power. Aside from recognizing that virtually all states have some sort of navy, however ramshackle, this minimum strength coding avoids the technical problem of ever having a "0" as the denominator of any sea power ratio.

A final coding concern with regard to sea power is that the importance of naval concentration must be recognized. A state may have a large navy, in aggregate; but if its component fleets are difficult to unite, or if united they are difficult to dispatch to distant theaters that have been left unprotected, its fighting naval strength suffers. To reflect this problem, this study adjusts Modelski and Thompson's figures in order to gauge the effects of separation. For example, at the outset of the Russo-Japanese War, Russia enjoyed a navy which comprised 10.8% of the world's total maritime strength. The Japanese possessed only 4.5%, giving the Russians a seeming 2.4:1 edge. When the dispersion of the larger Russian forces into components located in the Baltic and Black Seas, as well as in the Far East is considered, however, a divisor of "3" will be employed against the Russian figure.[14] Thus the adjusted ratio, from the Russian perspective, is .8:1, or 1.25:1 in favor of Japan. The measure, though imperfect, does depict situations in which the total naval force of a state is diminished by its difficulties in achieving concentration, or by its need to keep portions of the fleet in widely separated locations. Certainly the experience of Russia in its war with Japan reflects the problem. The concentrated Japanese fleet was able to defeat the isolated Russian Far East fleet first, then lie in wait for the arrival of the Baltic fleet (which it then virtually wiped out at Tsushima). All the while, the Russian Black Sea Fleet remained in home waters due to Russia's security requirements in that area.

No loss-of-strength gradient for distance to the theater of war is assessed by this model, primarily because the theory of command of the sea negates ordinary concerns regarding the length of lines of supply and communications.[15] The movement of large American forces across the Atlantic and Pacific Oceans in World War II, and the ability of the British to conquer the Falklands while maintaining an 8,000-mile-long line of supply are examples that distance, by itself, does not always diminish the resources which may be projected over great distances. Indeed, of the 25 interstate wars in this study that find one side fighting "overseas," the one participating far from home won nineteen times (76% of the time).[16] Traditional notions of the importance of distance as a "drag" on power projection capabilities should, therefore, be reconsidered.[17] Rather than having universal validity, distance should be viewed as a conditional variable, mattering less, if at all, when the side projecting its power is in command of the sea. As distance is a key variable in expected utility theory, this notion of its conditional importance should provide some impetus for a re-analysis of findings based on its equations, which incorporate the "loss-of-strength gradient."

For the analysis-of-variance qualitative model, which will be developed to provide an additional test of the theory developed in this study, a polychotomous rendering of sea power will be employed, constructed along the lines previously described. When the perspective of the side possessing greater naval strength is chosen for coding, a "2" score will be given. When neither side has predominant naval force, a "1" will be entered. When the perspective of the contending side that is weaker at sea is chosen, a "0" will be coded. Utilizing this method will enable the model to consider the maritime strength of other-than-great powers, moving beyond the scope of Modelski and Thompson's great power-oriented work. The Pacific War (1879–1883) of Chile against the materially stronger alliance of Peru and Bolivia[18] is a good example of a case in which the qualitative depiction of the sea power variable enlarges the scope of measurement. It is also vital to understanding how Chile won this war. Qualitative coding of sea power, when employed, will also be based on an examination of the naval balance existing at the outbreak of every war surveyed.

Strength

The two traditional dimensions of strength are economic and numerical. The former is composed of financial wealth, levels of commercial activity, and heavy industrial capabilities. The latter is oriented to standing armies and fully mobilized resources. It is possible to depict strength by constructing variables for each of these facets of its nature; but, given the need for parsimony in a statistical model characterized by relatively few (63) observations, a combination of the two would provide a better approach. The composite capabilities index, developed by the Correlates of War Project, captures both facets of the concept of strength, and will be employed in this study. Further, its index of military manpower and budgets, industrial production, and total population, along with the urban proportion, has come into generally accepted use as a quantitative measure of power.[19]

The economic and numerical aspects of strength will also be considered separately when alternative explanations are examined. Economic notions of power will be tested using GNP, while numerical strength will be looked at in terms of both sides' total populations, and of forces actually mobilized over the course of a given war. Both the composite and disaggregated measures of strength will be encoded in terms of relative ratios. However, when the qualitative model is constructed on an analysis-of-variance basis, for purposes of additional testing, strength measures will be converted to a polychotomous mode.

Skill

At the level-of-analysis concerned with the overall war outcome, superior skill may be manifested in many ways. Surprise, superior maneuver, more sagacious use of terrain and military intelligence, and better fighting qualities in generals and troops all contribute to greater relative skill. How is this to be measured? Because of its many component parts, skill is generally analyzed on a case-by-case, qualitative basis. Most histories of conflicts attempt to reach conclusions regarding relative skill, and some specialized studies have appeared that approach this matter in an effort to reach generalizable principles regarding combat effectiveness.[20] These various studies will be incorporated to guide the polychotomous approach (with its 2-1-0 coding scheme) to measuring skill, which forms one aspect of this study's testing of its models. However, it is also possible to consider a strictly quantitative representation of skill.

One might assume that, all other things being equal,[21] a side that possesses better troops and generals, and utilizes superior maneuver capabilities, will, generally, enjoy a favorable ratio of battle deaths inflicted to those suffered. This notion is hardly revolutionary, as previous efforts to understand historical war outcomes, and more recently, combat effectiveness itself, have utilized it;[22] and formal models that aim at calculating the chances for success in war routinely accept the importance of exchange ratios to victory.[23] There may be wars in which one side enjoys such a great superiority in numbers that it consistently takes greater casualties, knowing that it will triumph by attrition. The Allies of World War I and the Soviets of World War II, as well as the Iranians against Iraq in the "First Gulf War," come to mind. But generals who order their troops to make human wave frontal assaults, and the troops themselves, can hardly be credited with superior skill. Indeed, the conclusion, if any, to be reached by examples of this sort is that numbers may sometimes matter more than skill. Also, even strategists of attrition may be sensitive to their own losses. The U.S. military in the twentieth century provides a clear example of a power that has engaged in an attritional style of war-making while remaining concerned about the minimization of casualties.[24] The air campaign that preceded ground operations during the "Second Gulf War" affords a prime example of an attrition-oriented offensive, which, at the same time, is designed to minimize one's own casualties.

The quantitative aspect of the skill variable will be represented, therefore, by encoding the relative ratio of battle deaths per side in a given war. A simple preliminary test of its validity when compared to qualitative studies of skill may be made using the World War II case. The key comparative studies of combat effectiveness during that war give the German Wehrmacht a rating which is roughly double that of the Allies[25] (approximately 1.25:1 against Britain and the United States, and 2.5:1 against the Soviets, according to Dupuy). A relative battle death calculation of combat effectiveness, based on data from the Correlates of War, achieves a ratio of 2.03:1 in favor of the Germans.[26] This is close enough to demonstrate the general validity of the battle death ratio measurement technique. While this is a form of "external validity" obtained via only one comparative case, the differing approaches may be observed to obtain strikingly similar results when additional comparative analyses are made.

As formal comparative assessments of combat effectiveness that come to mathematically oriented conclusions are few, it is necessary to build further confidence in the battle death ratio by less formal means. One way is to consider historians' general opinions expressed regarding relative combat effectiveness, then to see how the battle death ratio compares. The Israelis, for example, have generally been considered much better soldiers than their Arab adversaries.[27] When the four wars in which Israel fought alone against the Arabs are considered, the ratio depiction of their superior skill seems very much in line with historians' impressions.[28] This is only the most dramatic example of the ratio's consistency with more traditionally descriptive historical views. Indeed, only one case finds the ratio in significant conflict with the consensus of historians, the Russo-Japanese War. The Japanese army is generally depicted as possessing greater skill than its Russian adversary,[29] while the battle death ratio measures its effectiveness at only slightly better than half that of the Russians (.53).

Some sensitivity to the issue of endogeneity must be expressed here, as was done earlier with the sea power variable. In this case, one must be concerned with the problem that the infliction of enough battle deaths may start to look a lot like the dependent variable, as one side may have insufficient manpower to continue the war. However, an examination of the total battle deaths suffered by every nation in every war of the post-Napoleonic era shows that the average battle deaths suffered as percentages of total population are exceedingly low.[30] Even the most extreme cases are of relatively small proportions of total population, except for Paraguay, whose battle death rates lead all others. A refinement of this analysis checks battle deaths against total armed forces size.

Because the Correlates of War dataset includes only standing forces at the outset of war, the denominator of this ratio is much smaller than one that would include total mobilization figures over an entire war.[31] Nonetheless, the overall average ratio of battle deaths to pre-war armed forces size for winners is only 9.5%. For losers, the related figure is 10.6%. Table 4.1 chronicles the average percentages of population and pre-war armed forces which winning and losing sides have lost in terms of battle deaths. The key point is that, when battle deaths are used as a measure of military effectiveness, it seems clear that casualty levels are almost never high enough (with the exception of the Lopez War of Paraguay), even when controlling for the segment of total population eligible for military service, to make war continuation unfeasible. The issue of civilian casualties is not included in this formulation, as it is only the validity of and possible endogeneity problems with the battle death measure that are being considered here.

The higher casualty rates, in terms of total population, of the losing sides do not necessarily support the notion of skill measurement which has been introduced. For example, in the Russo-Finnish Winter War of 1939–1940, the Finns enjoyed a skill ratio, as measured by this study, of 1.25:1. Yet, Finland lost,

Table 4.1
Battle Deaths as Percentages of Populations and Forces
(from 1815–1980)

Classification of wars	N =	Percentages		
		Winning sides	Losing sides	Combined
All	(63)	.132 (9.5)	.160 (10.6)	.144 (10.115)
Major	(19)	.600 (18.3)	.655 (14.5)	.632 (17.0)
Minor	(44)	.030 (8.4)	0.102 (9.0)	.060 (8.9)
Land	(30)	.436 (6.2)	.522 (14.2)	.498 (10.6)
Land-Sea	(33)	.305 (12.2)	.289 (8.6)	.301 (11.1)
Global*	(2)	.342 (17.2)	2.130 (15.1)	1.180 (16.4)

*Because of duration, intensity, and scope of the World Wars, the parenthesized percentages of forces killed in battle are based on total mobilized troop figures.

Notes. Parentheses around percentages denotes "Force" category.

Population outlier: Lopez War, 1864–1870, 40% (lost war); Chaco War, 1932–1935, 5.6% (won war).

World War II Germany is the only other population case over 5% (at 5.02). Only four other population cases fall between 1–5%.

Source: Correlates of War dataset for populations and battle deaths.

relatively, 36 times more of its population to the war than did the Soviet Union. Therefore, it might be argued that the figures shown in Table 4.1 may simply reflect a differential between the relative populations of larger and smaller sides. The big may just be defeating the small with regularity. The key point, again, is that the manner in which the skill variable is operationalized does not fall afoul of the problem of endogeneity.

Is the battle death ratio tautological? That is, does a measure based on information that is generated *by* the war simply explain that one side won "by winning"? This is also a question that must be asked of more qualitative approaches to understanding military skill, which are all written *ex post facto*. Logically, the "skill" hypothesis of victory is no different than the "strength" hypothesis. In the case of the latter, however, raw numbers of men and resources are fairly easy to gauge prior to a war. Skill, as has been previously mentioned in this study, is an "imponderable." Nonetheless, the hypothesis that the side that wins in (per this study, "land") war will inflict more casualties than it suffers is not inherently flawed. Since the battle death ratio is kept entirely as an independent variable, the risk of becoming tautological is minimized. Dupuy, on the other hand, has included, in his studies, a battle death ratio which acts both as an indicator of victory *and* as a measure of military skill.[32] Also, it must be noted that this study's dual theory of the paths to victory in war hypothesizes that the battle death ratio should influence only land war outcomes. Therefore, in land–sea wars, this ratio should be found statistically insignificant. If it is, then there will be some *prima facie* evidence that the ratio is not, intrinsically, tautological.

Finally, it should be noted that all data on battle deaths are estimates derived from the Correlates of War Project. This study has examined the secondary historical literature related to the wars being analyzed as a further check, and found that none of the figures from the dataset would have to be revised. This still does not ensure that the figures are "right," as historical sources may be imprecise with regard to casualties. It just means that, to the extent to which it errs, this study is in good company.

PRELIMINARY MODEL TESTING

In this section, two series of tests are developed. In the first, the theory that land wars are won primarily by "skill" is examined. In the second, the hypothesis that sea power has exerted a determining influence on war outcomes in land–sea wars is tested. The results of several tests of each type of war are reflected, demonstrating what happens when one or another variable is omitted. Also, the different measures of "strength" require separate testing. "Strength" is operationalized and analyzed in four different ways. First, the Correlates of War Project's composite capabilities index[33] is employed. Later, the raw population, military force, and economic measures[34] of the index are each tested separately.

Tables 4.2 and 4.3 reflect the results of testing across the two types of war. The first observation that may be made is that the hypothesized causal paths to victory in land and land–sea wars are very convincingly borne out by this analysis. Skill is strongly related to victory in land wars, while sea power determines the winner of land–sea wars. Each variable is necessary in order for the respective explanatory models to achieve statistical significance, both of which generate very high levels of prediction (93% in land and 88% in land–sea wars). The battle-death ratio (which is used to operationalize skill) works quite well in land wars, but fails to achieve significance in the land–sea category, as predicted by the theory advanced in this study. The overall results of the "strength" variables are poor. Only the composite capabilities index achieves a modest level of significance in each type of war. All other strength measures generate poor prediction (in the 70% range) when skill and sea power are omitted, and are unable to support explanatory models which have even the minimum 90% confidence level.

This study's notion that "skill" and "strength" have an interactive relationship in land wars, with skill predominating, is supported by the mildly significant results which the composite index operationalization of the latter concept achieved in testing. This finding suggests that both variables have some separate influences on outcome (in the case of strength, very small), and that they interact as well. However, it is important to note that their effects are not only, or even mostly, the product of interaction. Indeed, an explicit interaction variable was developed and tested. The results were insignificant.

Table 4.2
Analysis of Land Wars, 1815–1980

Variable strength measure used	Test		
	I COW index	II Population	III GNP
Intercept	.29**	.26*	.42
"Skill" (battle death ratio)	.52***	.52***	
"Strength I" (composite index)	.14*		
"Strength II" (population)		.09	
"Strength III" (GNP)			.11
Prediction	93%	80%	73%
Model chi-square	25.2***	13.01**	5.03

Significance levels: *p < .10; **p < .05; ***p < .01; N = 30.

This set of representative tests employs "relative ratio" quantitative variables. No significant changes in results occur when qualitative operationalizations are used, although Test I prediction reduces to 90%. Tests II and III employ varying measures of strength, neither of which becomes significant. When skill is omitted, as in Test III, the statistical model loses its significance (this holds true across a wide variety of tests of land wars).

Note. The intercept is the point at which the logistic curve meets the "y" axis (see Figure 4.1).

Table 4.3
Analysis of Land–Sea Wars

Strength measure	I Index	II Index, forces	III GNP	IV Population
Omitted variable(s)		Skill, sea power	Sea power	Sea power
Variables				
Intercept	.23**	.18**	.20	.06
Skill (battle deaths)	.02		.02	.02
Strength I (index)	.24*	.11		
Strength II (population)				.14
Strength III (forces)		.09		
Strength IV (GNP)			.15	
Sea power (ratio)	.49***			
Prediction	88%	67%	70%	67%
Model chi-square	17.53***	4.33	4.99	3.86

Significance levels: *p < .10; **p < .05; ***p < .01; N = 33.

This set of representative tests demonstrates the critical importance of sea power to victory in land–sea war. Equally important is the recognition that neither skill nor strength "matter" in this type of war. The Correlates of War index of strength is marginally significant though (see Test I). When the sea power variable was operationalized in a qualitative, polychotomous way, prediction improved to 94%.

Finally, in order to be sure that sea power and skill are not somehow "masking" other causally relevant variables, testing for the possible presence of multicollinearity was undertaken.[35] The correllogram analysis performed indicates that multicollinearity is not interfering with the proper working of any of the variables.

An additional form of sensitivity analysis was also performed. With regard to the regression coefficients derived from logistic regression analysis, it was hypothesized that they might not be "right." Therefore, each was modified, to the extent of one standard deviation, both up and down, and the regressions were re-run. While skill and sea power retained their powerful impacts, the composite index measure of the strength variable was no longer significant. Also, the correct prediction rate for land–sea wars dropped marginally, from 88% to 85%. Land war prediction dropped to 90%, down from 93%. These findings tend to support the robustness of the skill and sea power variables and, therefore, the notion that war does indeed have a dual nature. The relative "frailty" of the strength variable is not unexpected, and is consistent with what the theoretical discussion of its impact on war outcomes in Chapter 3 suggests.

Despite these excellent results, it is still possible that the models are not properly specified; and the two candidate alternative theories, which hypothesize that "technology" and/or "resolve" have powerful influences on war outcomes, must be examined.

Table 4.4
Analysis of Technology and War Outcomes

	Test		
	I	II All minus	III
Category of war	All	Great v. Minor Power	All
Variable(s) omitted	Strength	Strength	Skill, sea power
Intercept	.18*	.16*	.18*
Technology	.12*	.09	.05
Skill	.52***	.44***	
Sea power	.95***	.82***	
COW index (strength)			.14
Prediction	94%	90%	65%
Model chi-square	14.01***	12.25**	8.10

N = 63 in tests I & III. N = 39 in test II (the "fair fights").

TECHNOLOGY

The most succinct assessment of the importance of technology in war was made by J.F.C. Fuller, who argued that superior weaponry, from the time of the Hittites to the present, comprised "99% of victory."[36] Friedrich Engels, whose thinking ran as often to interstate as to class war, was also wedded to the notion that advanced types of arms would "always overcome the inventions of the mind of generals of genius."[37] Another sweeping generalization regarding technology was made by C. F. Cipolla, who avowed that the West's dominance of global politics during the last 500 years resulted from its superior naval architecture.[38] Each of these formulations supports the notion that victory goes to the technologically superior side, not necessarily to the "big battalions." Some dissent has been articulated,[39] but the basic notions of this form of technological "determinism" remain intellectually potent.

Testing the validity of the hypothesis that superior technology wins wars has to be done qualitatively.[40] Therefore, the polychotomous independent variable form will be used, with a "2" coded when the observed side is technologically superior, a "1" when neither side is, and a "0" when the other side holds the edge. What needs to be measured is the absence or presence of given types of weaponry on the two sides in any war. For example, a side that possessed an air force, while its enemy had none, would enjoy a technological edge. Similarly, armies with tanks have a qualitative edge over those who must do without. A side that possesses nuclear weapons has, in theory if not practice, a massive qualitative advantage over an opponent not similarly armed.

Table 4.4 reflects the results of testing the technology variable. The variable does achieve statistical significance in the universe of cases. However, when wars of Great versus Minor Powers are controlled for, technology ceases to be an important factor.[41] None of the global wars was fought with one side enjoying significant technological superiority over the other (at least at the outset).[42] Of the other "vertical" categories of war, those between minor powers even show some perverse tendencies toward victory on the part of the technological inferior. The Chaco and Palestine Wars offer good examples of ill-equipped and vastly outnumbered forces winning against their technologically superior foes. The Chaco War, in particular, witnessed an offensive by moderately mechanized Bolivian troops, supported by a sizeable (for the theater) air force, which failed completely against Paraguay's small infantry army.

Does technology determine the winner of interstate war? There are compelling logical arguments on both sides of the issue, making necessary its consideration as an alternative to the "dual theory" advanced in this study. Quantitative analysis, however, has found that, in wars between states at similar levels of the international hierarchy (Minor versus Minor or Great versus Great Powers), technology does not matter. In the subset of Great versus Minor Power Wars, the modest statistical significance which technology achieves is clouded by its multicollinearity with variables representing economic and maritime strength.[43] Also, in this latter class of wars, some troubling cases, mispredicted by the logistic regressions, crop up. France's defeat by Mexico in a war that ran from 1862–1867, Poland's victory over the Soviet Union in 1920,[44] and North Vietnam's successful conquest of the South, despite many years (1965-1973) of active American intervention, all suggest that there are serious problems with Fuller's notions about technology and war.

RESOLVE

The realm of conflict falls not only within the purview of social science, but also of ethology. With regard to "resolve" as a factor that influences the outcome of conflict, much insight may be derived from the work of those who have analyzed the purposive strife that dominates behavior throughout the animal kingdom. Since the appearance of Robert Ardrey's work on territoriality,[45] a spate of studies have confirmed many of his hypotheses regarding territorial behavior. Virtually all findings have been consistent, also, with his notions about who wins territorial fights in nature. Ardrey divided animal territory into a "heartland" and a periphery. He observed that animals defending their territories are virtually unbeatable in their heartland, weaken somewhat at the border, and generally fail to make new conquests. He could find no other reason for the high proportion of defender victories in nature than asymmetrical resolve. The attacker, who has a homeland to fall back on, will not risk all. The defender, who is in a "must win" situation, fights with reckless abandon, and wins.[46] Among humans, the many wars between Israel and the Arab coalitions which have sought its destruction provide examples that suggest that relative motivation may indeed play a vital role in the outcome of war. While not making explicit use of the findings of natural science, social scientist James

Morrow has also constructed a theory in which victory in war depends on resolve, or human choice.[47]

As with technology, resolve must be configured in qualitative terms. There is just no way of saying with accuracy that Side A's resolve is twice that of B. But there is a means of measuring whether or not it is greater or less. Therefore, a "2" is coded when the side from whose perspective the observation is made holds an advantage in resolve, a "1" when neither side does, and a "0" when the other side is more resolute. The basis for measurement is straight out of Ardrey: if a side is fighting a "total" war for its survival, it engages with maximum resolve—otherwise it is fighting a limited war, with limited resolve.[48]

Adding this variable to the regression analysis provided some interesting results, displayed in Table 4.5, with which Ardrey and Morrow would likely be unhappy. Resolve proved to be an inconsequential variable, even having a strong negative correlation with victory. When the class of Great versus Minor Power Wars (the by-now-usual "suspect"), in which the greatest cluster of cases of asymmetrical resolve exists, was controlled for, the results for the remainder were still poor. Superior resolve overcomes neither the interaction of skill and strength in land war nor sea power in land–sea war.

The finding of this study regarding the value of resolve is counterintuitive. While this runs against popular beliefs about the value of resolution, its unimportance is logically predicted by the "dual" theory of war advanced in this study. For if superior skill and sea power determine the respective outcomes of

Table 4.5

Analysis of Resolve and War

	Test		
	I	II	III
Category	All	All	Asymmetrical wars
Variables omitted	Index, technology	Skill, sea power	Index, technology
Intercept	.38**	.18	.42
Resolve	.02	.02	.01
Skill	.52***		.86***
Sea power	.92***		.90***
Strength (index)		.04	
Technology		.12	
Prediction	90%	73%	90%
Model chi-square	13.57***	8.02	12.66***

Tests I and II examined the universe (63) of cases. When technology and strength were substituted for skill and sea power in test II, the level of prediction dropped, and the variables and the model were statistically insignificant. Test III controlled for those cases in which Resolve was symmetrical, reducing the number tested to 39. The results were still negative. In addition to its performance in this representative set of tests, the Resolve variable failed to achieve statistical significance at any point in the testing process.

land and land–sea wars, then there is little room for resolve to make much of a difference.

FURTHER MODEL TESTING

Nuclear Weapons

Another possible problem in measurement might have arisen due to the absence of nuclear weapons from the models developed. Therefore, a polychotomous variable, representing conditions of nuclear dominance, inferiority and parity, was employed for cases during the nuclear era.

The variable performed quite poorly. Of the seventeen wars fought during the nuclear era (excluding World War II),[49] nations possessing nuclear weapons participated in five.[50] Of these, the "nuclear" side won twice (USSR versus Hungary and the Suez War of 1956), lost twice (first the United States, and later China versus Vietnam) and one unclear war outcome resulted (Korea).[51] These findings are quite consistent with recent work on extended deterrence that has also found that nuclear weapons have not tended to "matter."[52] In this regard, theorizing about future war will lead to the conclusion that a nuclear-armed state will not use weapons of mass destruction against a foe lacking similar arms.[53] Also, the strategic nuclear parity of the superpowers will create an inhibition of its own against the use of such weapons against a similarly armed enemy.[54]

Air Power

This study has contended that, though the capabilities of air weapons play important roles in both land and land–sea wars, they do not alter the causal path to victory, or create a separate class of war. Air weapons enhance combat effectiveness in both types of war, but they don't win the wars on their own. This reasoning runs counter to the classical formulations of air power's autonomous capabilities outlined in the works of Douhet and De Seversky.[55]

Because much strategic thought revolves around the importance of air power, leading to the likely comment that "sea power might have mattered once, but not since the advent of the plane," air power should also be tested as a key independent variable. The simplest response to an "air critique" is to observe that, though the tools of dominion over the sea may change, the importance of such command has remained undiminished. No one would say that the move from sail to steam had eliminated the need for sea command, nor should they say it in relation to the presence of aircraft. However, in the interest of methodological rigor, a separate air power variable, also polychotomous, was operationalized.[56]

As with the nuclear variable, air power performed very poorly in regression analysis, failing to achieve statistical significance. Thirty interstate wars have been fought since the advent of air power in World War I. Seventeen of these were characterized by the presence, at the outset, of one-side's superiority in the air. Of these, 10 possessors of air power won, and 7 lost. Appendix IV provides a detailed listing of these cases.

OTHER SENSITIVITY ANALYSIS

Mispredicted Cases

In this chapter, the theory of war's duality has been put to a rigorous set of statistical tests, and has been strongly upheld. Testing has employed, alternately, quantitative, qualitative, and mixed-variable operationalizations. Coding perspectives have been reversed, and one set of tests looked only from the point of view of the war initiator. Alternate candidate theories, of technology and resolve, have been considered. Through all these analyses, the skill and sea power variables have held up in, respectively, land and land–sea wars. Remarkably, only two cases of each type of war have been consistently mispredicted throughout the testing.

In land wars, the Franco-Thai (1940–1941) and Sino-Indian (1962) Wars are the only ones that the model consistently mispredicts. The Thais and the Chinese, the respective winners, had the same skill ratings (.50), suggesting that their military opponents were twice as skilled as they. How did they win? In the first case, the weakness of the Vichy regime is thought to have quite a bit to do with Thai success. The fact that this war was fought against a colonial power may also explain why military effectiveness alone does not predict the outcome. Finally, Japanese influence cannot be omitted from the analytical calculus either. By December 1940, the Vichy regime in Indochina was under considerable pressure from Japan, and was ordered, from home, to accede to Japanese requests.[57] In the Sino-Indian case, it may just be that this border dispute was won by the Chinese because they were willing to use superior numbers accepting heavy casualties as a tool of generalship. This concern was discussed earlier, in the analysis of the battle death ratio. The fact that the use of superior numbers as a "bludgeon" worked (statistically) for the winner only this once, in a very minor war, suggests the general validity of the ratio.

Of the land–sea wars, only the Franco-Mexican (1862–1867) and Vietnam (1965–1975) Wars are consistently mispredicted. Both have been characterized as efforts to defeat colonial rule or influence. In the first case, aside from Mexican persistence in adversity, the United States also made clear to France that, with the end of the Civil War, (1865), it would now oppose continued French support for the puppet regime of Maximilian. Louis Napoleon heeded the American warning, and stopped all support for his satrap. Soon, supplies were exhausted and, unreplenished, the "emperor" of Mexico was worn down to defeat.[58] The Vietnam case is, from the statistical point of view, at first most puzzling. Yet, when it is observed that massive Chinese and Soviet aid are not factored into the analysis, and that the United States withdrew from the war in 1973, and from the promise of continued naval and air support in 1975, the outcome seems less surprising. Also, the anti-colonial nature of the North's war aims must be recognized. Indeed, in wars against either colonial rule or indirect influence, there may be some room for the resolve variable to be reconstituted.

The most important finding of this review of mispredicted cases may be that three of the four saw resistance to colonial rule or influence emerge triumphant. An initial review of the universe of cases of interstate war reflects that, of the fifteen that have a "colonial" flavor, ten are won by the forces of "imperialism." The success rate is consistent with that enjoyed by other war initiators. If, however, a further subdivision into original conquests and wars of liberation from either occupation or influence is made, it may be seen that states fighting for their freedom, or to end residual colonial influence, win in three of four cases. The Chinese defeat in the Boxer War is the only one in which a war for "liberation" saw the colonial powers triumph (see Table 4.6). Perhaps, in this realm, the notion of resolve as important to victory in war may be more applicable than it is to interstate wars in general.

SUMMARY

Quantitative testing has strongly confirmed the hypotheses generated regarding the causal paths to victory in land and land–sea war, with skill and sea power, respectively, being the key variables. Testing of both quantitative and qualitative models was effected, with no change in results. There were also no changes

Table 4.6
"Colonial-Related" Interstate Wars, 1815–1980

War	Winner	"Imperialist"	"Liberation"
Anglo-Persian (1856–1857)	Britain	X	
Spanish-Moroccan (1859–1860)	Spain	X	
Franco-Mexican *1862–1867)	Mexico		X
Spanish-Chilean (1865–1866)	Chile	X	
Sino-French (1884–1885)	France	X	
Sino-French (1894–1895)	Japan	X	
Boxer War (1900)	Allies		X
Spanish-Moroccan (1909–1910)	Spain	X	
Manchurian (1931–1933)	Japan	X	
Italo-Ethiopian (1935–1936)	Italy	X	
Sino-Japanese (1937–1941)	Japan	X	
Changkuofeng (1938)	Japan	X	
Nomohan (1939)	Mongolia	X	
Franco-Thai (1940–1941)	Thailand		X
Vietnam (1965–1973)	North Vietnam		X

when the perspectives taken by each observation were reversed, with losers coded where winners had been, and vice versa. Two candidate alternative theories of victory were examined. In the first, technology's significance was found to be completely dependent upon the inclusion of great versus minor power wars. In the second, relative resolve had a surprisingly poor showing. Separate tests of nuclear and air power variables also failed to cloud the initial findings.

What of the notion that the outcome of war is the product of chance factors, that conflict is so uncertain as to be, as Clausewitz put it, a "game of cards"?[59] The results of the tests employed here have delineated strong, recurring patterns across all wars, suggesting that their outcomes are not random. This "physiocratic" explanation of war must, therefore, be seen as posing a serious challenge to all who hold that "friction" and the "fog of war" make *a priori* correct predictions of its outcome a most difficult, if not impossible, task. This does not mean that chance events never occur in war. It simply suggests that such occurrences have an insignificant causal impact on the war's outcome.

The quantitative testing employed in this chapter has solved only a part of the puzzle of loser initiation. Victory in land war has been demonstrated to be dependent on "skill." Therefore, it should be unsurprising that so many war initiators lose, because it is virtually impossible to tell with certainty, before a war begins, which side will fight more skillfully. In this regard, a proper understanding of the path to victory in land war might help to foster peace, as it highlights the terrible uncertainties of war. Mechanistic notions of the use of some form of "greater positive utility," as a sign that the "necessary conditions" for war initiation have been achieved, should be discarded.[60] Finally, a serious challenge has been mounted to the validity of the Lanchester laws of attrition, which emphasize the importance of numerical strength over skill. Instead, it has been demonstrated that, in land wars, skill is more important than strength.

The finding that sea power is crucial to achieving victory in land–sea wars provides the foundation for the detailed case studies that follow. The decisions of Louis XIV and Kaiser Wilhelm II to start wars with maritime powers will be reexamined, with a special focus on the behavior of their respective naval leaders. The previous chapter's hypotheses, derived from organizational and bureaucratic politics theories, will be employed in the effort to unravel the final part of the puzzle.

NOTES

1. Bearing in mind that the dominant sea powers of the last 400 years have been democracies, one would have also to explore the possibility that war initiators based their decisions on an assessment that the sea power, because of its domestic political structure, would lack the "will" to pursue a fight to the end. This issue will be more fully explored when the alternative theory that greater relative resolve wins wars is examined.

2. These number 63 according to the Correlates of War dataset, available from the Inter-University Consortium for Political and Social Research. The only interstate war from this period excluded in this study is the Korean War, due to the indecisiveness of its conclusion. Even though the original invasion was defeated, it could reasonably be argued that the US expanded its aims to encompass conquest of North Korea, in which endeavor it failed. See Appendix I for the full listing of wars.

3. That is, those which may be described qualitatively, such as in terms of "win" or "lose."

4. Gary King, "Event Count Models for International Relations: Generalizations and Applications," *International Studies Quarterly,* vol. 33, no. 2 (June 1989), argues the case in favor of logistic as opposed to linear regression for purposes of modeling international interactions, such as wars.

5. F. W. Lanchester, *Aircraft in Warfare* (London: Constable and Co., 1916), introduced the notion that force in war consisted of the product of combat effectiveness and the *squared* value of the number of forces engaged. His famous "squared" law, which extols the primacy of quantitative strength, retains its hold on formal models of attrition in war, particularly modern war. John W. R. Lepingwell, "The Laws of Combat? Lanchester Reexamined," *International Security,* vol. 12 (1987):89–133 accepts the conditional validity of the squared law, and posits that the linear law, which holds skill to be as important as strength, is at times also valid. In the previous chapter, both of Lanchester's laws were challenged, and the notion that skill ought to be "squared" when interacting with strength was advanced.

6. Which will also be considered viable alternative explanations for victory in land wars.

7. Melvin Small and J. David Singer, *Resort to Arms: International and Civil Wars, 1816–1980* (Beverly Hills: Sage Publications, 1982), pp. 297–329, contains an annotated listing of the historical literature used to support the coding of the Correlates of War Project. This study has utilized many of the works referred to by Singer and Small, but has also employed additional sources. These latter references are included in the Selected References to this study. In this chapter, historical references are cited when specific wars are discussed.

8. China initiated this war to "punish" Vietnam for its continued occupation of Cambodia. Not only was it unclear exactly which party to the conflict was being punished, but China's use of force failed to achieve its aim of hastening Vietnam's withdrawal from Cambodia. See Appendix I for the full listings.

9. Thirty-eight wars (60%) featured only two combatants. See Appendix I.

10. Damodar Gujarati, *Basic Econometrics* (New York: McGraw-Hill, 1978), pp. 287–303, discusses the properties of all-qualitative and "mixed-variable" (or analysis-of-covariance) models. The point here is that some variables can't be represented by ratios, but all of them can be depicted in a qualitative sense. In this regard, a qualitative rendering of the sea power variable will give it greater richness as, for example, the naval supremacy of Chile over Peru and Bolivia (which was not yet landlocked at the outset of the Pacific War in 1879) may be measured. Ratio measures are exclusively limited to the great powers.

11. George Modelski and William R. Thompson, *Seapower in Global Politics, 1494–1993* (Seattle: University of Washington Press, 1988), pp. 50–96, describe a rigorous procedure for gauging each nation's relative share of global naval power over a 500-year period. Unfortunately, their ship counting measures during the Age of Sail,

based on state ownership until 1655, and a 30-, 40-, and later 50-gun minimum until 1860, lead to severe distortions. Privateers are never properly accounted for as part of global seapower assets, as components of battlefleets, or in their primary, but vitally important roles as scouts and raiders. Thus Modelski and Thompson give Spain a 2.12:1 (70 to 33 state-owned warships) edge in naval power over Britain at the outset of the War of the Armada. No differentiation is made between heavily armed galleons and lightly armed transports. Nor are Drake's 60 privateers mustered for the battle in any way reflected. See Julian Corbett, *Drake* (London: Macmillan Publishing Company, Ltd., 1911), p. 141, for an assessment of the actual fighting strength of the rival fleets which reflects Spanish quantitative and qualitative inferiority. See Chapter 2 of this study for a fuller discussion of relative naval power in the Armada Campaign.

12. Modelski and Thompson, *Seapower in Global Politics*, p. 122 provides the raw data on Russian, French and British naval power. The ratios cited are "adjusted," based on the force minimum and divisor effects discussed below.

13. This is not to suggest that warring states neglect to estimate their enemies' production capacities. However, it is important, if sea power is to be a predictor, to measure it before one side's fleet gets sunk. In the Armada case, for example, Spain went from having a navy (according to Modelski and Thompson's figures) more than twice Britain's in 1588, to one which could claim bare numerical parity in 1589. As the war raged on past the turn of the century, the ratio grew ever worse, due to Spanish losses. The only interstate war whose naval ratios were affected by production was World War II, because of American shipbuilding. Therefore, it seems reasonable to code in a fashion that minimizes the problem of endogeneity, since the problem of differential rates of intrawar naval construction causes little statistical "noise."

14. For the Crimean War, Russia's divisor was "2," as the Far East Squadron was quite small at that time. During the period covered by this study, France, the United States, and Britain are subjected to a divisor factor of "2." Germany and Japan are not subject to divisors, as their respective fleets were not divided by either land masses or global requirements (in the British case).

15. The point is made most succinctly by Bernard Brodie, *A Guide to Naval Strategy* (Princeton: Princeton University Press, 1944), p. 171: "One of the great differences between naval warfare and land warfare is that in the latter an advance upon the enemy's communications usually tends to expose one's own, but in naval warfare that is not the case. A fleet at sea is highly mobile and largely self-contained. It is therefore free of a rigid supply line which may be menaced."

16. See Appendix II.

17. Kenneth Boulding, *Conflict and Defense* (New York: Harper & Brothers, 1962), pp. 229–242, introduced the general concept of distance causing "loss of strength." Bruce Bueno de Mesquita, *The War Trap* (New Haven: Yale University Press, 1981), p. 83, makes the "loss of strength gradient" an explicit parameter of his modeling of expected utility. This study suggests that distance's impact on strength is conditional, not general.

18. According to the Correlates of War dataset, at the outset of the Pacific War, Peru and Bolivia possessed, combined, .32% of the world's composite capabilities (a mix of demographic, industrial and military factors, discussed below) to Chile's .14%. From Chile's perspective, its quantitative inferiority could be expressed as .44:1. Qualitative analysis of the naval balance in 1879, however, shows Chile with a substantial edge. Indeed, Chile's amphibious invasion of Peru is viewed as the war-winning blow. See

Luis Galdames' discussion in *A History of Peru* (Chapel Hill, NC: University of North Carolina Press, 1941).

19. See J. David Singer, S. Bremer and J. Stuckey, "Capability Distribution, Uncertainty and Major Power War, 1820-1965," and "Status, Formal Organization, and Arms Levels as Factors Leading to the Onset of War," both in *Peace, War and Numbers,* Bruce Russett, ed. (Beverly Hills: Sage Publications, Inc., 1972); J. Ray, *Global Politics* (Boston: Houghton Mifflin, 1979); and Bueno de Mesquita's many works on expected utility theory. Richard L. Merritt and Dina A. Zinnes, "Validity of Power Indices," *International Interactions,* vol. 14 (1988):141–151, catalogue and assess the values of the many power measures in use, according the composite capabilities index a prominent position.

20. Trevor N. Dupuy, in *Numbers, Predictions and War* (Fairfax, Va.: HERO Books, 1985, and *Understanding War* (New York: Paragon House, 1987) attempts to generalize a "quantified judgment model" of combat effectiveness, derived from campaign studies of WWII and the Arab-Israeli Wars. Williamson Murray and Allan Millett, *Military Efficiency,* 3 vols. (Boston: Unwin Hyman, 1989) is grounded in the experience of World Wars I and II, but also strives to develop generalizable conclusions regarding proficiency.

21. That other factors are seldom "equal" requires that the impacts of lopsided numerical or technological balances be assessed. These variables, and another (economic strength), are controlled for in the regression analyses that follow.

22. Implied in the introduction to J. F. C. Fuller, *The Conduct of War, 1789-1961* (New Brunswick, N.J.: Rutgers University Press, 1961), the notion that increased combat effectiveness achieves, overall, favorable casualty "exchange ratios," and victory, is propounded more fully in Frank L. Klingberg, "Predicting the Termination of War: Battle Casualties and Population Losses," *Journal of Conflict Resolution,* vol. 10 (1966):129–171. Klingberg also searches out the level of civilian "suffering" which, in theory, would have to be inflicted to induce surrender of one's enemy. More recently, the United States Army Concepts Analysis Agency has completed a study, "Do Battles and Wars Have a Common Relationship Between Casualties and Victory" (Technical Paper CAA-TP-87-16, 1987), which finds that battle death ratios afford a reasonable measure of both combat effectiveness and chances of victory in war. Dupuy, *Numbers, Predictions and War,* and *Understanding War* both incorporate a battle death ratio as a measure of military effectiveness.

23. In recent years, the intense analysis of the conventional balance in Europe frequently focused on the expected "exchange rates" which could be achieved in favor of the numerically inferior NATO forces. Occasionally, the relationship between skill and the ability to inflict greater casualties was explicitly recognized, as in John J. Mearsheimer, "Numbers, Strategy, and the European Balance," *International Security,* vol. 12:174–185, especially p. 176fn.

24. Until the latter part of the Civil War, US military doctrine stressed maneuver over attrition. From the closing campaigns of Grant, to Pershing in WWI, attritional war-fighting was espoused, with concerns about casualties being overridden. From WWII to the present, the US has accommodated a national sensitivity to casualty levels, with an emphasis on close support firepower and mechanization, to its still-dominant attritional approach to warfare. See Russell F. Weigley, *The American Way of War: A History of United States Military Strategy and Policy* (New York: Macmillan Publishers, 1973).

25. See Trevor N. Dupuy, *Understanding War: History and Theory in Combat.* Allan Millett and Williamson Murray, *Military Efficiency,* also give the Germans high marks, though their approach is considerably less quantitative than Dupuy's.

26. Small and Singer, *Resort to Arms,* p. 91, also reflects this overall ratio. Dupuy, *Numbers, Predictions and War,* pp. 98–110, provides enough data on battle deaths by front to show that the Germans enjoyed a nearly 3:1 battle death exchange ratio versus the Russians. The comparable figure versus the Allies in the West is 1.05:1.

27. Non-Israeli assessments have been provided by: John B. Glubb, *A Soldier With the Arabs* (London: Hodder and Stoughton, 1956); Edgar O'Ballance, *The Arab-Israeli War* (London: Faber and Faber, 1956); and Lawrence L. Whetten, *The Canal War* (Cambridge: MIT Press, 1974).

28. The wars and ratios are: Palestine (1948)—2.67, Six-Day (1967)—18.6, War of Attrition (1969-70)—13.59, and Yom Kippur (1973)—4.47. The Suez War is excluded because of British and French participation, which would cloud a judgment solely of the Israelis.

29. A reputable estimate of military effectiveness in this war is provided by Christopher Martin, *The Russo-Japanese War* (New York: Abelard Schulman, 1967).

30. All of the averages fall between one tenth and one twentieth of one percent. Even when population outliers who generally fought small wars, such as China, are excluded, the averages rise only minimally (still under one sixth of one percent with China and India deleted).

31. Total mobilization data *is* readily available for World Wars I and II, and the percentages for these cases reflect this.

32. See Dupuy, *Numbers, Predictions and War,* pp. 47–50.

33. Made available through the Inter-University Consortium for Political and Social Research (ICPSR). The index is composed of military, industrial and demographic factors. Its general acceptance and common usage are discussed earlier in this chapter.

34. Much of the economic data employed in these tests is generated from B. R. Mitchell, *European Historical Statistics, 1750-1970* (New York: Columbia University Press, 1976); *Statistical Yearbook* (New York: United Nations, 1948-81); and *World Tables* (Baltimore: The Johns Hopkins University Press, 1971-80). Country-specific data sources are listed in "References."

35. See Appendix III.

36. See his *Armaments and History* (London: Eyre and Spottiswoode, 1945), p. ii.

37. Friedrich Engels, *Anti-Duhring* (New York: International Publishers, Inc., 1939 ed.), p. 185. The interaction of raw industrial might with technological advances was the key element of the "force theory" which he developed.

38. In *Guns and Sails in the Early Phase of European Expansion, 1400-1700* (London: Collins Publishing, 1965), Cipolla credits the "marriage of gun and sail," a technological innovation, as the cause of the West's dominance over the international system.

39. Martin Van Creveld, *Technology and War: From 2000 B.C. to the Present* (New York: Free Press, 1989), offers a counterargument, supported by his analysis of history, that the logic of war is frequently opposed to the logic of technology. A good example of the conflict he describes is offered by modern aircraft carriers. Van Creveld holds that the logic of technology has led to the creation of a small number of large carriers, while the logic of war dictates that a large number of smaller carriers, decreasing the vulnerability of the carrier arm to countermeasures, should be constructed. Andrew C. Hess,

"The Evolution of the Ottoman Seaborne Empire in the Age of the Oceanic Discoveries, 1453–1525," *American Historical Review,* vol. 75 (1970):1892-1919, takes sharp issue with Cipolla's theory of European dominance. Ottoman technological inferiority is acknowledged by Hess, but their ability to rebuff invasions of their vulnerable Southeastern borders through vigorous defense of coastal waters by their galley fleets, was nonetheless quite evident. Also, despite their technological backwardness, they remained a dominant player in European power politics, continuing their expansion until nearly 1700.

40. The technology hypothesis postulates that the side in possession of more modern *types* of weapons will prevail, even against vastly superior numbers. The archtypical example would be the successful defense of Rorke's Drift, in the Zulu Wars, in which less than a hundred rifle-armed British soldiers defeated a spear-carrying native army of some 6000. English possession of the longbow at Agincourt is another example. Any variable representing "technology" must strive to capture this qualitative essence.

41. And in this subset of wars, the Great Power's technological edge is frequently highly collinear with greater composite capabilities and superior naval strength. These results also hold when separate tests of land and land–sea wars are made.

42. The closest one can come to a definable technological edge at the outset of Great Power wars is in an examination of radar in the early phases of World War II. In the European theater, the British air defense radar is rightly credited with improving the RAF's capabilities against the Luftwaffe. But this point relates rather to the inherent defensive advantages of a radar-equipped defender, not to the technology itself. In fact, German radar technology was quite sophisticated, especially in relation to naval gunnery, in which a considerable edge was held throughout much of the war. In the Pacific theater, the United States had ship-borne detection radar from the outset, the Japanese had none. Yet, in night surface actions, the Japanese overcame this disadvantage, inflicting several punishing defeats on sometimes larger American battle groups.

43. Technological superiority is also mildly correlated (.29, p < .05) with skill. However, when the Great versus minor power conflicts are controlled for, the intercorrelation drops to .09, and is statistically insignificant. Not only are Great Powers generally stronger than minor powers on land and sea. It seems that they also have better troops, better led, in most cases of this uneven category of war.

44. The technological edge of the loser was smallest in this war. However, the Soviets possessed an abundance of artillery which vastly outranged and outperformed anything which could be mustered by the newly founded Polish state, which relied heavily on cavalry for its national defense. Piotr S. Wandycz, *Soviet-Polish Relations, 1917-1921* (Cambridge: Harvard University Press, 1969), points out that the Poles stayed scrupulously out of the Russian civil war, and fought only to keep from being overrun by a Soviet invasion aimed at spreading Marxism "at the point of a bayonet." Norman Davies, *White Eagle, Red Star: The Polish-Soviet War, 1919-1920* (New York: St. Martin's, 1972), chronicles the Soviet technological advantage, as well as the significant edge its forces had in combat experience.

45. Robert Ardrey, *The Territorial Imperative* (New York: Atheneum, 1966).

46. Ardrey even tries to make the connection with human warfare: "The principal cause of modern warfare arises from the failure of an intruding power correctly to estimate the defensive resources of a territorial defender. The enhancement of energy engendered in the defending proprietor; the union of partners welded by the first sound of gunfire; the biological morality demanding individual sacrifice, even of life; all of the

innate commands of the territorial imperative act to multiply the apparent resources of a defending nation" (pp. 236–237).

47. James D. Morrow, "Social Choice and System Structure in World Politics," *World Politics,* vol. 41 (1989):75–97.

48. Jane Holl, *From the Streets of Washington to the Roofs of Saigon: Domestic Politics and the Termination of the Vietnam War* (Stanford: Ph.D. Dissertation, 1989), focuses on the importance of domestic politics to the war termination process, but also builds into her model the explicit assumption (pp. 6–7) that asymmetrical motivation is a key determinant of outcome. A side which is fighting a "total" war will generally be able to overcome a side engaged in a "limited" war. This is really quite similar to Ardrey's ethology generated ideas.

49. World War II should be excluded, as the war in Europe was ended and the Japanese decisively defeated before nuclear weapons were possessed (or employed).

50. The Yom Kippur War is excluded because of official uncertainty about Israeli possession of these weapons. In any event, the war was won by Israel's superior application of conventional force. However, even when Israel is included in this set, because Israel might have had these weapons in 1973, the nuclear variable still does not become significant.

51. Because of the indecisive outcome of this war, it was excluded. The ambiguous nature of the war's outcome is accepted by the COW Project, and by Bueno de Mesquita, *The War Trap,* p. 209. Harry G. Summers, *On Strategy* (New York: Dell Publishing, 1982), p. 239 suggests that *both* sides won in Korea. A. F. K. Organski and Jacek Kugler, *The War Ledger* (Chicago: University of Chicago Press, 1980), p. 3 calls the war a "stalemate."

52. See Paul Huth and Bruce Russett, "Deterrence Failure and Crisis Escalation," *International Studies Quarterly,* vol. 32 (1988):29–45, which states: "Irrelevant to deterrence outcomes were both the defender's possession of nuclear weapons and an overt threat by the defender to use such weapons" (p. 38).

53. Ibid., p. 38. Huth and Russett describe this situation as ruled by "normative inhibition."

54. Kenneth N. Waltz, *Man, the State and War* (New York: Columbia University Press, 1954), p. 236, describes this condition as one of "mutual fear of big weapons[.]" His further caution is that such fear "may produce, instead of peace, a spate of smaller wars" (p. 236). From 1985 to the present, the average number of ongoing wars during any year was, according to Brassey's *War Annuals,* thirty-one. Wars go on, despite nuclear weapons; and the path to victory in them relies more on the considerations outlined by this study than on fission or fusion weapons.

55. Giulio Douhet, *Command of the Air,* Ferrari translation (New York: Coward-McCann, 1942); and Alexander P. De Seversky, *Victory Through Air Power* (New York: Simon and Schuster, 1942). A perceptive critique of airpower's "claims of autonomy" is offered by Edward N. Luttwak, *Strategy: The Logic of War and Peace* (Cambridge: Harvard University Press, 1987), pp.164–168.

56. It should be noted that the "Technology" variable does not adequately address the notion of air superiority. Superior technology refers, for example, to having an air force when the other side does not, or to having jets against an enemy's biplanes (or tanks vs. cavalry). The technology variable does not reflect one side's preponderance of planes against its enemy, requiring the use of a separate variable. Subsequent regressions were run both with and without the technology variable in the model.

57. The anti-colonial "flavor" of this case comes from Thailand's history of resistance to Western interlopers. Though never colonized by France, it had strongly resisted British control, and could be expected to do the same against a neighboring colonial "puppet" regime. Robert Paxton, *Vichy France* (New York: Alfred A. Knopf, 1972), pp. 89–101, provides a good overview of this case.

58. Daniel Dawson, *The Mexican Adventure* (London: G. Bell and Sons, 1935) is a comprehensive study that is quite sensitive to Maximilian's growing military and diplomatic isolation.

59. Carl von Clausewitz, *On War,* ed. and trans. by Michael Howard and Peter Paret (Princeton: Princeton University Press, 1976), p. 86.

60. This study specifically challenges Bueno de Mesquita's contention, in *The War Trap,* p. 92, that "[g]enerally, the side with the larger positive expected utility—and hence the greater incentive and pool of resources with which to keep on fighting—will win." A review of his 76 cases of interstate war (pp. 208–209) reflects that only 38 (50%) had "larger" expected utility.

Chapter 5

Why "Losers" Start Wars

War can protect; it cannot create. —Alfred North Whitehead

Armed with the insight regarding war's dual nature developed by this study, how is one to move from an explanation of the varying paths to victory to an understanding of why "losing" wars are begun? The quantitative testing employed in the previous chapter confirmed that "skill" and sea power are, respectively, the key ingredients needed in order to win land and land–sea wars. But if the decision makers of potential aggressor states are substantially, even if imperfectly, rational, why do they start wars against nations with better troops or bigger navies? The answer, as applied to land wars, is that accurate foreknowledge of which side has more skilled forces, and is led by superior generals, is very difficult to obtain. Therefore, if the "skill" theory of victory is accepted, the fact that many land wars are begun by the side which loses should be somewhat unsurprising. Further, if leaders contemplating the initiation of land wars believe that "strength" is the key to victory, then the "loser" phenomenon grows even less puzzling. History is full of examples of the quantifiably "weak" triumphing over the strong. In the 30 land wars analyzed by this study, 13 (43%) were won by the side clearly inferior in quantifiable strength. In this same set of wars, the initiator won only 15 (50%), while the side with superior skill won 26 (87%).

The simple solution to the land war puzzle is not easily applied to land-sea wars, upon which the cases examined in this chapter focus. Naval mastery has been identified in this study as the crucial factor leading to victory in wars with significant maritime aspects. However, unlike "skill," which is hard to measure before a war, the relative sea power of potential adversaries is generally well known. Indeed, the cases in which there is even a modicum of opposing naval "balance" are quite few. Why, then, if information is not a problem, are land-sea wars started by those who are clearly inferior in naval strength? The idea that the leaders of land powers do not fully understand the importance of naval strength is an important one, which merits investigation; but a complete answer to this second part of the "loser" puzzle requires an examination of key organizational and bureaucratic actors as well.

In the last part of Chapter 3, some modifications to existing theories of organizational and bureaucratic behavior were introduced. In particular, the notion that military organizations are driven by self-interest to espouse offensive doctrines was considered a proposition of *conditional* validity. Navies of continental powers, the key organizational actors in this study, were theorized to have differing perceptions of their interests in peace and war. While offensive doctrines might make the best sense for the organization in peacetime, favoring bigger budgets and building programs, the onset of war should be seen as compelling the navies of land powers to switch to a doctrine that ensures their organization's survival by avoiding the risk of their hard-won fleet's destruction.

The foregoing may be summarized in two testable hypotheses designed to explain why "losers" start land–sea wars:

1. Leaders of continental powers have substantial but imperfect understanding of maritime affairs, which significantly lessens their inhibitions about starting land-sea wars.
2. The naval doctrine of continental powers will be offensive in peacetime, encouraging aggression, but will switch precipitately to the defensive with the onset of war.

If these hypotheses are found to be true, then the puzzling phenomenon of "loser" initiation of land–sea wars will have finally been explained. Land powers start "losing" land–sea wars because their political leaders do not fully appreciate the importance of sea power. Also, their naval leaders have convinced them that whatever threat they face from the sea can be dealt with successfully. The harsh reality that soon intrudes informs the aggressor that his war plans failed to consider the exigencies of land–sea warfare, and that he commands a timid war navy, radically differing from the confident, aggressive one upon which he relied to contest for command of the sea with a reasonable chance of success.

There are two possible approaches to testing these hypotheses. The first would employ the "case study" method, requiring the examination of all "loser" initiations of land-sea war during the period surveyed. The results of the studies could then be statistically tabulated, and a judgment could be made as to the causal impact of the variables being tested. There are only ten such cases between 1815 and 1980, a number so small as to make any statistical-correlational finding subject to some doubt. Therefore, a second approach, the "counterfactual case method," will be employed.

It has recently been pointed out that counterfactual logic is widely employed in both historical and political analyses.[1] Essentially, it argues that, in the absence of some key variable, the course of events would have been radically altered. "Proof" is obtained not by testing against a large number of comparable cases, but by relying, for analytic purposes, on the behavior predicted by other theories.[2] In this chapter, two cases of "loser" initiation will be examined in some detail. The hypothesized behaviors of key decision makers and organizational actors will be searched out. If the above hypotheses are borne out, then a counterfactual analysis, employing the "rational actor" theory, as well as some limited historical examples, for comparative purposes, will demonstrate that, absent the hypothesized actions, "loser" war initiation would not have occurred.[3]

For the purposes of the cases to be examined, the first steps will be to identify the leader's imperfect understanding of land-sea war, and the organizational pathology that leads to precipitate doctrinal shifting. Then, the cases will be compared to what they would have been like if the leader's understanding of maritime considerations was a full one, and if organizational influences had abated with the onset of war. It is important to note that counterfactual logic will not necessarily result in the finding that war would have been avoided. Rather, it will demonstrate that a "losing war" would not have been begun. This result might be achieved either by the continuance of peace, or by the initiation and waging of a war with single-minded determination to achieve command of the sea.[4]

CASE SELECTION

Throughout this study, global wars have come under continual scrutiny. They are conflicts in which the continental powers that start them always lose (see Chapter 1, Table 1.1, and the discussion of global war in Chapter 2). At the heart of the puzzle of "loser" war initiation, they also have the greatest and longest-lasting impact on the international system, and upon the quality of life within it. They also offer the opportunity to test rigorously both hypotheses of "loser" behavior—leadership's imperfect understanding of land–sea wars, and precipitate shifting of naval doctrine, resulting from undue organizational influences.

Of the global wars begun by land powers, which should be examined? To some degree, each must be considered. Otherwise, it might be contended that land-bound thinking and self-serving naval bureaucracies existed in just one or two cases. The best way to proceed, therefore, is to look for some general indicators that the hypothesized behaviors consistently appear. Then the "toughest" cases, those in which the land power has posed the most potent challenge to its foe's naval mastery, which also imply the greatest understanding of the importance of sea power, will be selected for detailed examination. These would be what Eckstein has called "least likely" cases.[5] If there are any instances in which land powers should *not* shift away from an offensive sea control doctrine, these should be the ones.

In considering general indicators, this study has fixed upon three measures that should give some sense of whether or not naval challenges are being systematically mounted and then abandoned. First, the absolute growth of the naval strength of continental powers in the 10 years preceding their war initiations will be examined. Substantial growth rates will tend to confirm that a sensitivity to the importance of naval matters did exist. Second, the corresponding ratio of naval power relative to the maritime hegemon will be examined, also at 10 years' prior to war and at its outbreak. Finally, the issue of doctrinal shifting will be considered. Naval doctrine prior to and after war's outbreak will be characterized as offensive or defensive, with shifts noted. Offensive sea fights, started in an effort to gain sea command, will also be noted.

The results of this preliminary testing for case selection purposes confirm that all of the land powers were striving mightily to improve their ability to "go to sea" during the decade preceding the launching of their wars. Their absolute growth rates are uniformly high (see Table 5.1), with the exception of France in the decade between the end of the American War of Independence and the onset of the Napoleonic Wars. In terms of their naval strength relative to the incumbent sea powers, there is also much improvement across the board. The challenges posed by Louis XIV, Napoleon, and Kaiser Wilhelm II are the most robust. While the French navy under Louis XIV achieved actual numerical superiority, the 1.15:1 advantage in relative naval power that the Kaiser's High Sea Fleet enjoyed over the Royal Navy includes the effects of a "divisor," which affected British naval concentration capability.[6] Every land power espoused offensive sea control doctrines, except for the Habsburg navy at the outset of the Italian Wars, and each one shifted to commerce raiding soon after war began. However, the navies of Philip II, Louis, and Wilhelm each made one effort to obtain command of the sea (at, respectively, the battles of: the Armada, Beachy Head and Jutland).

On balance, though, it appears that only the global wars of Louis and Wilhelm qualify as truly "tough" tests of the theory advanced by this study. Their relative strengths drew the closest to the leading maritime power's. They even sought battles for sea control, and won them at the tactical level. They had the least reason, therefore, to abandon their offensive doctrines for commerce raiding. Napoleon's naval challenge looks strong on its face, but his navy never really sought a sea control battle. Even Trafalgar was fought with his fleet trying to run away. The numerical ratios in this latter case are also deceiving because they fail to account for the purge of naval officers from the *ancien regime,* which went on at the outset of the French Revolution. These losses were never made good, as most naval commanders were chosen for their political reliability rather than their nautical skill. Even the Royalist officers who remained were those who had held very low rank in pre-Revolutionary days.[7] Therefore, Louis and Wilhelm are the "losers" who most merit more detailed study.

Table 5.1
Naval Growth of Continental Powers Prior to Global Wars

(War)/ nation	Relevant 10-year prewar period	Initiator's battle fleet growth rate	Relative* prewar	Naval power at outbreak
(League of Cambrai)**			1499	1508
France	1499–1508	400%	.05	.16
Spain		633%	.05	.32
Portugal		1,625%	.08	1.30
(Armada)	1578–1587		1578	1587
Spain		300%	.23	.61
(Louis XIV)	1678–1688		1678	1688
France		17%***	1.72	1.66
(Napoleonic)	1783–1792		1783	1792
France		6%	.98	.99
(World War I)	1904–1913		1904	1913
Germany		114%	.74	1.15
(World War II)	1930–1939		1930	1939
Germany		500%	.10	.71

*Relative strength is measured against the continental power's maritime opponent in the global war, adjusted for dispersion factors (e.g., France always has a divisor of "2," because of its historic split beween Atlantic and Mediterranean fleets, which were often subject to defeat in detail before they could unite). The "dispersion dilemma" cannot be solved by simply concentrating all forces in one theater, as the enemy would then be ceded control of the other at very low cost.

**The naval strengths of France and Spain are measured against Venice. Portugal's foe was the Ottoman Empire.

***A deceptive figure, as it masks Louis's earlier decades of great naval expansion. There was no need for feverish growth at this point because of a favorable existing balance. The key decade to examine is the period 1661–1670, which coincides with Louis taking active control of the reins of government. During this period, naval growth aggregated over 300%. Also, if Dutch naval power is added to British in 1688 (because of the alliance created by Wiliam's joint rule of these countries), French relative naval strength reduces to .96:1.

Source: George Modelski and William R. Thompson, *Seapower in Global Politics* (Seattle: University of Washington Press, 1988).

THE CASES

1. The Global War of Louis XIV

Historical narrative. Reigning over France for 72 years, Louis XIV matched his unparalleled longevity as a ruler with a ferociously single-minded determination to expand French power. He ascended the throne at the age of four, in 1643, and was soon indoctrinated for life in the militant nationalism of his prime minister, Cardinal Mazarin. This cleric preached a gospel of territorial expansion, buttressed by balanced land and naval forces. By the time Louis took primary control over French policy in 1660, Mazarin's vision had become his own.[8] He began systematically to expand his military might under the stewardship of his gifted state secretaries for the army and navy, Louvois and Colbert.[9]

After more than a decade of buildup, an outstanding opportunity for expansion presented itself in the form of the weakened United Provinces. The Dutch had received rather the worst of it in two wars with Britain when, in 1672, the English began yet another conflict with them. Louis seized the chance to join in the plunder of the Dutch, and his 400,000-man army was soon sweeping through the Low Countries.[10] In the Mediterranean, his battle fleet sought out weak Dutch formations, routinely thrashing them. However, in 1674, the Dutch purchased Britain's exit from the war by ceding their holdings in North America, which included what would be renamed New York. France continued the war alone, battering Dutch armies in Flanders and what was left of de Ruyter's proud navy. In 1676, the legendary Admiral de Ruyter, who had once led a raid up the Thames, would die in action against a vastly superior French fleet at Stromboli.[11]

When the war was at its bleakest, however, the Dutch called upon 21-year-old William, Prince of Orange, whose ancestor had led the revolt against Spain nearly a century before. In a grim enactment of his family motto, "we shall maintain," William led Dutch forces from one defeat to another. Finally, with the French closing in upon Amsterdam, William opened the dikes that held back the sea, turning his capital into an unassailable island. The waters were too shallow for the French navy to negotiate, while the Dutch were past masters of naval movement under such conditions. Though the Dutch had been militarily defeated, and their country laid waste, William refused to surrender. Louis, frustrated, agreed to a negotiated peace that granted him limited territorial gains and some indemnities.

Something else that he gained was the lifelong enmity of William, who proceeded to build the foundation of a "grand alliance" designed to thwart Louis's ambitions. Louis was ambitious. He continued to probe for weakness in the United Provinces, expanded his eastern frontier beyond the Rhine, and pursued control over the Spanish throne. At sea, he continued to expand a navy whose outlook was increasingly global.[12] In the face of this aggressiveness, William sought to align the United Provinces with various German states and Britain. He was third-in-line to the British throne and, in 1688, when James II was deposed because he had been favored with an heir who would continue his barely tolerated Catholic ways, William was invited to assume the kingship.

Louis was extremely concerned by this development, knowing well that the new alliance of Britain and Holland under William could severely constrict his ability to expand. Two other matters had been exerting pressure on Louis to act decisively. First, the archbishopric of Cologne had been given to an anti-French candidate, limiting Louis's control over this satellite. Additionally, Austria had just won a convincing victory over the Turks. Soon, it would be free to oppose his eastward expansion. Sensing that his aims would never have a better chance of success, Louis invaded the Palatinate in September of 1688, and declared war on the United Provinces and Britain a month later. This latter action was precipitated by his decision to assist his co-religionist James in regaining his throne. To some extent, French aggression may thus be characterized as "preventive."

Because of French depredations in the Palatinate, and incursions into Spain, the war soon expanded to include most of Europe among France's enemies. Seemingly endless indecisive land campaigns ensued, with the French winning tactical victories and William's coalition armies avoiding strategic defeat. At sea, France opened the war as the leading naval power. Strangely, it made no move to assert naval mastery. While Louis strove to overthrow William by engineering James II's invasion of Ireland a few months after the war's start, Seignelay, Colbert's son and successor as state secretary of the navy, saw fit to support this venture initially with only three frigates, adding only modest reinforcements later.[13] Soon, lacking supplies, the expedition turned into a complete disaster.

Louis exerted pressure on Seignelay to engage the Allies' battle fleet, and was joined by Louvois, the state secretary for the army. Louvois, unhappy with the indecisiveness of the land campaigns, and the growing numbers which his forces faced, clamored for either aggressive naval action or the disbanding of the navy.[14] In 1690, the French fleet finally put to sea looking for battle. It consisted of 75 ships-of-the-line under the command of Admiral de Tourville. At Beachy Head it encountered and defeated an allied fleet of 59 sail under Admiral Torrington. The French navy returned triumphantly to port, and stayed there.

For the balance of Louis's global war, the French battle fleet would strive to avoid pitched battles. Portions of de Tourville's command would be coaxed out a few times, suffering a tactical defeat at La Hogue in 1692, and winning a small victory off of Lagos in 1693. After that, the battle fleet simply remained "in being," with the naval war directed against allied commerce, and prosecuted almost entirely by frigates and privateers, the most famous of which was commanded by Jean Bart. A complete switch was made, from an offensive *guerre d'escadre* sea control doctrine to what has been called an "inherently defeatist"[15] commerce raiding doctrine of the *guerre de course*.

On land, the pattern of indecisive campaigning would continue. At the treaty of Ryswick in 1697, a temporary peace was achieved on the basis of the *status quo ante bellum*. Soon, however, the war heated up again, with Louis's primary aim shifting to control of Spain. In this last half of his global war, Louis's navy made no effort to contest for sea control, and his armies were finally defeated by coalition forces under the command of the Duke of Marlborough. The war ended with France bankrupt, having failed to achieve any of its grandiose aims.

Hypothesis testing and analysis. With regard to the first hypothesized cause of "loser initiation," that the leaders of continental powers have an imperfect understanding of land–sea war, there appears to be considerable supporting evidence in the case of Louis XIV. The issue is not his failure to accept the importance of sea power, but rather his flawed reasoning regarding its workings. Mahan provides the best and most extensive analysis of Louis's inherent maritime failings. First, he notes that Louis's notion of sea power was entirely military, lacking the understanding that a vigorous merchant marine provided the economic nourishment which a navy requires. His refusal to support French maritime commerce is viewed, by Mahan, to be the root cause of the later French naval collapse.[16] Also, Louis was insensitive to all advice that counseled him to achieve naval mastery before attempting further continental expansion. Indeed, the philosopher Leibnitz proposed a "sea first" grand strategy to Louis, which predicted disaster if territorial aggrandizement were to precede maritime dominion. His admonition had no effect.[17]

In addition to pre-war indications of Louis's incomplete understanding of sea power, Mahan finds a body of perplexing, inconsistent behavior in his wartime actions. Though Louis had spent decades building a navy, which outnumbered the combined fleet strength of Britain and Holland at the outbreak of war in 1688, Louis failed to call for a general fleet action. When one occurred, at Beachy Head in 1690, the French were victorious. Again, Louis did no prodding for follow-on operations. His strategic decision to support James's plan to invade his former realm, the proximate cause of France's declaration of war on Britain, was completely undermined by Louis's dispatch of only light naval elements to back the combined operation.

Mahan views Louis's failure to capitalize on the victory at Beachy Head as the gravest strategic blunder of his long career, greater than his failure to provide adequate naval support for James's invasion of Ireland.[18] Yet, it's unfair to lay the entire blame for failure on Louis. After all, it was he who single-mindedly pursued naval expansion, building fleets, ports, and bringing able naval advisors to his side. That he ultimately acceded to requests to abandon the naval offensive, though, replacing it with expanded operations on land and a commerce raiding strategy at sea, resulted both from his perception of sea power and from the advice of his senior military and naval leaders.

The final decision to abandon the *guerre d'escadre* was made by Louis only after a heated debate within the French policy establishment, in which organizational influences figured prominently. The navy, which had espoused an offensive sea control doctrine since the early days of Colbert's administration, had oddly avoided combat from the outset of the war against the Grand Alliance. Indeed, its tactical doctrine made an almost immediate shift to the defensive, ordering ships-of-the-line to seek only positions from which they maintained an unimpaired ability to escape action. During the policy debates, the navy contended that it had to remain "in being," ready to strike counterblows against any invasion attempts by the coalition.[19]

The army position, championed by Louvois, was that the navy should be disbanded, its guns and crews mustered into the army. A fast cavalry force would be created to meet any threat of coastal depredations. One of Colbert's disciples, Bonrepaus, refuted the argument that cavalry could supplant a fleet for defensive purposes; but the navy was clearly in trouble. The French economy was suffering, as the harvest had been poor, and Louis had been compelled to impose a capitation tax to fund the war. Resources were growing scarce, and hard choices had to made about military spending.

At this critical juncture, a bureaucratic compromise was reached that pleased the army and the navy, even though it guaranteed defeat in the war by ending the French challenge for naval mastery. Vauban, the renowned master builder of fortresses, entered the debate by suggesting that the existing battle fleet should be retained for defensive purposes, but that all future naval efforts should be focused on commerce raiding. This, he argued, could be achieved largely by means of non-governmental investment in privateers. The army was pleased because the lion's share of the military budget was freed up for its use. The navy was pleased by the preservation of its battle fleet, and the chance to pursue an active naval war at little risk to its capital assets. Pontchartrain, the successor to Colbert's son, the Marquis de Seignelay, who had died of cancer shortly after the victory at Beachy Head, recommended this course to Louis, who accepted it.[20]

The *guerre de course* was extremely popular among French admirals, several of whom made fortunes by leading syndicates that invested in privateers.[21] Unfortunately, commerce raiding did nothing to knock Britain or Holland out of the war, and could not keep the British from fielding armies on the continent, one of which finally defeated the French. The additional funds freed up by the neglect of the battle fleet, the benefit of which the French army received, could only prolong a bitter attritional struggle in a land–sea war that could never be won.

While it is clear that Louis had, at best, a "bounded" sort of rationality with regard to land–sea war, and that the French navy behaved as this study's findings regarding organizational theory suggest (offensive doctrine in peace, defensive in war), further analysis is required in order to demonstrate that these factors caused a "loser" to start the war. According to the counterfactual analytic method described earlier in this chapter, it is necessary now to consider how a rational actor would have behaved in Louis's circumstances. For if a rational actor's better understanding of land–sea war, along with the abatement of organizational influences, would have resulted either in the keeping of the peace, or in the more successful waging of a war, then the cause of "loser" initiation will have been demonstrated.[22]

Would a rational actor have begun this conflict? If he lacked confidence in the ability of the French navy to achieve sea control, then he would not have started the war against Holland and England. Louis had complete confidence in his navy's ability to win command of the sea. It had decisively defeated the Dutch navy in the most recent war, and was much larger and better equipped than the Royal Navy, which had suffered from budgetary constraints since the end of the Third Anglo-Dutch War.[23]

On the other hand, the continuance of peace would by no means have made

France susceptible to conquest. Neither Spain nor the Low Countries had the ability, even in alliance with Britain, to conquer France; and Austria would always have to worry about the Turks in its rear. France had maintained cordial relations with the "Sublime Porte" for decades, with just this notion of its value as a counterweight in mind.[24] However, France's aims were expansionist, and a rational actor who saw the reasonable chance to win command of the sea would have begun this war.

The war would have been waged in a strikingly different fashion, however. First, James II's invasion of Ireland would have been given full naval support, preventing the disaster that ensued. Second, the French battle fleet would have sought out confrontation sooner rather than later, and would have followed up its victory with more aggressive action. In short, a rational actor would *never* have allowed the fatal switch to the *guerre de course*. The avoidance of an early fleet confrontation, and the inadequate naval support given to James's restoration effort are each quite inconsistent with pre-war fleet development and planning. Consistency is one of the hallmarks of rationality.

The organizational and bureaucratic "pulling and hauling" which dragged naval doctrine away from offensive sea control would have been overcome by a rational leader's unquestionable authority (certainly Louis XIV had sufficient executive power) to set policy. Finally, the land war would not have been expanded into the Palatinate and Spain until command of the sea had been achieved, and the British and Dutch defeated. Also, it is interesting to note that Louis's expansion of the land war is consistent with the theory, which this study has propounded, that continental aggressors tend to "create" the balances arrayed against them. France's enemies all entered this war by virtue of either French invasion or declaration of war upon them.

To some extent, the analysis of this case confirms existing theories about why Louis lost this war. His lack of understanding of the requirements for successful combined operations has been well chronicled; and he must be largely blamed for the disastrous failure of the Irish expedition. Beyond this, though, Louis emerges as one aware of the need for command of the sea. This was instilled in him very early on by Mazarin. He spent decades building a first-rate fleet, faced always by the opposition of the Army and its chief civil administrator, Louvois. During the war, he continued to push for fleet confrontation until, after long, heated debate, his army and navy leaders both called for an official change in doctrine. That Louis acceded to the request for a shift to the *guerre de course* is in itself evidence that organizational influences persist well beyond the onset of war. It also suggests that the "bureaucratic politics" model of decision making does a better job of explaining intra- rather than pre-war decisional outputs. The army, as the senior service, should have prevailed in peacetime bureaucratic "pulling and hauling," but did not. In war, civilian intervention should have overcome army opposition to the battle fleet, but also did not.

Interestingly, William also called for a debate regarding commerce raiding versus sea control. Initially, he leaned toward a vigorous *guerre de course* against the French. In this case, however, the British army was not included in the debate. The Royal Navy, steeped in the offensive doctrine that it had developed during the three Anglo-Dutch Wars, and unthreatened by army interests, convinced William that sea control was their prime mission. William acceded to the Navy's point of view, the consequence being that sea control was never compromised, though French commerce suffered only slightly during the war.[25]

Finally, it is necessary to consider whether or not the explanation of the precipitate French naval doctrinal shift offered in this study is more convincing than that developed by previous theories. The French shift away from a sea control doctrine in this war is quite well known, though its importance to the outcome has been undervalued. There are two major explanations. First, Louis's "naval myopia" has been held to blame for the change. However, as the examination of this case has shown, Louis was an ardent supporter of an active battle fleet, and agreed to the change only after the weight of bureaucratic opposition became too great for him to resist. The other theory that has, to some extent, supplanted the direct critique of Louis, is that there was simply no choice for the French but to change doctrines. The worsening economy, the increasing cost of the field armies, and several bad harvests all conspired, according to this theory, to make it impossible for France to match allied naval growth. The *guerre de course* offered France its best opportunity in an inevitably eroding situation at sea.[26]

Certainly there is no question but that Symcox is right about the pressures on the French economy at this point, and about the allied naval buildup that was underway. But fiscal pressures in no way explain why the French battle fleet waited nearly two years from the start of the war before it challenged the allies. Only under Louis's prodding did it go to sea looking to fight. Then, in the face of the allies' naval resurgence, why should fiscal distress logically call for French *naval* reductions? If command of the sea was crucial to the successful prosecution of the war, shouldn't these financial straits have resulted in some "belt tightening" by the army? The rational actor model used in the counterfactual analytic aspect of this case would definitely call for continued sustenance of the French naval effort. This is especially the case because the situation on land still greatly favored the French. They had the finest and largest army in Europe, and could choose to escalate or de-escalate the pace of operations at will during this period of the war. Indeed, the army's offensive actions in the Palatinate and Spain incurred Louis's stern displeasure. So, while it may be said that Symcox's facts are correct, his conclusion does seem open to question, especially when viewed from the counterfactual perspective of the "rational actor."

2. The Kaiser's War

The developments leading up to the outbreak of World War I, particularly the activities of the relevant parties during the "July Crisis" of 1914, are certainly among the most comprehensively reported and examined events in history. Perhaps this is so because of the general sense that no party involved preferred a major war, and that its onset and outcome brought great hardship to both victor and vanquished alike. Some may also find reason to study these events in the hope that a fuller understanding of this period will assist in the formulation of plans, procedures, and safeguards that would prevent the recurrence of such a tragedy. At this point, is there anything new to be added to the study of this conflagration's origins and conduct? Despite the mountainous body of work that already exists, this study suggests that there is still much which may be uncovered.

The insight into war's duality developed in the preceding chapters suggests that, with the assistance of a new theory of the importance of naval power to victory in land-sea war, and hypotheses generated from theories of individual, organizational and bureaucratic behavior, explanation of this war's onset and its outcome may be greatly enhanced. In particular, the powerful influences that led to the German challenge for command of the sea, and its precipitate abandonment, will be closely examined for their causal impact on the Kaiser's initiation of a "losing" war. Thus, the possibilities that Wilhelm's understanding of sea power was flawed, and that organizational and bureaucratic influences contributed significantly to the disastrous decision to change naval doctrine early in the war, must be carefully considered.

Historical narrative. Unlike the France of Louis XIV, which had been at the time of his birth a cohesive nation for centuries already, the modern German state did not even exist when Wilhelm Hohenzollern came into the world in 1859. Full unification would only be achieved by the time of his early adolescence in 1871, at the end of Chancellor Otto von Bismarck's string of victories in limited wars. After the crushing blow delivered against France in the Franco-Prussian War, Bismarck set about the business of consolidating his gains. Germany would be, in his vision, a Great Power, but one interested in maintaining the *status quo*.[27]

Wilhelm, on the other hand, would grow to maturity with a strong sense that Germany's position in the international system was below what it merited, and that its era of expansion lay ahead of rather than behind it. His domineering mother and stern tutors inculcated a vision of German greatness not unlike that which Mazarin cultivated in Louis XIV with regard to France. By the time he became Kaiser in 1888, Wilhelm's view of Germany's place in the world was fully formulated, and considerably at variance with Bismarck's.[28] This fundamental difference in world views was one factor in the chancellor's soon being driven from office by Wilhelm in March of 1890. The Kaiser would then have nearly a quarter of a century to pursue his aspirations for German world power, before beginning the disastrous "losing" war that would end in his abdication.

From the earliest years of his reign, the Kaiser sought to create a first-rate navy, which would move Germany away from its one-dimensional image as a continental power. In 1890, the German navy was stunted whereas the army was robust. The army was quite happy with the existing relationship between the services and, though the navy desired growth, it lacked the bureaucratic strength to win funds for expansion. However, the Kaiser's personal interest in naval affairs, fueled by his enthrallment with the recently published work of Mahan, led him to intervene in favor of the navy.[29]

Soon, the Kaiser found his latter-day counterpart to Louis's Colbert in the person of Admiral Alfred von Tirpitz. Tirpitz was also a dedicated Mahanian, and an ardent lobbyist for the creation of a battle fleet. Tirpitz would use Mahan's arguments about sea control to critique the idea of building light forces for cruiser warfare or commerce raiding. He was an enormously capable administrator, as comfortable analyzing ship specifications as with lobbying the *Reichstag* to pass his costly Navy Bills. With the Kaiser's support, he overcame all bureaucratic opposition, and a vigorous German naval expansion was soon underway.

How large a fleet needed to be built? Here Tirpitz had a clever idea, based on his insights regarding British naval power. He reasoned that the Royal Navy, with its many global commitments, could never muster all of its forces to oppose a German naval threat. Therefore, if only a battle fleet two thirds the size of the Royal Navy's could be constructed, the British would never chance a fight with Germany. Thus the famous "risk theory" was born. Its central formulation was that, once the critical overall force ratio was reached, Germany had a reasonable chance of defeating the Royal Navy. Because of this possibility, and the probability that, even if defeated, the German navy would inflict mortal damage to the British, Tirpitz argued that Britain would avoid conflict with Germany. A freer hand in both colonial and continental affairs could be won by these means. In this way, German naval expansion may be seen to have powerful impact across a broad range of foreign policy plans.[30]

Naval doctrine began to evolve as the fleet-building program was prosecuted. From the very outset, it maintained a strong offensive tilt. A variety of plans for the defeat of Britain's Grand Fleet by Germany's High Sea Fleet were developed. Plans were also elaborated for the period after command of the sea was achieved. They ranged from additional colonial conquests, to the invasion of England.[31] These plans, including those for invasion, were widely accepted, though Tirpitz expressed his opinion that the latter notion of invasion was a ridiculous proposition.[32] Army opposition to becoming a "projectile fired by the navy" was also pronounced. The interservice rivalry spilled over to the foreign policy arena, in which the navy took a "global" perspective, while the army's vision was almost completely restricted to continental affairs.[33] Indeed, the rivalry hampered interservice cooperation so greatly that the army's Schlieffen Plan completely neglected to develop any sort of role for the navy.[34]

Shorn of its more outrageous aspects, German naval doctrine continued doggedly to espouse an offensive which would fight to achieve positive sea control, driving the Royal Navy from the North Sea. The high water mark of the offensive naval doctrine was reached in 1908, when Vice Admiral Baudissin's plan for an immediate naval offensive at war's outset was enthusiastically embraced by the Kaiser, who noted that "the explicit offensive only corresponded with his wishes."[35] Actually, the Kaiser contended that he had always *wanted* to be able to launch a naval offensive at the outset of a war with Britain, but that he had waited until the right time (10 years into the naval buildup) and plan (Baudissin's) had come along before granting his unqualified support.[36]

Further impetus for offensive plans was provided by deep German concern that the British would perceive the true nature of the German threat and elect to strike it down preventively. A popular analogy of the time was drawn between the present German situation and that of the Danes nearly a century earlier.[37] Denmark had joined in Napoleon's continental alliance against Britain; and its fleet, if added to French and Spanish naval forces, might have tipped the balance against the Royal Navy. To avoid this eventuality, the British struck a crippling preventive blow to the Danes in 1807.

The pervasive idea that the British would come after the German fleet at war's outset led to some flexibility in planning. There might be no need to steam to the British coast in search of combat. If the Royal Navy was coming, better for the High Sea Fleet to fight in "home" waters. A variety of "trapping" plans were developed with this in mind. However, the possibility that the British would not be coming was also addressed. Distant blockade by the dominant sea power was envisioned, with the only way to break it the pursuit of a vigorous offensive. By 1912, the notion of an initial waiting period was firmly established, though the offensive was still the explicit strategy. The exact time to be allotted to the "waiting offensive" was never specified, as it was left to the commander of the High Sea Fleet to seize upon the *gluecksfall*, or "lucky chance," which would give the best prospects for success.[38]

To provide some credibility for these offensive doctrines, the German fleet underwent a massive expansion during the first 20 years of Wilhelm's reign. But build as they might, the Germans had great difficulty in even beginning to approach the 2:3 (or 67%) ratio versus the British, which Tirpitz held to be a necessary condition for engagement with a reasonable chance of victory.[39] The problem was that the British had begun the naval arms race with a substantial advantage, and were capable of building new ships to maintain enough of their numerical advantage to keep the Germans in what Tirpitz called the "danger zone."[40] At any point below the two thirds level, the British could "Copenhagen" the High Sea Fleet. Because of British shipbuilding capacity, this "zone" was, as Steinberg has pointed out, "theoretically infinite."

However, in 1906, the launching of the first dreadnought, or all-big-gun, ship, had the effect of wiping out the initial British advantage in the naval arms race. Previous capital ships had maintained a balanced array of large- through small-caliber guns, giving them the theoretical capability to deal with a variety of levels of threat. With the growing realization that destroyers and cruisers had the speed and armament which made them better suited to the "lighter" tasks of naval warfare, the battleship moved inexorably to the specialized role of fighting other capital ships. Because of its powerful armament, a dreadnought could make short work of the previous generation of mixed-caliber battleships. Tirpitz was quick to seize upon this innovation as the path out of the "danger zone," and by 1912, the German navy had two thirds as many dreadnoughts as the British.[41] In the opening months of the war in 1914, the relative numbers of capital ships opposing each other in the North Sea was quite close to quantitative parity, at 15:17.[42]

With regard to the war that Wilhelm precipitated in August of 1914, it is not the place of this study to recapitulate the many causes so well chronicled in the major works on its origins.[43] It will be assumed that Germany's drive for *weltmacht* and the related naval rivalry with Britain, the many entangling alliances, and the fractious and oftimes misleading domestic politics of the key nations involved were all important factors that contributed to the war's outbreak. At the same time, in relating the events in a manner focused by this study's theory of land–sea war, an emphasis on maritime matters is necessary.

Aside from the abovementioned underlying causes of the war's outbreak, the notion that its proximate cause was "accidental" has also been advanced.[44] The prime causes of accident are seen as misperception, miscalculation and undue organizational influence (of armies). Some qualification and rebuttal to these arguments have been advanced.[45] To the extent that a month of crisis ensued after the assassination of the Archduke Franz Ferdinand and prior to any declarations of war, this study contends that there was sufficient time for Germany to weigh its chances for victory before plunging into conflict. Further, the Kaiser's limited understanding of naval matters, and the German Navy's organizational interests, are seen as factors which caused Germany to miscalculate its probability for winning the war.

Germany's opening moves in World War I were very much in line with its pre-war planning, at least on land. The strategic defensive in the East culminated in a crushing victory at Tannenberg, delivered by counterpunches against two sizeable invading Russian armies. The offensive in the West came within an ace of knocking France out of the war in the first six weeks, barely failing. Nonetheless, substantial territory had been gained, and the tactical advantages of a defensive by entrenched men firing machine guns from behind belts of barbed wire was soon well appreciated by the Germans. The General Staff switched to its "fallback" plan of a defensive in the West, with an offensive in the East. First, Russia was to be defeated, then it would be possible to resume the offensive in the West.

At sea, things proceeded in a markedly different fashion from the way in which they had been envisioned. The first surprise was that there was no "Copenhagen." The expected British attack from the sea failed to materialize, as a strategy of "distant blockade" was adopted. Nonetheless, the Germans were doctrinally prepared for this eventuality. Their "waiting offensive" had been designed to cope with such seeming passivity on the part of the British. So the

Germans "waited." And waited. In fact, there appeared to be little interest, once war had begun, in seeking the Mahanian fleet confrontation which would break British sea power. Instead, a new-found fascination with the early success of an untried new weapon, the submarine, resulted in an amazingly rapid turnabout in German naval doctrine.

Credit for catching the German Admiralty's eye must go to Lieutenant Otto Weddigen, commander of the kerosene-burning *U-9*, one of the first generation of submarines. On one August morning, Weddigen, with his crew of 28, and full complement (six) of torpedoes, sank three British cruisers, the *Aboukir*, *Hogue*, and the *Cressy*. He achieved this feat by remaining in the position from which he had struck the first while the second came to the scene. He torpedoed it as well, and gave the next rescuer a similar rough treatment. His feat became an immediate sensation, both with the German public and the leaders of the navy. What was needed now, the latter argued, was more submarines.[46]

That Germany had only 28 U-boats in total at the war's outset did not seem to bother the Admiralty. The submarine was quickly and closely embraced, and championed as the means by which the war could be won, even though it was soon clear that Weddigen's feat would probably never be repeated, due to British learning and countermeasures. Admiral Tirpitz and his advisors understood that the submarine's ability to attack battle fleets was quite limited. The submarine suffered from the weakness that, once detected, there was no way for it to maintain tactically offensive operations, a problem which persists to this day.[47] There was simply no way for it to fight for command of the sea. It could, however, prey upon commerce, and this is exactly the role in which it was soon cast.

The shift in German doctrine from sea control to commerce raiding was stark and swift. Even Admiral Tirpitz, who had spent his entire career inveighing against advocates of the *guerre de course* and other forms of "light warfare," or *kleinkrieg*, was soon prompted to support commerce raiding.[48] Indeed, the German naval bureaucracy was soon pressuring the Kaiser to expand the range and scope of commerce raiding operations. The Kaiser was reluctant to sanction such actions, on the grounds that unrestricted submarine attacks violated the laws of war, and might also bring the Americans in on the side of the Allies. Chancellor Bethmann-Hollweg also fought against the expansion of the submarine campaign for like reasons. The navy continued to push, supporting their argument with studies that showed that, even if the Americans entered the war, unrestricted submarine attacks could achieve victory before the United States could muster its great strength against Germany. By early 1917, with the Army supporting its request, the Navy was given the go-ahead to wage unrestricted submarine war. In April, the United States entered the war against Germany and, after six months of operations, it was clear that the war was far from won by the U-boats.

What happened to the High Sea Fleet during this period? Not very much. It remained "in being," which meant mostly in port. Morale grew bad, and naval officers in large numbers were asking for transfers to the Army (particularly to the cavalry).[49] From time to time, the Kaiser would inquire about its going into action,[50] and Bethmann-Hollweg encouraged a fight for sea control as a way to avert what he thought would be a disastrous submarine campaign.[51] The Army also called for battle fleet action, in fact for *any* action, as its dismal prospects in a long attrition war were becoming ever clearer. Resolutions calling for action were drawn up in the *Reichstag*. Tirpitz himself came back to his intellectual roots, arguing for fleet confrontation.

In late May 1916, under increasing pressure from all sides, Admiral Scheer, the High Sea Fleet's third war-time commander, ordered a sortie that would both quiet his critics and give him some opportunity to inflict damage on the British.[52] He hoped that some portion of the Grand Fleet might chase him back toward Germany, at which time he would turn on his pursuer. As matters turned out, the British found him and gave chase. A savage, confused naval battle ensued at Jutland, off the Danish coast. The Germans definitely won at the tactical level, sinking more ships and killing more men.[53] Yet, when the fleets returned to their respective bases, a different strategic outcome seemed to be evident. British Admiral Beatty got off a signal to London that the Grand Fleet could return to sea in 48 hours. Scheer cabled the Kaiser that he needed a minimum of three months to prepare his fleet for a return to sea.[54] Though the High Sea Fleet had suffered little relative to the damage done to the Royal Navy, Scheer wanted time for repairs. However, his behavior on his next sortie indicated that he had little relish left for fighting the British.

Two months and 20 days after Jutland, Scheer took his fleet out again. As happened during his previous sortie, he was detected and chased by the British. This time, however, there was no fight left in Scheer. He scurried directly back to base. For the rest of the war (more than two years), the High Sea Fleet stayed in port. In October 1918, a last-ditch surface naval offensive was ordered. Instead of going back to sea, the navy mutinied. Within weeks Germany surrendered, and the High Sea Fleet sailed to the British naval base at Scapa Flow in Scotland. There it was scuttled, no longer "in being."

Hypothesis testing and analysis. Kaiser Wilhelm was extremely interested in naval matters. He often went to sea, dreamed of innovations in naval architecture, and ultimately made himself Supreme Commander of the navy, with its six divisions reporting directly to him. Soon after he came to power, Mahan's works began to appear. They had a profound effect on the Kaiser, convincing him that naval expansion was crucial to Germany's future success.[55] Despite army opposition, he approved ever larger naval budgets, as the army share of military spending continued to decline.[56] Here was a leader of a continental power who had an appreciation of maritime concerns.

His avid interest in naval affairs did not, however, bespeak a mature understanding of land–sea war. Despite his devotion to the teachings of Mahan, which emphasized the importance of battle fleets, the Kaiser would be heard advocating the rapid build-up of *light* naval forces.[57] He made absolutely no effort to encourage joint planning between army and navy staffs. The services, left to their own devices, made independent plans, each of which neglected to consider possible contributions by the other.[58]

On balance, the Kaiser's sensitivity to maritime concerns may be seen as the driving force behind successful German naval expansion. He overrode peacetime bureaucratic opposition to a battle fleet, and brought forth a naval administrator, Tirpitz, whose vision and skill were every bit as refined and effective as Colbert's had been in the service of Louis. What the Kaiser failed to do was compel the type of interservice cooperation that is so vital to success in land–sea war. The separate command structures and lack of coordinated planning that he allowed are sure signs of his inability to grasp fully the requirements of land–sea war. For if his understanding of this type of war were "purely" rational, he would certainly have availed himself of the benefits of combined operations. With regard to the doctrinal shift away from offensive sea control, no rational actor fighting a land–sea war would allow this.

Did the Kaiser's imperfect understanding contribute to this "loser" war initiation? By means of the counterfactual analysis which employs a "rational actor" alternative, one must see that his flawed perception of the nature of land–sea war did contribute to his willingness to begin this "losing" effort. A rational actor would have either refrained from starting such a war, or would have begun and waged it with absolute devotion to both combined operations and offensive naval doctrine. In terms of "consistency" as a hallmark of rationality, it is clear that the Kaiser had spent decades preparing to challenge the British at sea. Yet, with the onset of war, he failed to insist that his High Sea Fleet go out to contest for the command of the sea which he believed was so vital to his success. The case against the Kaiser must not be overstated, though. He did ask (rather than command) the fleet to go out and fight. For a variety of reasons, examined below, his naval leaders stalled and prevaricated, and ultimately resorted to a highly questionable study that purported to demonstrate how an unrestricted U-boat campaign could win the war in six months.

How does the German naval organization fare in this analysis? Certainly it behaved as this study's hypotheses have predicted. In peacetime, the most grandiose offensive doctrines were espoused and articulated. Invasion of England was a common theme, as was the conquest of distant parts of the globe. The Far East and Madagascar were frequently voiced objects of desire. As one German army leader put it, navy officers tended to "dream in continents."[59] They would also stop at nothing to maintain the pace of naval expansion. For example, when, a few years before the war, First Lord of the Admiralty Churchill called for a "holiday" from the naval arms race, the Kaiser was initially interested in taking up the offer. He was persuaded by Tirpitz to wait for an analysis of the proposal that would be prepared by the naval attache in London. In the meantime, Tirpitz, in collusion with Muller, chief of the naval cabinet, secretly instructed the attache to portray the offer as one which had grown out of British fear of inevitable German success in the arms race. The report was duly crafted, and the Kaiser, pleased by his apparent success, rejected the idea of a "holiday."[60]

As war approached, however, offensive naval doctrine slipped a notch to a "waiting offensive." Soon it became apparent that the "waiting period" was intended by naval leaders to run indefinitely. That the shift in doctrine came from persistent organizational influences is beyond question. Though Tirpitz, throughout his *Memoirs*, contends that he always championed a Mahanian view of sea control, Muller points out that it was Tirpitz who articulated the navy's most compelling reason for avoiding a fight. He reports a lunchtime conversation with Tirpitz during which the latter argued against naval confrontation because "[i]t would be highly desirable that, at the eventual peace discussions that we should be in possession . . . of the fleet."[61]

Did the naval doctrinal shift contribute to "loser" initiation? Again, in terms of the counterfactual analysis employed in this study, the answer is that it did. The shift to the defensive at sea guaranteed defeat in a land-sea war. The Kaiser wasn't a complete "loser" until this shift, to which he acquiesced, occurred. Until then, he had a chance of winning the war at sea, and his decision to initiate hostilities could be rationally defended. Once the doctrinal change was made, though, and Germany turned away from the path to victory in land-sea war, its "loser" status became evident.

Some alternative explanations. While Germany's naval doctrine prior to and during World War I has been subjected to a scrutiny more intense than that focused on the navy of Louis XIV, the explanations generated follow similar paths—of personality and necessity. Where Louis has been held to be largely ignorant of naval matters, the Kaiser has been depicted as an ardent navalist. He loved going to sea, wearing naval uniforms, and even dreaming up innovations in naval architecture. In short, he is seen as being "romantically attached" to his navy, unwilling to risk its loss.[62] Other "personality" arguments center around the operational command of the High Sea Fleet. Admiral von Ingenohl, its first war-time commander, was thought to be reluctant to fight the Grand Fleet because of his British-born wife. His successor, Admiral von Pohl, was terminally ill with cancer, thought to lack the energy to fight.[63]

The argument that German naval doctrine shifted out of strategic "necessity" differs from the "fiscal constraint" theory of French naval doctrinal change advanced by Symcox. In the German case, it has been argued that the "need" for change arose when the capabilities of the U-boat were unveiled in the opening weeks of the war. The naval high command is argued to have been resistant, in peacetime, to a shift toward greater emphasis on submarine warfare. Its doctrinal stagnation was overcome, according to this theory, only when war imposed a set of new foreign policy requirements upon the navy. While the battle fleet may have been appropriate for peacetime deterrent purposes, only submarines could ensure that the naval war could be waged in a manner that would be a continuation of political policy. The rapidity of change in naval doctrine is the result of "top-down" pressures exerted by a political policy that had shifted from deterrence to the drive for victory.[64]

As with explanations of the French doctrinal shift, the foregoing fail to withstand close analysis. That the Kaiser had a great interest in naval affairs is unquestionably true. That this interest evolved into a clear understanding of the means by which sea power affects war outcomes is dubious. Indeed, the Kaiser's willingness to allow the army-navy feud to keep the High Sea Fleet from interdicting the British Expeditionary Force on its way to France is solid evidence of his imperfect understanding.[65] Nonetheless, rated with Louis, the Kaiser receives higher marks as a navalist. The contention that he was too emotionally involved to allow the risk of his beloved fleet in action is simply not supported by the facts. The Kaiser's operational orders to the fleet *always* included conditions under which it could seek battle.[66]

As to the personal situations of Admirals von Ingenohl and Pohl, the former was married to a woman of British descent, the latter did have cancer. Whatever effects these matters had on the admirals, they could not have been greater than the stern admonitions of Admiral von Tirpitz to keep out of harm's way. Despite Tirpitz's lamentations, in his *Memoirs*, that he was restrained by the Kaiser from launching a naval offensive, this study's investigation has shown that it was Tirpitz, during the period of the doctrinal shift, who championed the preservation rather than the risking in battle of the fleet.[67] How were Ingenohl and Pohl to overcome this opposition?

Was the shift to an emphasis on commerce raiding and a battle fleet defensive the result of the Kaiser and his advisors overcoming the navy's organizational inertia? Was a *guerre de course* run by U-boats Germany's best chance for success? Again the historical record seems clearly to indicate negative answers to both of these questions. First, it must be reemphasized that the doctrinal shift recommendation came *from* the navy, without pressure from the outside. Onlookers, including the Kaiser, were completely surprised by Tirpitz's switch.[68]

With regard to its winning chances, the German High Sea Fleet could muster 15 dreadnoughts to the Grand Fleet's 17, from the war's outset to early in 1915, a ratio far better than Tirpitz's two thirds "threshold" for offensive action. Indeed, between drydocking, refitting and repairing mine damage, eight of the Grand Fleet's capital ships were unavailable, leading Professor Arthur Marder to conclude that "the prospects of German success were greatest in the first months."[69] Additionally, the German navy had the tremendous advantage of better armed and armored warships, as would be strikingly borne out at Jutland. There is simply no reason to contend that the British material advantage was so great that the German navy was restricted to a defensive stance. Again, Jutland makes this point dramatically, as the Germans won a tactical victory over the Royal Navy despite an unfavorable battleship ratio of 16:28.

What about the notion that submarines offered the best chance for victory?

The Kaiser himself was quite wary about the uses of submarines for commerce raiding. He and his chancellor, Bethmann-Hollweg, were strongly opposed to unrestricted submarine warfare, which the navy contended was the only effective way of waging the *guerre de course*. From the fall of 1914, the navy continued its "full court press" for authority to expand the submarine campaign and was, ironically, supported by the army, which was growing increasingly weary of the grinding attritional struggle in which it was mired. Reluctant to the end, the Kaiser continued to call for another fleet confrontation in the wake of Jutland.[70]

Wilhelm's opinion was only changed after a study, prepared by the Admiralty Staff, concluded that six months of unrestricted submarine campaigning against commerce would win the war. The army and navy were vigorously lobbying him at this point, and even Bethmann-Hollweg, after long resistance, had given in. To the Chancellor's remonstrance that the campaign would bring in the Americans against Germany, the navy responded that it would sink most of the US troop transports. In actuality, none was sunk during the war. The Kaiser finally approved the plan on January 9, 1917, agreeing with the Chancellor that "in view of the opinions of the General Staff and the Admiralty he could not oppose unrestricted U-boat warfare."[71]

Since it was the Admiralty study that finally persuaded the Kaiser to give up on his idea of achieving positive sea control, some discussion of it is merited. Its governing assumption was that Britain had only 10 million tons of merchant shipping that it could devote to supplying the homeland. Based on this figure, a sinking rate of between 500,000–600,000 tons per month for six months would provide for a sufficient decline in British food imports to starve them into submission. Bethmann initially challenged this formula, noting that the whole scheme depended on the ten million ton shipping allocation limit. He noted that the British controlled *20* million tons, and that "England will sacrifice its last man and last shilling before capitulating to German sea power."[72] Aside from the allocation issue, the matter of American merchant shipping was not included, though the virtual certainty of U.S. entry into the war as a result of the campaign was considered.[73]

While the "50% allocation rule" and the gross error of excluding the American merchant shipping factor may imply some attempt to "cook the books," in order to put the best light on a plan the navy desperately wanted approved, there is no documentary evidence that proves these distortions and omissions were intentionally ordered with deception in mind. However, in one crucial area, that of world wheat supply, there is a clear example of disseminating favorable and concealing damaging information. When British vulnerability to the "wheat weapon" was first disclosed in a report, Bethmann called for the information, which he had helped to generate, to be classified "top secret." Instead, Admiral Muller made 500 copies, circulating them to over 200 military and naval posts. When, on the other hand, intelligence information came in from neutral countries, indicating that they would respond to unrestricted warfare by increasing their wheat exports to Britain, these reports were suppressed.[74]

The most interesting, and puzzling, aspect of the German navy's precipitate shift to the advocacy of submarines was that it entered the war completely unprepared to wage such a U-boat campaign.[75] Therefore, it is exceedingly difficult to argue that the shift was a rational choice based on switching to a weapon proven to be more effective than a battleship. Finally, where the effects of U-boat depredations would be felt only over time, resulting from a form of maritime attrition, battle fleet action offered a timely decision. For this reason, Churchill referred to Admiral Jellicoe, commander of the Grand Fleet, as "the man who could lose the war in an afternoon." The German abandonment of offensive sea control just does not add up to a consistent "rational" choice.

There is even some evidence that the submarine campaign was simply an effort by naval leaders to evade the pressure for battle fleet action which the Kaiser and the Army had been exerting. That there was little sincere belief in or desire to continue the use of the submarine in the long run seems evident from Admiral von Capelle's (Tirpitz's successor) comment in January of 1917 that "we have already discussed in the Navy Office . . . creating after the war a special cemetery for our existing submarines."[76] The reason for this position was that a future emphasis on submarines, which were commanded by Lieutenant Commanders (and below) would make promotion to flag rank "superfluous."[77]

A final alternative explanation for the Kaiser's "loser" war initiation is that he did not think that he was getting into a land-sea war with Britain. He may have thought that Britain would remain neutral while war raged on the Continent. Without recapitulating the many analyses of the few fateful days when the British position may have been somewhat in doubt, one can at least say that Germany had good reason to expect British opposition to its designs for *Weltmacht*, or world power.[78] Amid the diplomatic flurries of the first two days of August 1914, there was some confusion about the precise British position. Tirpitz used the occasion to tell Muller that the "risk theory" worked and would keep Britain out of the war. Muller found Tirpitz's remark to be "tactless" and incorrect. In his diary, dated August 2, 1914, Muller noted that he had voiced a contrary view:

> In view of the general political position, England had no grounds for avoiding the risk of her Navy being engaged against us in a war. Rather the contrary![79]

Germany may have preferred a war without England among its enemies at this point; but it was quite willing to fight the British, and had long made plans to do so. The general view of historians on this matter of German readiness for major war remains that "Germany did not plan for a general war in August 1914, but she welcomed it when the opportunity occurred."[80] Since war with the British was contemplated and prepared for by the Kaiser, witness his decades long naval buildup, it cannot be convincingly argued that British participation caused the Kaiser inadvertently to initiate a "losing" war.[81]

CONCLUSION

The hypotheses tested in the foregoing cases have been strongly confirmed. The two political leaders examined each had an awareness, but also an imperfect understanding, of sea power and its role in land-sea war. Their naval organizations espoused offensive doctrines during peacetime, which they abandoned with the onset of war. These are the reasons for "loser" initiation of land-sea war. The "rational actor" model of decision making, utilized in the counterfactual analytic aspect of this study, confirmed that loser initiation would not have occurred in the absence of these two problems. Either peace would have been continued, or the wars of Louis and the Kaiser would have been started and fought employing combined operations and a strict offensive doctrine. In either case, the "loser" phenomenon would have been absent.

Would Germany have won the war if the Kaiser's behavior with regard to the matter of sea control had been consistent, and if the naval organizational "pull" to the defensive had not occurred? Several crucial differences would have arisen. First, as has been discussed, the naval balance in the North Sea at the war's outset was nearly equal. Had the Germans fought then, they would likely have won an even greater victory than they did at Jutland nearly two years later, where they were outnumbered almost two to one. If they had avoided a general battle fleet confrontation, and only gone after the antiquated warships covering the transports of the BEF in the Channel,[82] the disruption of these reinforcements would likely have had a crucial impact on the "Miracle of the Marne." [83] Finally, the abatement of organizational influences would likely have kept the unrestricted submarine campaign from being waged, removing much of the impetus for American entry into the war.

Other findings of these case studies have also tended to confirm that bureaucratic politics are more effective in determining an outcome during a war rather than in peacetime. Thus, it has been seen that, before the global wars of Louis and Wilhelm, the nascent navies of France and Germany overcame the entrenched opposition of their respective army counterparts. Their successes resulted from intervention by their rulers, in a sort of *"regis ex machina."* In wartime, however, the bureaucratic strength of the French and German armies underwent a resurgence.

Where war effected a favorable change in the ability of army bureaucracies to flex their long-bound-up muscles, its onset had little effect on abating naval organizational influences. A key theory of military organizations suggests that their influence is strong in peacetime, but weakens in crisis and war.[84] The case studies in this chapter have pointed out that organizational influences persist well into wartime.[85] Indeed they have a critical impact on war's outcome.

Finally, the use made of counterfactual analysis, and its implications, must be noted. The key point is that the actions of Louis and Wilhelm are held up against those which a rational actor would have taken under similar circumstances. Also, the counterfactual finding doesn't always suggest that there would have been peace instead of war. Rather, the findings are that peace might have prevailed; but land–sea war could just as easily have occurred, and would have been waged in a more efficient manner by the continental aggressor. In either case, there would have been no war initiation by a "loser."

NOTES

1. See James D. Fearon, "Counterfactuals and Hypothesis Testing in Political Science," *World Politics,* vol. 43 (1991):169–195.

2. Ibid., p. 177.

3. As Fearon notes (p. 177), Stephen Van Evera, "The Cult of the Offensive and the Origins of the First World War," *International Security,* vol. 9 (1984):58–107 explicitly adopts the "rational actor" theory for counterfactual comparative purposes. The need to rely on behavior suggested by other, generally accepted theories in counterfactual analysis is identified in David Lewis, *Counterfactuals* (Cambridge: Cambridge University Press, 1973), pp. 62–67.

4. Van Evera, "The Cult of the Offensive and the Origins of the First World War;" and Jack Snyder, *The Ideology of the Offensive: Military Decision Making and the Disasters of 1914* (Ithaca: Cornell University Press, 1984), apply the counterfactual approach to point out that, had German leaders correctly understood the tactical defensive advantages of barbed wire backed by machine guns, World War I would either have been averted or fought differently. Specifically, they posit Germany's initiation of an "Eastern-oriented" war against Russia, which it was highly likely to win.

5. See Harry Eckstein, "Case Study and Theory in Political Science." In *Handbook of Political Science,* Vol. V, *Strategies of Inquiry* (Reading, MA: Addison-Wesley, 1975), pp. 117–120.

6. See Chapter 5's section on measuring sea power for a more complete discussion of naval "divisors."

7. John Keegan, *The Price of Admiralty* (New York: Viking, 1989), pp. 31–33, describes the disarray in the officer corps caused by the Revolutionary purge. The best example is provided by Admiral Villaret-Joyeuse, who commanded the French fleet at the "Glorious (for the British) First of June" in 1794. Just three years earlier, he had been a lieutenant.

8. Olivier Bernier, *Louis XIV: A Royal Life* (New York: Doubleday, 1987), p. 54, describes the importance of Mazarin's role: "[F]rom 1653 on, the ill-educated King received his political education as he watched the wiliest of living statesmen."

Voltaire, *The Age of Louis XIV* (London: Dent, [1756] 1926), p. 66, offers another view of Mazarin's value: "Mazarin only served his own interests and those that concerned his family. Eight years of absolute and undisturbed power from his last return to the time of his death were marked by not a single glorious or useful achievement."

9. The latter was closely involved with Mazarin on a day-to-day basis. See Ines Murat, *Colbert* (Charlottesville: University Press of Virginia, 1984), pp. 21–34, for a discussion of their working relationship. The influence of Mazarin's predecessor, Cardi-

nal Richelieu, on Colbert's view of sea power is summed up in this saying of Richelieu's, which Colbert was wont to repeat to Louis: "Whoever is master of the seas has great power on land" (cited on p. 171).

10. Paul Sonnino, *Louis XIV and the Origins of the Dutch War* (Cambridge: Cambridge University Press, 1988) describes Louis's vision of continental expansion as the determining influence on his decision to join the British in this war. This ambition would fuel the later drive for hegemony that started his period of global war. Interestingly, Colbert was very concerned about the depletion of French assets in a war with the Dutch. His early opposition to beginning this war was reversed when, after he told Louis that there was no way to finance the war, the king responded: "Think about it. If you can't do it, there will always be someone who can" (p. 172). Colbert quickly reworked his maritime mercantilist plans, assuring Louis that he could indeed "do it."

11. Alfred T. Mahan, *The Influence of Sea Power Upon History, 1660–1783* (Boston: Little, Brown and Company, 1890), pp. 143–172, provides a lucid analysis of this conflict, and of the profound positive effect that limited naval successes against the Dutch in the Mediterranean had upon the prospects for further French naval expansion.

12. Bonrepaus, a protege of Colbert, wrote a powerful doctrinal statement "Concerning the Utility of the Navy," analyzed at length in Geoffrey Symcox, *The Crisis of French Sea Power 1688–1697* (The Hague: Martinus Nijhoff, 1974). One citation (p. 106) from Bonrepaus, describing the benefits of naval mastery, is particularly revealing: "[His royal highness] has imperceptibly become master of trade and navigation . . . increasing the commerce of his subjects and consequently reducing that of the other nations of Europe; the renown of his great name, and his glory, have been borne by the fleet even into the remote corners of the globe."

13. Mahan, *The Influence of Sea Power Upon History, 1660–1783,* pp. 178–180, describes the strong political but weak naval support which France offered to James's cause.

14. Symcox, *The Crisis of French Sea Power,* p. 106.

15. See R. E. and T. N. Dupuy, *The Encyclopedia of Military History* (New York: Harper & Row Publishers, 1970), p. 533.

16. Mahan, *The Influence of Sea Power Upon History, 1660–1783,* pp. 72–74, describes this situation. Sonnino, *Louis XIV and the Origins of the Dutch War,* p. 172, points out that, when confronted by Colbert with the economic constraints on his army and navy, Louis's response was simply to threaten his minister with dismissal.

17. Mahan, *The Influence of Sea Power Upon History,* pp. 141–142, details Leibnitz's proposal and Louis's truculent response.

18. Ibid., pp. 186–187 puts it thus: "The success of William, and with it the success of Europe against Louis XIV . . . was due to the mistakes and failure of the French naval campaign of 1690, though in that campaign was won the most conspicuous single success the French have ever gained over the English."

19. Symcox, *The Crisis of French Sea Power 1688–1697,* pp. 103–107 provides the insight that it was Louis who encouraged the debate, which was then pursued with great vigor on each side.

20. Ibid., pp. 177–190, describes Vauban's compromise proposal, as well as the eagerness and relief with which it was greeted.

21. Ibid., p. 76, notes that even bitter bureaucratic rivalries could be set aside when there was a profit to be turned. Thus, the state secretary of the navy was joint owner of four privateers with Louvois, the civil chief of the Army.

22. See Chapter 3 for a discussion of the "rational actor" model.

23. Mahan, *The Influence of Sea Power Upon History,* pp. 176–180, describes Louis's confidence, Dutch fear, and the British state of naval disrepair. Murat, *Colbert,* pp. 197–218, describes the French navy's success in the Dutch War, and the profound impact which this had on Louis's willingness to fight Britain and Holland. Harold E. Jenkins, *A History of the French Navy* (London: Jane's, 1973), pp. 88–90, provides further confirmation of this view.

24. Ludwig Dehio, *The Precarious Balance* (New York: Alfred A. Knopf, 1962), pp. 77–83, describes France's excellent security from invasion. It possessed a standing army larger than all others in Europe combined, and could count on the cooperation of the Turks to tie down Austria. Dehio thus views France's secure continental position as encouraging further expansion.

25. See Paul Kennedy, *The Rise and Fall of British Naval Mastery* (London: Ashfield Press, 1976), pp. 77–81. Also, G. N. Clark, *The Dutch Alliance and the War against French Trade, 1688-1697* (New York: Columbia University Press, 1971 ed.).

26. Symcox, *The Crisis of French Sea Power 1688-1697,* pp. 221–222, sums the situation up: "Louis XIV's deteriorating financial situation compelled him to reduce his war-expenditure, and in view of the fleet's disappointing performance it became a primary target for budgetary retrenchment." The French navy's "disappointing performance" was not in combat, in which it acquitted itself so well; but rather in its reluctance to engage in sea fights with the British.

27. W. N. Medlicott, *Bismarck and Modern Germany* (New York: Harper & Row Publishers, 1965), p. 184, expresses the general view that German aims under the "Iron Chancellor" were strictly delimited by "Bismarck's circumspect use of force, his opposition to preventive wars, his religious faith, his indifference to *grossdeutsch* or pangerman ambitions, his satisfaction after 1870 with Germany's place in a European balance of power, and his determination to maintain the supremacy of the political over the military authority."

28. Lamar Cecil, *Wilhelm II: Prince and Emperor, 1859-1900* (Chapel Hill: University of North Carolina Press, 1989), offers a comprehensive current view of the early influences upon the Kaiser.

29. Barbara Tuchman, *The Proud Tower* (New York: Macmillan, 1966), p. 152, refers to the Kaiser as Mahan's "most enthusiastic disciple." The dinner which Mahan attended on the Kaiser's yacht *Hohenzollern* in 1893 resulted in the latter ordering German-language translations of all of the former's works for the on-board libraries of all German ships of war. The Kaiser also determined, in the wake of this contact with Mahan, to embark upon a vigorous naval expansion.

30. Jonathan Steinberg, *Yesterday's Deterrent: Tirpitz and the Birth of the German Battle Fleet* (London: Oxford University Press, 1965), provides an comprehensive analysis of "risk theory," and the means by which Tirpitz calculated the "2/3 requirement" for offensive action.

31. See Paul Kennedy, "The Development of German Naval Operations Plans against England, 1896-1914," *The English Historical Review,* vol. 99 (1974):48–76.

32. Ibid., pp. 54–55.

33. See Holger Herwig, "Admirals *versus* Generals: The War Aims of the Imperial German Navy," *Central European History,* vol. 5 (1971):208–233.

34. Gerhard Ritter, *The Schlieffen Plan: Critique of a Myth* (New York: Frederick A. Praeger, 1958), p. 72, puts the matter succinctly: "Schlieffen had not the least use for

the German Navy. . . . It was to be used neither as an offensive weapon to support the Western Front, nor in the Baltic, where its superiority was already unquestioned and where one might have thought its task was to secure sea lanes and enable the German Army to operate in the Baltic coastal provinces. . . . "

Holger Herwig, *"Luxury" Fleet* (London: George Allen & Unwin, 1980), p. 148, reports that when Army chief Moltke was offered naval assistance in stopping the arrival of the British land forces, "Moltke . . . coolly informed the Navy that he desired no actions in the Channel, preferring instead to mop up Sir John French's Expeditionary Force along with the French Army."

35. Kennedy, "The Development of German Naval Operations Plans Against England, 1896–1914, p. 65. Kennedy's assessment is that, by 1908, the Kaiser was "completely won over" to the offensive doctrine.

36. Ibid., pp. 65–66.

37. See Jonathan Steinberg, "The Copenhagen Complex," *Journal of Contemporary History,* vol. 1 (1966):23–46.

38. Kennedy, "The Development of German Naval Operations Plans Against England, 1896–1914," p. 68 describes the "waiting offensive" in some detail. Also, Kennedy delineates (p. 75) the overarching necessity for a strategically offensive naval doctrine: "[t]he German Admiralty Staff recognized the key strategical fact of the Anglo-German naval race—that since it was Germany that was challenging Britain's naval predominance, it was also up to the High Sea Fleet to go out and give battle if this aim were ever to be realized."

39. In 1897, the German battle fleet stood at 17% of its British counterpart. By 1907, this had improved only to 40%. Source: George Modelski and William Thompson, *Sea Power in Global Politics, 1494–1993* (Seattle: University of Washington Press, 1988), p. 76, Table 4.2.

40. Jonathan Steinberg, "Germany and the Russo-Japanese War," *American Historical Review,* vol. 75 (1970):1965–1986 points out (p. 1981) that the problem was chronic: "The navy's difficulties arose not because the (navy bills) were not yet carried out but because the danger zone was theoretically infinite. Tirpitz argued that Germany had to build a navy to deter an attack by Britain, the principal naval power, but as long as that power continued to expand its own fleet, the gap between the two competitors, and thus the danger zone, would remain forever."

41. The High Sea Fleet had 14 dreadnoughts to the Grand Fleet's 21. Source: Modelski and Thompson, *Seapower in Global Politics,* p. 78, table 4.3.

42. See Herwig, *"Luxury" Fleet,* p. 147.

43. Sidney B. Fay, *The Origins of the World War* (New York: The Macmillan Company, 1928); Luigi Albertini, *The Origins of the War of 1914,* 3 vols. Trans. by I. M. Massey (London: Oxford University Press, 1957); and Fritz Fischer, *Germany's Aims in the First World War* (New York: W. W. Norton, 1961) all offer rich, comprehensive views of the start of World War One. All agree that the naval rivarlry between Britain and Germany was an important cause of the war. Paul M. Kennedy, *The Rise of the Anglo-German Antagonism 1860–1914* (London: George Allen & Unwin, 1980) focuses in great detail on the importance of the naval arms competition to the war's outbreak.

44. For "accidental" theories, see Van Evera, "The Cult of the Offensive and the Origins of the First World War"; Jack Snyder, *The Ideology of the Offensive* (Ithaca: Cornell University Press, 1984); Jack S. Levy, "Organizational Routines and the Causes of War," *International Studies Quarterly,* vol. 30 (1986):193–222, and "Preferences,

Constraints, and Choices in July 1914," *International Security,* vol. 15 (Winter 1990/1991):151–186.

45. Scott D. Sagan, "1914 Revisited: Allies, Offense and Instability," *International Security,* vol. 11 (Fall 1986):151–176, offers the view that offensive doctrines may have resulted from alliance commitments and their resultant strategic requirements rather than from military "cults." Marc Trachtenberg, "The Meaning of Mobilization in 1914," *International Security,* vol. 15 (Winter 1990/1991):120–150, reexamines much of the evidence that supports the "accidental" explanation of war, and purports to rebut it.

46. Herwig, *"Luxury" Fleet,* p. 163, points out that Weddigen's exploit "greatly encouraged the adherents of the *guerre de course.*"

47. Karl Lautenschlager, "The Submarine in Naval Warfare, 1901–2001," *International Security,* vol. 11 (1986):94–140, points out that sea control is the mission for which the submarine is "least capable."

48. Admiral G. A. von Muller, *The Kaiser and His Court* (New York: Harcourt, Brace & World, Inc., 1964), ed. by Walter Gorlitz, indicates Muller's "surprise" (p. 58) when he first read (on January 27, 1915) the memo in which Tirpitz called for "aggressive submarine raids," and which noted " the extraordinary importance of trade disruption" by the U-boats. Muller headed the German naval cabinet throughout the war.

49. Ibid., p. 44. Muller notes the serious morale problem in a letter, dated November 8, 1914, to his friend Adolf von Trotha, commanding officer of the battleship *Kaiser.*

50. Ibid., pp. 97–99. Admiral Pohl, the second wartime commander of the High Sea Fleet, wrote to Muller to complain about the Kaiser's impatience for battle fleet action. Muller's response, dated August 6, 1915, is very supportive:
"Dear Pohl!
. . . I fully agree with you that the idea of a Supreme Commander . . . who says to his Commander (of the fleet), 'Go out tomorrow and engage the enemy in battle,' is monstrous."

51. Karl Birnbaum, *Peace Moves and U-Boat Warfare* (Stockholm: Almqvist and Wiksell, 1958), chronicles the chancellor's consistent, if ever-weakening, fight against the *guerre de course* in its most virulent form. Also, Pohl is identified as the leading naval proponent of unrestricted submarine warfare (p. 24).

Geoffrey Bennett, *The Battle of Jutland* (London: Batsford Ltd., 1964), p. 56, points out Bethmann-Hollweg's attempt to characterize even limited High Sea Fleet surface raids as "evidence that British command of the sea was incomplete, and that the blockade could be broken." Certainly Pohl would have thought the Chancellor's interpretation of surface actions as inimical to his own interests. His almost complete curtailment of action might well have sprung from his fear of the use Bethmann would make of any positive reports of raids.

52. By this point the pressure for action had become intense. Captain Baron von Maltzahn, who had close personal ties to leaders in both the military and the nobility put it this way: "Even if today large parts of our battle fleet were lying at the bottom of the sea, our fleet would have accomplished more than it does now by lying well preserved in our ports."

Vice Admiral von Hipper, second-in-command of the High Sea Fleet responded to the pressure of which Maltzahn's comments were indicative: "For this reason alone, I wish that we may soon be able to do battle." Both cited in Herwig, *'Luxury' Fleet,* pp. 175–177.

53. Keegan, *The Price of Admiralty,* p. 151, notes that the British dead in this battle totalled 6000, to the German 2500. A rough 3:1 ratio applies to ship losses: three British dreadnoughts were sunk, to one German. Losses in lighter forces (pre-dreadnoughts, cruisers, destroyers and torpedo boats) just about balanced out.

54. Ibid., pp. 131, 151.

55. Barbara Tuchman, *The Guns of August* (New York: Macmillan, 1962), p. 329, puts it this way: "If the Kaiser had confined his reading to *The Golden Age,* Kenneth Grahame's dreamlike story of English boyhood in a world of cold adults, which he kept on the bed-table of his yacht, it is possible there might have been no war. He was eclectic, however, and read an American book that appeared in 1890 with the same impact in its realm as the *Origin of Species* or *Das Kapital* in theirs. In *The Influence of Sea Power on History* Admiral Mahan demonstrated that he who controls communications by sea controls his fate; the master of the seas is master of the situation. Instantly an immense vision opened before the impressionable Wilhelm: Germany must be a major power upon the oceans as upon land."

56. V. R. Bergrahn, *Germany and the Approach of War in 1914* (New York: St. Martin's Press, 1973), pp. 5–6 describes the situation: "When, on 4 August 1914, the German Empire entered the First World War it had at its disposal two formidable military instruments, the Army and the Navy." Yet, ". . . the German Empire fought the war against the Triple Entente almost exclusively with its land forces."

"The minor role played by the Navy in World War I may not appear to be worth emphasizing to someone who is accustomed to seeing the German Empire as a continental power. The fact that the Hohenzollern Monarchy, during World War I, acted solely as a land power gains significance only if it is related to the Reich's armaments policy in the two decades preceding that war. One would expect a nation which, by virtue of its geographical position alone, is constantly confronted with the possibility of a war on land to neglect the Navy. But a glance at German armaments expenditure will show the opposite to be true. From the mid-1890s onwards, naval expenditure increased enormously while, at the same time, the expansion of the Army came to a virtual standstill."

57. Tuchman is no doubt right regarding the Kaiser's "enthusiastic" discipleship of Mahan. However, Wilhelm's emotional commitment to sea power would never make up for an imperfect understanding of the way to and workings of naval mastery. For example, in an 1896 address to the *Kriegsakademie,* the Kaiser called for the rapid build-up of *light* forces rather than battleships. Cited in Philip Crowl, "Mahan," in Peter Paret, ed., *Makers of Modern Strategy* (Princeton: Princeton University Press, 1986), p. 473.

58. See Ritter, *The Schlieffen Plan,* p. 72.

59. Holger Herwig, "Miscalculated Risks: The German Declaration of War against the United States, 1917 and 1941," *Naval War College Review,* vol. 39 (1986):88–100. Herwig's "Generals *versus* Admirals: The War Aims of the Imperial German Navy, 1914–1918," pp. 214–221, points out that, as late as December 1916, the navy was calling for the incorporation of plans to seize the Faeroes, Cape Verde, the Canaries, Tahiti (!), and especially Madagascar. All this from a navy whose battlefleet would never again appear at sea during the war.

60. Alfred von Tirpitz, *Memoirs,* 2 Vols. (New York: Dodd, Mead, 1919), i, pp. 395–397, is quite frank about relating the episode. This matter was investigated and

confirmed in Gordon Craig, *The Politics of the Prussian Army 1640–1945* (London: Oxford University Press, 1955), p. 298.

61. Muller, *The Kaiser and His Court*, p. 22. Muller is quite clear that Tirpitz was thinking of the good of the Navy rather than of Germany in his fleet preservation remark. Muller's diary entry for August 19, 1914 notes that "[o]ur senior naval officers . . . are of the opinion that our fleet should take no risks. . . . Tirpitz found it necessary to justify the passive waiting game played by our fleet."

62. William II, in *My Early Life* (New York: George Doran Co., 1926), pp. 229–239, dwells on what he describes as his "peculiar passion" for naval affairs. He writes of his strongly-felt bond with the Vikings and Hanseatic pirates of the Middle Ages, contending that the cultural "naval memory" of Germany begins with these raiders.

63. These arguments are advanced in Herwig, *'Luxury' Fleet*, Bennett, *The Battle of Jutland*, and Correlli Barnett, *The Swordbearers* (London: Eyre and Spottiswoode, 1963), especially Part II.

64. Robert Art, *The Influence of Foreign Policy on Seapower: New Weapons and Weltpolitik in Wilhelminian Germany* (Beverly Hills: Sage Publications, 1973), advances this notion.

65. Muller, *The Kaiser and his Court*, p. 17, points out that the Kaiser actually ordered the High Sea Fleet, on August 8, 1914, to attack the British Expeditionary Force while it crossed the Channel. That it did not set sail was the result of Army chief von Moltke's insistence that he could "handle" the British, and the High Sea Fleet's sudden interest in "guarding" the Baltic (pp. 18–19).

66. Ibid., p. 54. Muller writes in retrospect that on only one occasion during the war did he feel the need to suggest to the Kaiser that the latter should press for "more energetic" battle fleet behavior (this one-time "urging" took place in January of 1915).

67. Ibid., p. 22. Muller quotes Tirpitz as saying that the fleet should take "no risks."

68. Ibid., pp. 58–60. Muller notes in his diary the surprise which greeted Tirpitz's memo (of January 27, 1915), because it sided with the senior naval officers (most prominently Pohl) who were calling for the switch to the *guerre de course*.

69. See Arthur J. Marder, *From the Dreadnought to Scapa Flow*, Vol. II, *The War Years* (London: Oxford University Press, 1965), p.43.

70. Ibid., p. 170. Muller quotes the Kaiser in a speech at Wilhelmshaven naval base on June 5, 1916 (six days after the battle): "The spell of Trafalgar has been broken." George S. Viereck, *The Kaiser on Trial* (Richmond, VA: Byrd Press, 1937), p. 305 accredits this comment on Britain's vulnerability to the Kaiser: "Another blow, like the Battle of Jutland, and the Trident would have dropped from her hands."

71. Muller, *The Kaiser and His Court*, p. 230.

72. Cited in Philip K. Lundeberg, "The German Naval Critique of the U-Boat Campaign, 1915–1918," *Military Affairs*, vol. 27 (1963):105–118. Konrad Jarausch, *The Enigmatic Chancellor* (New Haven: Yale University Press, 1973), gives a continuing account of Bethmann's struggle against the navy's call for unrestricted submarine warfare, and of his eventual acquiescence.

73. Herwig, *'Luxury' Fleet*, p. 197, views this omission as "incredible."

74. Ibid., pp. 195–197.

75. Lundeberg, "The German Naval Critique of the U-Boat Campaign, 1915–1918," p. 105, points out that Germany entered World War I with "neither the capability nor the intention of launching a submarine offensive against merchant shipping of the Entente."

76. Herwig, *'Luxury' Fleet,* p. 224.

77. Ibid., p. 224. Herwig also notes that one lieutenant commander even had the temerity to write to Admiral von Trotha, of the Naval Staff, that "[t]he executive officers sit around, eat, drink, politicize, intrigue, and even believe that they are being patriotic in trying by sordid means to bring about the adoption of unrestricted submarine warfare. Submarine warfare is supposed to cover up the stupidities in the fleet construction and in the wartime deployment of the fleet. The bad conscience of the executive officers emerges in this forbidden propaganda for it" (cited on p. 195).

78. Paul Kennedy, *The Rise of the Anglo-German Antagonism 1860–1914,* considers the conflicting aims of Germany and Britain one of the major causes of the war, and that British participation against Germany was in no way surprising.

79. Muller, *The Kaiser and His Court,* p. 12 (diary entry of August 2, 1914).

80. Brian Bond, *War and Society in Europe 1870–1970* (Leicester: Leicester University Press, 1984), p. 95.

81. It should be noted that the alternative explanation of uncertainty about British participation relates even less to the global war of Louis XIV, who began the conflict by declaring war against the United Provinces and England. Indeed, one of the preventive pressures at work on Louis was the problem of unified Anglo-Dutch strength under the single rule and guiding hand of his arch-enemy William. Louis sought to strike before William could consolidate his rule.

82. Herwig, *'Luxury' Fleet,* p. 147, contends that the Germans "would have had no difficulty in disposing of the . . . elderly battleships" which were protecting the transports.

83. Of the 100,000 British troops which were ferried over during the first week of the war, it has been noted, in E. B. Potter, ed., *Sea Power: A Naval History* (Englewood Cliffs, NJ: Prentice-Hall, Inc., 1960), p. 400, after puzzling over the German failure to attack in the Channel, that "the British troops . . . provided the thin margin of successful resistance to the initial German surge."

84. Barry Posen, *The Sources of Military Doctrine* (Ithaca: Cornell University Press, 1984), develops this notion. See especially pp. 239–240 for conclusions about the abatement of organizational influence in crisis and war.

85. Which suggests that organizational influences on military doctrine may be more powerful than its *realpolitik* sources. Posen's suggestion that these latter considerations are more important than organizational factors should perhaps be reexamined in the light of these findings.

Chapter 6

Summary and Conclusions

Wisdom is better than weapons of war. —Ecclesiastes 9:18

This study began by asking why, if wars arise from the reasonable calculations of decision makers, do those who start them so often lose? The defeat of one out of every three initiators of interstate war (two out of three in Great Power wars)[1] starkly challenges the many formulations about decision-making rationality that characterize a major strand of reasoning about the onset of war.[2] The alternative notion, that decision-making processes tend to be fatally flawed by misperception and bureaucratic pathologies,[3] is equally dissatisfying. After all, most wars *are* won by the side that starts them. If cognitive problems are common among war initiators, wouldn't more of them be starting "losing" wars?

Because of the sharp rise in the rate of initiator defeats when Great Power wars are considered on their own, an effort was made to determine whether or not existing structural theories of the international system could provide an explanation for the phenomenon of "loser initiation." The structural theories break down into two broad categories: one that predicts "balancing" to maintain or restore a systemic equilibrium,[4] and the many notions of the "transitional," or cyclical interplay of the most powerful states.[5]

The defeat of war initiators is predictable from the hypotheses of each of the structural theories. Under the balance of power, aggressors ought to be opposed by coalitions of the relatively weaker, whose aggregate strength is theorized to be adequate to halt them. Transitional situations are characterized by either the premature challenge of an aggressor, the preventive war of an incumbent hegemon, or a mature challenge defeated by balancing behavior.[6]

In Chapter 2, the key hypotheses of these theories were tested against the universe of cases of global war, in which the "loser" phenomenon is quite well known, and were found wanting. More often than not, balancing behavior was absent from this "most-likely" set of cases; and some *de facto* balances arose, in the absence of balancing behavior, due to the initiator's decisions to widen an ongoing war. Power transitions simply could not be identified with either the onset or the outcome of global wars, with the possible exception of the outbreak of World War I. Also, transitional theories were found to be complementary, in some respects, to balance of power theory. Time and again, transitional theories hypothesized that initiator defeats in global war were the result of the defender's better balancing talents.[7]

Finally, the initial focus on global wars resulted in this study's assertion that the Anglo-Dutch (1652–1674) and the Seven Years'/ Revolutionary (1756– 1783) Wars merited inclusion in this category. Both of these conflicts were characterized by successful initiators and an almost total absence of balancing behavior. In the former, Britain was guided by the grim determination of Cromwell to break the power of the United Provinces. Over the course of three wars, Dutch maritime power was broken. The United Provinces were never aided by allies. Indeed, France joined in with Britain at the outset of the last of these wars. One hundred years later, Britain determined to drive France from North America and India. In these endeavors it was wildly successful, and withstood, in the latter half (1776–1783) of this global conflict, the efforts of a vast coalition to strip it of its gains. The identification of these cases of successful global war initiation (initiators lost all other global wars) should allow for the future employment of "structured focused" comparison techniques[8] designed to illuminate the conditions under which global aggression succeeds or fails. Specific hypotheses to guide such studies would concentrate on the awareness and full understanding of maritime affairs which these aggressors exhibited. Also, the unswerving dedication of their naval organizations to offensive doctrines of positive sea control should be examined. These points should then be considered, with the same hypotheses tested, in the cases of global war in which the initiator lost.[9]

MODIFICATIONS TO EXISTING THEORIES

The fundamental insight developed by this study is that "all wars are not created equal." There are two kinds of war: those fought only on land, and those that include a significant maritime aspect. Each has its own causal path to victory. Land wars will generally be won[10] by the side which demonstrates greater "skill," a complex attribute composed of superior leadership, troop quality, intelligence, and surprise. This notion is quite consistent with and supportive of the theories of Jomini and Clausewitz, and a host of others who have thought about the art of winning wars.[11] It also challenges the thinking of those who have emphasized the notion of victory tending to go to the "big battalions," particularly Lanchester and his intellectual descendants. For them, winning at war is more science than art.[12]

In land–sea wars, however, this study has demonstrated that neither superior "skill" nor "strength" on land matters. Instead, victory can be won by the application of sea control. While this formulation draws considerably on the work of Mahan, it goes well beyond his primary emphasis on the economic warfare capabilities of sea power.[13] Where Mahan saw limited utility for amphibious operations, this study portrays them as vital to the maritime power's ability to generate a force "multiplier-divisor" effect. Indeed, Mahan's vision of war is in many ways consistent with the "strength" school of thought, as he posits the chief value of sea power to be its ability more successfully to supply and maintain a war of attrition. The image of sea power developed in this study, on the other hand, views its economic aspect as but one part of an integrated whole. The same forces that impose an economic blockade also prevent hostile invasion while allowing friendly forces to invade at their site of choice, isolate distant enemy outposts, subjecting them to swift attrition, and compel enemy force dispersion while enabling friendly force concentration. An excellent recent example of this last point is provided by the war against Iraq. Two U.S. Marine Corps brigades, totalling 18,000 troops, were, from their positions afloat, able to tie down roughly 125,000 Iraqi troops in a line down the Kuwaiti coast.

Based on these insights, how should the structural theories of the international system be modified? First, power should be reconfigured, with extra weight given to naval strength. The important work of Modelski and Thompson, despite some conceptual and technical flaws,[14] goes a long way toward making a "maritime reinterpretation" of the history of the last 500 years possible. With regard to balancing, this study suggests that aggressors often *create* the balances that oppose them, in their hapless attempts to "conquer the sea by conquering the land." This is a striking reversal of traditional notions of the balance of power, explaining a way in which balances may arise in the absence of defensive balancing behavior. Instead of states banding together to ward off another's "growing power" or "rising threat," it is the powerful and threatening whose repeated use of force *creates* new adversaries by the act of attacking them. Generally, the states which create opposing coalitions in this fashion are continental powers, pursuing strategies of conquest which are reasonable in land war, but self-destructive in land–sea war. Until the sea power is beaten, additional aggressions merely add to the land power's enemies, and disperse its forces, making it more vulnerable to counterblows from the sea.[15] At the level of global conflict, the wars of Philip II, Louis XIV, Napoleon, and Hitler come quickly to mind as cases that confirm this pattern.

As to power transitions, an emphasis on the naval aspects of power should serve to "smooth out" the curves that make up most notions of cyclical change. Even "long cycles," which are to some degree measured in terms of sea power, should be modified according to the "concentration adjustment" made in this study.[16] If this is done, then power transitions and cycling behavior are virtually nonexistent. Instead of the "fragile" international system envisioned by one of the transitional theorists,[17] global politics should be viewed as operating under a hardy maritime order, one capable of withstanding great stresses.

Do these insights into war's duality assist in the effort to explain the phenomenon of "loser" initiation? Only partially. In land wars, where "skill" reigns supreme, it is impossible ever to know with certainty which side will "fight better." Therefore, the defeat of a land war initiator should not be surprising. Since victory is such an imponderable prior to the start of a war, decisions to initiate should also be more understandable. The chance to win did exist, and was taken. The foregoing reasoning is supported by noting that, of the 30 land wars examined in this study, initiators won only 15 (50%).[18]

In land–sea conflicts, the calculus of war is much clearer. The relative naval strength of the contending sides is well known and, because of the time it takes to build and equip fleets, changes in relative strength develop only quite slowly. Though a theory of maritime preeminence may explain why an initiator would lose, some doubt remains as to why he would initiate. Notions of the duality of war suggest that a land power unduly discounts the impact of its maritime foe's strength; and it is at this point that the investigation moved away from structural considerations to a closer examination of the aggressor's decision-making process.

Using Allison's seminal study of decision making during the Cuban Missile Crisis[19] as a guide, this study reexamined existing bureaucratic politics and organizational theories, with an eye for their relevance to the war initiation process. Specifically, these theories were projected upon the decision-making processes of land powers (who initiated many and lost almost all land–sea wars). In terms of bureaucratic politics, the armies and navies of land powers were theorized, respectively, to be the senior and junior services. Bureaucratic politics theory suggests that interservice rivalry will be evident, and also that the more powerful service will prevail in disputes. While this study accepts the theoretical notion that bureaucratic friction occurs, the outcome of such conflict should be seen as beyond bureaucratic control. Krasner's notion of the importance of the leader to the decisional output is adopted at this point,[20] suggesting that, whatever the relative strengths of the rival services, the leader will hear both sides and decide a course on his own. It is crucial to note, though, that the leader of a continental power is viewed as having an imperfect understanding of war's duality, and of the preeminence of sea power. To summarize, the various military services will behave as rivals, according to Allison and other theorists, but decisional outputs will be controlled by the leader in a boundedly rational manner.[21] Thus, a junior service will feel compelled to fight for resources with its older "brother," but has good chances of "winning" the bureaucratic struggle because of the leader's importance to the decisional output.

On the organizational side, a rich body of theory has already been applied to professional militaries. They are generally viewed as wedded to offensive doctrines and averse to change.[22] This study returned to the major early works of organizational theory,[23] searching for insights that might illuminate the behavior of the navies of continental powers. The key theoretical insight, for purposes of this study, was that organizations will change if their existence is threatened. Applied to continental powers' navies, this formulation opened up the possibility of doctrinal shifts away from the offensive as war neared. Indeed, in the interest of self-preservation, organizational theory suggests that these navies would have little choice *but* to advocate switching from offense to defense. Merrily sailing out to challenge the ruling naval power runs wholly contrary to theory.

This study has also suggested that naval organizations, like all others, will manipulate the flow and interpretation of information to their benefit. Strong examples that this occurs have been noted. The German naval attache's deliberately distorted analysis of Churchill's call for a halt to the pre-World War I arms race as a sign of British weakness, and the German Naval Staff's overstated claims of the efficacy of the U-boat, based on Otto Weddigen's sinking of three cruisers in August 1914, convincingly demonstrate this point.[24] Also, as discussed in the preceding chapter, the German navy's statistical studies of the likely effects of unrestricted submarine warfare contain glaring evidence of "cooking the books." The failure to incorporate any production value for American industry and agriculture, and the setting of an unrealistically low percentage of total British shipping (50%), which was calculated as available for supplying the home islands are the most obvious examples of this sort of accounting sleight-of-hand.

Aside from challenging the conventional notion of militaries as blindly pursuing offensive doctrines, this study has argued that navies comprise a different sort of military organization, due to their heavy capital requirements, and the difficulty with which lost assets may be replaced. Previous work has not attempted to differentiate naval from other military organizations in this way, creating a theoretical "gap."[25] A final point of great importance is that the notion of military organizations bowing to civilian intervention in crisis and war cannot be derived from organizational theory.[26] Therefore, this study has assumed that militaries continue to work their influence upon decision makers with a degree of success comparable to or better than that which they achieved in peacetime.

QUANTITATIVE ANALYSIS

To determine whether or not war does exhibit a dual nature, and the preeminence of "skill" and sea power, respectively, in land and land–sea war, a quantitative analysis of the universe of cases from 1815-1980 was performed.[27] In addition to the primary objectives of the analysis, the testing of important alternative theories was also effected. The results of testing via logistic regression strongly confirmed both the duality of war and the hypothesized causal paths to victory in each of the two fundamental types of military conflict. Further, theories suggesting that "chance," superior technology, and greater resolve were keys to the riddle of victory were all found to be lacking in explanatory power. The finding with regard to resolve was especially counterintuitive.

While Chapter 4 reflects some of the regression results achieved, they should simply be viewed as representative. Hundreds of possible variable permutations and mixes were tested, none of which could shake the finding that skill reigned in land war and sea power in land–sea war. A key observation is that skill, though an extremely powerful variable in the set of land wars, was reduced to insignificance when land–sea wars were tested (as the dual theory predicts). All of the coded dataset generated by this study's research has been reproduced in Appendix I, allowing others to perform additional tests, for purposes of duplicating, challenging, or expanding upon the conclusions arrived at herein.

How definitive are the claims to be made by the quantitative analysis? What is their scope? These questions run to the heart of issues regarding the value of quantitative methods in political science and historical research. This study has employed logistic regression analysis as a preliminary form of hypothesis testing which, if successful, would justify and serve to focus the ensuing case studies. The regressions were not meant to stand alone, but to assist in solving the puzzle of "loser initiation." In this endeavor they were supremely useful, demonstrating the complementarity of quantitative and detailed case study methods. As to their indications about what, generally, causes wars to be won and lost, the regressions should be viewed as a suggestive, meaningful first step in the right direction. However, in order to demonstrate convincingly the hypothesized dual causal paths to victory in war, it is necessary to engage in historical case studies which "process trace" the key variables throughout the course of the conflicts examined.

CASE STUDIES

The global wars initiated and lost by Louis XIV and Wilhelm II were examined, with the focus of attention on each directed by hypotheses regarding their imperfect understanding of war's dual nature, and by theorizing that modified some organizational and bureaucratic political notions. In particular, naval doctrinal shifts from offensive to defensive "tilts," and the ability of the bureaucratically weaker service to achieve its budgetary and programmatic aims were searched out. These particular cases were chosen because they offered the "toughest" tests available of the hypotheses that had been formulated.[28] The navy in each had to overcome entrenched opposition from the heads of highly successful armies who had the attentive ear of their sovereigns. Also, these navies were the best ever fielded by a continental challenger for global hegemony. Thus, the reasons for doctrinal shifting to the defensive were minimized.

The findings in each case strongly bore out the hypotheses that were tested. The two rulers accepted the importance of strong navies, and overruled army opposition to naval expansion. Their navies dutifully espoused offensive sea control doctrines in peacetime. However, with the onset of war, both navies wavered, and their doctrines took on an almost completely defensive tenor with regard to sea control. Thus, the rug was completely pulled out from under Louis and Wilhelm, who each went to war thinking that they had some chance to defeat their maritime enemy. The subsequent (and disastrous) doctrinal shift to the *guerre de course* in each case was the product of both continuing bureaucratic pressures on these navies to contribute to the war effort, and of persistent organizational influences, which continued to work their will on the decision-making calculus of Louis and Wilhelm.

Aside from confirming the validity of the hypotheses generated by this study, the results of examining these cases should lead to the modification of some thinking regarding both bureaucracies and organizations (particularly those of a military nature). The political chief executive's role should be seen as enhanced *in peacetime*, with bureaucracies "mattering" less. Military (naval here) organizations should be viewed as quite capable of innovation and change; and their ability to influence the decision-making process after the onset of crisis and war should be recognized. Finally, these studies have suggested that current historical understanding of the events surrounding the onset and conduct of two global wars has some need of "mending." Notions that the doctrinal shifts away from sea control occurred for fiscal and technological reasons have been seriously challenged, and must be reevaluated in light of these findings.

Have these case studies "proved" why Louis and Wilhelm began their wars? The global wars of each ruler had myriad causes, which have been well and exhaustively documented by able historians. This study's contribution has been to point out that the machinations and misunderstandings surrounding the naval affairs of these continental powers provided a *necessary* cause for their becoming cases of "loser" war initiation. Neither Louis nor Wilhelm would have launched global conflicts if they knew that their navies would not fight for sea control. All of their behavior prior to these wars, and much during them, supports this conclusion. Indeed, both Louis and Wilhelm consistently maintained, in their operating orders, the mandate to seek, under favorable terms, decisive fleet engagements.

The case studies employed a form of counterfactual analysis, testing the behavior of Louis and Wilhelm against hypothesized "rational actors."[29] Specifically, one of the important measures of rationality was the search for "consistent" behavior. Also, some "third-party" testing was done to unearth evidence that the behavior of the navies of continental powers, in peace and war, followed similar patterns. The key finding of the case studies was that purely rational actors, aware of the duality of war and the overarching need for positive sea control, and free of organizational influences, would not launch wars unless they had good chances for achieving naval mastery. However, if the opportunity for success at sea was substantial, rational actors with expansionist aims would have gone to war. They would then have made sure to maintain offensive sea control doctrines, and would have avoided the organizational and bureaucratic beartraps which might swerve them from this maritime imperative. In either instance, continued peace or the launching and informed waging of war, "loser initiation" would have been avoided.[30]

SOME LINGERING QUESTIONS

While the major objective of this study, explaining the phenomenon of "loser" war initiation, has been achieved, the nature of the answer provokes both a critical re-appraisal of previous thinking about the functioning of the international system, which has been discussed, and a new set of questions. There are three of the latter, two related to the systemic aspects of the dual theory, and one which is directed at the national/organizational level:

1. Do "Skill" and Sea Power Have Relevance in the Nuclear Age?

It would be quite natural for the reader of this study to pause, at its conclusion, agree that two fundamental types of war may have existed, indeed may still exist, but question whether or not any of this matters when nuclear weapons are factored in. Bernard Brodie, who spent much of his life grappling with the (figurative) impact of nuclear weapons upon strategy and warfare, began with the twin formulations that these armaments "existed," and that they were "enormously destructive." Three decades and much intellectual effort later, he returned to these observations, finding no way around them. They had changed strategy and war, inevitably and unalterably.[31] Is not Brodie's "dilemma" applicable, in a critical way, to this study? Does it matter any more that "sea lines of communication" may be controlled, if entire societies may be devastated by nuclear-tipped missiles?

Sea control and good generalship in land wars still matter because, oddly enough, Brodie was *right*. Near the end of his career, Brodie saw a world in which superpower nuclear parity had made any war utilizing weapons of this sort more "unthinkable" than it had ever been before. But, if this were true, and both current scholarship and trends in nuclear arms control seem to bear Brodie out,[32] then are not the conflicts that do arise likely to be conventional?[33] If this is true, then the strategic experiences of the last 500 years, even of the preceding millennia, retain their value. Indeed, Samuel Huntington has even gone so far as to call for the "renewal of strategy."[34] Another scholar has suggested that nuclear weapons have always had limited utility, and that traditional strategic thinking never lost its validity.[35] Though the existence of nuclear weapons may have a limiting effect on aims, "smaller wars" will be started, fought, and won or lost on the basis of traditional strategic thinking. In this regard, the dual theory advanced by this study shall doubtless have much value and, sadly, future opportunities for practical application.[36]

2. If Leaders Believe the Dual Theory, Will There Be More Wars?

This question calls to mind the abuses which some of Clausewitz's self-anointed disciples made of his most important formulations about war. His idea that war was simply a continuation of state policy made it, in some eyes, a far more "thinkable" option, providing solid intellectual support for both militarism and imperialism. Though Clausewitz cautioned his readers to make no mistake, that war could only be won by bloody battle, he would doubtless have recoiled, in horror and disdain, from the mindless attritional slaughter invoked in his name during World War I. Nonetheless, the battle-minded offensive doctrines which have sprung up in most of the world's professional armies are unquestionably Clausewitzian.

Will acceptance of the dual theory make war more "thinkable"? Will states which enjoy a naval advantage over their potential enemies go to war confidently, perhaps more frequently? Will even small states feel little worry about attacking a larger neighbor if they believe that they can limit conflict to a land war, allowing the superior qualities of their own forces to triumph, even against long numerical odds? The essence of the problem is that delineation of the *necessary* conditions for launching a successful war may encourage the use of force, once these conditions obtain, in periods of high tension or crisis.

With regard to land wars, the logical impact of this study should be that their occurrence will grow less likely. Though the key to victory, "skill," has been identified, its relative value in any potential warring dyad or coalition is virtually unknowable, with any precision, prior to the outbreak of substantial fighting. The resulting uncertainty about military effectiveness should act as a force for peace. Even potential aggressors with significant quantitative advantages will be given pause, if their contemplation of the dual theory causes some discounting of the importance of numbers. For example, the Arab-Israeli Wars might have stopped after 1948, once superior Israeli "skill" was demonstrated, if discounting of Arab material advantages had occurred.[37] Of course, "skill" does remain an imponderable, and some potential aggressors may have an appetite for gambling that would be encouraged by this notion. These possible war initiators would be operating in what prospect theory calls the "domain of losses," and would be quite willing to risk all. On the other hand, cases of this sort might be offset by those in the "domain of gains," who seek to minimize their risks.[38] The point here is that general human psychology, which tends to favor risk averse behavior when in a materially comfortable, stable position, and risk acceptance when trying to recoup "losses," may interact with the inherently murky factor of military "skill" in a way which may *either* promote or discourage war initiation.

That possession of superior naval strength may encourage bellicosity has some small support from the cases examined in this study. Of the 33 land–sea wars analyzed, 2 of every 3 were begun by a maritime power;[39] and virtually all of these consist of victorious examples of a Great Power attacking a minor power. Where sea powers may go astray, however, is in thinking that their naval strength offers sufficient support for wars that are largely delimited to land operations. A good example of this is provided by the behavior of Charles XII of Sweden during the Great Northern War (1700–1720) with Russia. Sweden entered the war with undeniable naval mastery of the Baltic, which Charles used as a springboard for his invasion of the Russian heartland. Unfortunately, his superior fleet was of little use to him at Poltava, located in the middle of the Ukraine. Disaster ensued, as Charles's winning edge in a land–sea war was squandered by his decision to fight a land war. This may be the reason that sea powers have never striven for continental hegemony: their peculiar form of strength, which protects the maritime homeland, and gives them mastery over the littoral, is dissipated as they move away from the sea. It is a nautical version of the story of Antaeus, the mythological wrestler who could never be defeated while his feet remained on the ground.

On balance, it seems that acceptance of the dual theory of war may decrease the chances for outbreaks of major or global wars, though maritime powers, savoring "easy pickings," and those in the "domain of losses" contemplating land wars, might derive some encouragement from the findings of this study. That two thirds of the land–sea war initiators from 1815–1980 were maritime powers attacking the small and the weak suggests that any new change caused by the dual theory might simply be at the margin. Certainly this is outweighed by the benefit of decreased chances for global war. For, if all believed in the dual theory, land powers would stop warring with maritime powers; and the latter would avoid conflicts that drew them away from their favored element.

3. Why Are Not Navies of Sea Powers Doctrinally Defensive in War?

If the modified applications of organizational theory that this study has employed are valid for the navies of continental states, should not they apply equally to those of maritime powers? Are not lost fleets just as hard to replace for the maritime hegemon? Though defensive instincts in war should exist even in the navy of the lustiest maritime power, there are several reasons why they are muted. First, the navy of a maritime power is generally the senior service. Its position is entrenched and well accepted. Moreover, there is a clear understanding that the navy is *necessary* for the maritime power's security, not what is, for a continental power, a "luxury."[40] Finally, the maritime power's navy will have a "tradition of victory" upon which to draw, one which will spur its leaders to offensive action. Indeed, the prevailing attitude in the Royal Navy of 1914 was one of eagerness for war, as it had been "a long time since Trafalgar." New legends were waiting to be carved out.[41]

SOME POLICY IMPLICATIONS

While this study has operated throughout on a largely theoretical level, it is hoped that the insights derived therefrom will have significant policy relevance. From the perspective of the United States, the dual theory should prove to be a catalyst for discussion and reappraisal of both military doctrinal and international policy matters. The differing requirements for successful defense and for deterrence of limited aggression must also be highlighted.

NAVAL MASTERY AND SUCCESSFUL DEFENSE

The United States is, and has been since at least 1945, the world's leading maritime power. This study has suggested that the international order fostered by maritime hegemony is of a quite sturdy, long-lasting sort, on the order of some 400 years per cycle. But the longevity of this position is not guaranteed by default or inertia. The British had to face Spanish, Dutch, French, and German challenges during their tenure and, no doubt, the United States will also face challengers. It is, therefore, incumbent upon U.S. policy planners to act in a fashion that will maximize the chances that maritime supremacy will be sustained. When the resources available for defense are apportioned to the various services, each must be evaluated on the basis of its ability to contribute to this broad grand strategic goal. This sensitivity may end up affecting not only budgetary considerations, but those surrounding force structure and doctrine as well.

Aside from mandating self-examination, the dual theory suggests also that a close eye should be kept on potential challengers. For example, the naval capabilities of the Former Soviet Union (FSU), even amid domestic chaos and international retrenchment, should still be a cause for concern. In many respects, Soviet naval development resembles the pattern followed by other continental powers that have striven for influence at sea. Where France had Colbert, and Germany Tirpitz, the USSR's Gorshkov performed a similar role, with a tenure as long as the former two. His call for naval expansion resulted in the tremendous growth of Soviet naval capabilities though, at his retirement, he was still calling for a larger, more diverse navy.[42] His success, it should be noted, was achieved in a bureaucratic environment heavily weighted in favor of the Soviet Army.[43] That Soviet naval expansion could be attained in a hostile administrative milieu is a prediction that may be drawn from the hypotheses developed in this study.

The call to monitor naval matters closely should encourage reexamination of current analyses of the navy of the FSU. Traditionally, two schools of thought, depicting it variously as a "strong threat" or as a "weak threat,"[44] have been elucidated.[45] The dominance of "weak threat" thinking is based primarily upon perceptions that it lacks, in Gorshkov's terms, "balance."[46] Particularly, the absence of carrier battle groups, the capital naval assets of our day, is held against it. Additionally, the FSU's geographical position is still judged to be a significant liability, limiting its navy's ability to concentrate. But are these reassuring formulations the right ways to be assessing a potential threat to American naval mastery?

The "weak threat" assessment is based, it seems to this writer, upon the assumption that submarines cannot achieve positive sea control.[47] If this is true, and the Russians, who have inherited virtually all of the Soviet Navy's assets, are following a doctrine of *guerre de course*, they are as doomed to failure as all the "corsairs" who have preceded them. However, if one accepts the foregoing, the Russians must also be perceived as differing radically from all previous continental challengers for naval mastery. The French, from Louis XIV to Napoleon, entered their wars with sea control through battle fleet action (the *guerre d'escadre*) as their explicit doctrine. Likewise, the German naval challenge was based on the battle fleet. Doctrinal shifts occurred, as this study has pointed out, for complex organizational and bureaucratic reasons.

The insight that might be derived from this study is that the Russians may be no different from previous naval challengers. They may be emphasizing submarines, not because they have "learned" something new about the chances for success of the *guerre de course*, but because they think that submarines offer them the best future chance to achieve positive sea control. In this regard, Lautenschlager's notion that submarines cannot fight fleet actions must be reconsidered. The South Atlantic War of 1982 offers some evidence, in the performance of *HMS Spartan*, of the submarine's growing ability to fight successfully against a battle fleet and to control the sea, not just to prey on commerce. Future analyses, therefore, must be oriented toward an evaluation of the fleet-fighting capabilities afforded by the latest submarines.

With this in mind, it should be noted that the Russian impulse to avoid copying the navy of the incumbent maritime hegemon has some tradition. When, in the years following his victory at Poltava, Peter the Great sought to build a navy that could defeat the Swedes, he eschewed the construction of ships-of-the-line. Instead, he built galleys, whose oars could take maximum advantage of those frequent occasions on which the Baltic suffered from "light airs." The Swedes, who had dominated the Baltic for centuries (lately with British acquiescence), maintained a sail-only fleet of warships, and were decisively defeated by Peter's unconventional challenge.[48] This resourcefulness, and the willingness to avoid copying the leading navy, should give the United States pause when considering its own unilateral policies to remove nuclear weapons from its naval vessels. Unless Russian reciprocity can be absolutely verified, no chance should be taken that the U.S. Navy might one day put to sea against a foe armed with nuclear torpedoes and missiles.

In terms of defense planning, this study provides strong support for the "maritime strategy" that has been the object of much debate in recent years.[49] The "firebreak" between conventional and nuclear war is being widened and strengthened, an inevitable result of both superpower nuclear parity and normative inhibitions regarding threatening the use of nuclear weapons against only conventionally armed foes. Therefore, it makes great good sense for the leading maritime power to be thinking strategically about the means by which it intends to employ its most useful tool of force, its navy. Keeping away from the threat of nuclear weapons use is so beneficial for the maritime power, maintaining its land–sea war advantages intact, that adherence to a doctrine of "no first use" is also eminently reasonable.[50]

IMPLICATIONS FOR DETERRENCE

The abovementioned policy implications of the dual theory are directed toward guaranteeing that the United States and its allies emerge the winner from any future war in which they become embroiled. But are the steps necessary to maintain adequate defenses the same that should be taken to lessen the likelihood of war's outbreak? After all, this study has pointed out that land powers, for a variety of structural, bureaucratic and organizational reasons, never realize *ahead of time* that they face losing situations in land–sea conflict. So they start wars against maritime powers. Huth and Russett's studies of the conditions under which deterrence works or fails implicitly support this very notion.[51] One of their key observations is that

> we found that successful deterrence was associated with an immediate balance of forces, or a short-term balance of forces, favoring the defender. Where these balances were tipped against the defender, the attacker was likely to seize the chance for a quick takeover of territory. As we also expected, the long-term balance of forces, affecting the probable outcome of a war of attrition, was only weakly associated with deterrence outcomes.[52]

What better description is there of the problems that a maritime power faces in its efforts to deter a continental power's aggressive acts? A recent example of this phenomenon may be seen in Iraq's invasion of Kuwait, which tends to confirm the idea that maritime power is not as good for deterrence as having ground and air forces on the spot. It is hard to know Saddam Hussein's exact thinking on the impact of American intervention (as opposed to its likelihood), but his public comment to Egypt's leader Mubarak that "we are not ones to be intimidated by navies"[53] is highly suggestive.

The fact must be faced that, while the diminishing utility of nuclear weapons may enhance the intrinsic value of sea power, the latter may well have poor deterrent capabilities. Historically, sea power has not done well as a deterrent.[54] However, Barry Posen, commenting on the nineteenth-century *Pax Britannica*, has suggested that maritime powers "dissuade" rather than deter.[55] With "the best that can be managed" in mind, the United States should take steps to make such a posture credible. Perhaps a set of treaties with nations in areas of vital interest to the United States would be appropriate. If the United States were committed by treaty to the use of force in defense of an ally, its deterrent efforts would be more convincing.[56] At the very least, the domestic political problems which a democracy has in gearing up to fight would be lessened by such treaties.

Of course, the United States still has the option to deploy its forces on the ground to act as a deterrent in areas of vital interest. No doubt deployments of this sort, which have occurred in Korea and Western Europe, will continue in the future. Certainly southwest Asia is a strong candidate for continuing U.S. presence on the ground as a deterrent. But the acceptance of further troop commitments in troubled areas must be seen as a strategically risky posture, spreading U.S. resources ever thinner. A "cleaner" solution would couple resolve-signaling treaties with vastly improved sea and airlift capabilities. Nonetheless, one cannot evade the conclusion that, as much as sea power does to ensure successful defense, its inconspicuous presence makes successful deterrence a very difficult enterprise. Finally, the United States must resist the temptation to solve this "deterrence dilemma" by making even implicit nuclear threats against regional powers. Such a course would either prod them to pursue nuclear weapons of their own, or to seek the shelter of some other power's (such as China or the FSU) nuclear umbrella.

CONCLUSION

What began as a search for the answer to one puzzling aspect of international relations, the phenomenon of "loser" war initiation, turned into a varied intellectual journey. Several long-standing formulations, regarding the workings of the international system, the nature of power, and the character of war, were held up to scrutiny through the new lens of the dual theory. While the initial puzzle was solved, the means by which solution was effected created several new images. First, the international system may be seen as enjoying a hardy "maritime order." There is much conflict, but no continental hegemony. Next, Clausewitz and Jomini turned out to be right about generalship in land wars, while, in other wars, sea power reemerged as Mahan's "marvelous force." Finally, new light was shed on the way in which leaders think, bureaucracies interact, and organizations pursue their self-interest.

E. H. Carr was right. New theories do "change" history,[57] in that the facts of any sequence of events must be given different reasons for their occurrence if the theories are correct. In this respect, looking first through the "lens" of war outcomes has produced an abundance of new insights, a few of which, when tested, have confirmed long-held formulations. But so many other entrenched notions have been toppled that new studies, informed by the dual theory, must follow. It is this writer's sincerest hope, though, that, more than providing new illumination on the past, the findings of this study may help to guide the way safely through a future as likely to be fraught with peril as it will be full of opportunity for peaceful progress.

NOTES

1. See Chapter 1, Table 1.1, and Appendix I for detailed listings.

2. Major articulations of this point of view, cited in more detail in Chapter 1 are to be found in: Geoffrey Blainey, *The Causes of War* (New York: The Free Press, 1973); Bruce Bueno de Mesquita, *The War Trap* (New Haven: Yale University Press, 1981); and Michael Howard, *The Causes of Wars* (London: Temple Smith, 1983).

3. Robert Jervis, in *Perception and Misperception in International Politics* (Princeton: Princeton University Press, 1976), and "War and Misperception," *Journal of Interdisciplinary History,* vol. 18(1988):675–700 suggests that perceptual problems are rampant, while R.N. Lebow purports to confirm this in *Between Peace and War* (Baltimore: Johns Hopkins University Press, 1981). J.S. Levy, "Misperception and the Causes of War," *World Politics,* vol. 35 (1983):76–99 provides a comprehensive look at the phenomenon. John Stoessinger, *Why Nations Go to War* (New York: St. Martin's Press, 5th ed., 1990), p. 210, takes the position that *all* wars are begun because of misperception.

4. As formulated in Kenneth N. Waltz, *Theory of International Politics* (New York: Random House, 1979). Stephen M. Walt, *The Origins of Alliances* (Ithaca: Cornell University Press, 1987), argues that balances arise against "threat" rather "power." If Walt's formulation is correct, then the defeat of war initiators should be even less surprising, as those who threaten may have much less power than the coalitions whose rise their threats spark.

5. The major "transitional" approaches evaluated by this study include: A. F. K. Organski and Jacek Kugler, *The War Ledger* (Chicago: University of Chicago Press, 1980); Charles F. Doran and Wes Parsons, "War and the Cycle of Relative Power," *American Political Science Review,* vol. 74 (1980):947–965; Robert Gilpin, *War and Change in World Politics* (Cambridge: Cambridge University Press, 1981); and George Modelski, *Long Cycles in World Politics* (Seattle: University of Washington Press, 1987).

6. Jack S. Levy, "The Causes of War: A Review of Theories and Evidence," in Philip Tetlock, J. L. Husbands, Robert Jervis, P. C. Stern and Charles Tilly, eds. *Behavior, Society and Nuclear War,* Vol. I (New York: Oxford University Press, 1989), particularly pp. 252–8, summarizes the predictions of what this study has labeled "transitional" theories. With regard to premature challenges, Levy notes that they are predicted by theory but that "[i]t is not clear why the challenger should fight rather than wait until the trends in underlying power . . . propel it into the stronger position" (p. 253). Perhaps Gilpin's observation, in *War and Change in World Politics* (Cambridge: Cambridge University Press, 1981), p. 191, that preventive war is a declining hegemon's "first and most attractive response" serves to hurry the challenger. Finally, Organski and Kugler, *The War Ledger,* p. 62, point out that, despite the importance of power transitions, "the coalition with the dominant nation is stronger than the coalition shaped by the challenger to unseat the leader and recast the international order." See Chapter 2 of this study for more extensive analysis of the predictions of these theories.

7. Levy, "The Causes of War . . . ", p. 255, observes this in his own survey of "transitional thinking."

8. Alexander L. George and Richard Smoke, *Deterrence in American Foreign Policy* (New York: Columbia University Press, 1974), serves as a model for this type of analysis.

9. Much as was done in Chapter 5 of this study.

10. Of the 30 land wars examined in Chapter 4, the side with superior skill, as measured in terms of relative battle deaths, won in 27. Of the seven major land wars included, the more skillful side always won.

11. John I. Alger, *The Quest for Victory: The History of the Principles of War* (Westport, Connecticut: Greenwood Press, 1982), offers a most comprehensive survey of strategic thinking. It finds an overwhelming tendency of theorists to emphasize "skill" over strength as the key to victory.

12. F. W. Lanchester, *Aircraft in Warfare* (London: Constable and Co., 1916), introduced the first formal model of attritional warfare in which the overarching importance of numerical strength was purported to be demonstrated. John W. R. Lepingwell, "The Laws of Combat? Lanchester Reexamined," *International Security,* vol. 12 (1987):89–133, surveys and updates this line of thinking. Perhaps the most articulate and sweeping argument in favor of strength over skill is presented in Paul Kennedy, *The Rise and Fall of the Great Powers: Economic Change and Military Conflict from 1500 to 2000* (New York: Random House, 1987).

13. A.T. Mahan, *The Influence of Sea Power Upon History, 1660–1783* (Boston: Little, Brown, 1890), and, particularly, *The Influence of Sea Power Upon the French Revolution and Empire, 1793–1812* (Boston: Little, Brown, 1894) both focus inordinate attention on economic warfare through blockade. In the former work, Mahan's critique of amphibious warfare in the Seven Years' War is nothing less than scathing. In the latter, his analysis of the Peninsular War, which did so much to bring Napoleon down, is almost nonexistent, covering one-and-a-half pages.

14. George Modelski and William R. Thompson, *Seapower in Global Politics, 1494–1993* (Seattle:University of Washington Press, 1988). See the discussion, in Chapter Two of this study, of the problems that their counting techniques face by limiting their calculations to "government-owned" ships. In the Age of Sail, rife with privateers, serious distortions may occur.

15. See Chapter 3 for a more detailed discussion of this modification to traditional notions of balancing.

16. See the discussion of this concept in Chapter 3.

17. See Joshua Goldstein, *Long Cycles* (New Haven: Yale University Press, 1988), p. 348.

18. See Appendix I.

19. See Graham T. Allison, *Essence of Decision: Explaining the Cuban Missile Crisis* (Boston: Little, Brown, 1971).

20. See Stephen D. Krasner, "Are Bureaucracies Important? (Or Allison Wonderland)" *Foreign Policy,* vol. 7 (1972):159–179.

21. Herbert A. Simon, *Models of Bounded Rationality* (Cambridge: MIT Press, 1982) has been an important source for developing the concept of "imperfect understanding" of sea power.

22. Major efforts to apply classical organizational theory to professional militaries include: Jack Snyder, *The Ideology of the Offensive: Military Decision Making and the Disasters of 1914* (Ithaca: Cornell University Press, 1984); Stephen Van Evera, "The Cult of the Offensive and the Origins of the First World War," *International Security,* vol. 9 (1984):58–107; and Barry Posen, *The Sources of Military Doctrine* (Ithaca: Cornell University Press, 1984). None of these efforts, however, examines the naval organizations of the relevant actors.

23. Particular use was made of Herbert A. Simon, *Administrative Behavior* (New

York: The Macmillan Company, 1945); and Richard M. Cyert and James G. March, *A Behavioral Theory of the Firm* (Englewood Cliffs, NJ: Prentice-Hall, Inc., 1963).

24. See Chapter 5 for a fuller discussion of these events. Harold L. Wilensky, *Organizational Intelligence: Knowledge and Policy in Government and Industry* (New York: Basic Books, 1967) offers a comprehensive analysis of the ways in which organizations use information to advance their positions against competing organizations, and to influence decisional outputs.

25. Though he does not address the capital intensive nature of navies, Samuel P. Huntington, *The Common Defense* (New York: Columbia University Press, 1961), does point out one striking difference between naval and other military organizations: the former's flexibility to perform a wide variety of missions on land, sea and air, has allowed it "smooth sailing" (pp. 423–424) through interservice conflicts. Harvey M. Sapolsky, *The Polaris System Development: Bureaucratic and Programmatic Success in Government* (Cambridge: Harvard University Press, 1972) adds to this notion of mission flexibility, and points out that, in the case of the Polaris, limitations on accuracy were dealt with by espousing an "assured destruction doctrine" that would neatly fit the navy's capabilities (p. 141).

26. In this respect, Allison's *Essence of Decision,* which holds that organizational and bureaucratic influences persist in crisis and war, is viewed by this study as having more relevance to the issue of civilian intervention than Posen's *The Sources of Military Doctrine,* which holds that organizational influences ineluctably abate due to civilian intervention (see especially pp. 239–241).

27. This was the object of Chapter 4.

28. The doctrinal shifting of the navies of continental powers, and the imperfect maritime understanding of their political leaders, are unquestionably "constants" in the set of global wars. Louis XIV and Wilhelm II were chosen for closer study because, of all the continental challengers, they had the best understanding of sea power, the time to take action, and navies best suited to challenge the incumbent maritime hegemon.

29. James D. Fearon, "Counterfactuals and Hypothesis Testing in Political Science," *World Politics,* vol. 43 (1991):169–195, provided much guidance in the application of counterfactual methods. Stephen Van Evera, "The Cult of the Offensive and the Origins of the First World War," which explicitly adopts the "rational actor" model for counterfactual testing purposes, was also relied upon. Finally, Scott D. Sagan, "1914 Revisited," *International Security,* vol. 11 (1986):151–176, points out that conclusions must be carefully drawn. He suggests that even without a "cult of the offensive," conflicting aims and treaty requirements might have led even rational actors to both war and strategic offensives. He also engaged in "third-party" testing to demonstrate that states that had offensive doctrines, but less onerous alliance commitments, entered the war in defensive postures. With regard to "loser" initiation, therefore, this study argues that pure rationality on the decision maker's part could lead to either peace *or* war. However, war would be waged quite differently by a decision maker fully aware of the exigencies of land–sea conflicts.

30. With regard to the First World War, Holger Herwig, *'Luxury' Fleet* (London: George Allen & Unwin, 1980), pp. 147–148, raises the tantalizing possibility that a "rationally" aggressive German naval doctrine could have interdicted the British Expeditionary Force on its way to France: "Ingenohl [then commander of the German High

Sea Fleet] would have had no difficulty in disposing of the 19 elderly battleships and 20 cruisers that made up a joint Anglo-French Channel Fleet."

Herwig goes on to point out that such a maneuver would be fraught with risk for the Germans. Yet, the impact of preventing the British from joining the battle in France would have been enormous; and the High Sea Fleet was much closer in numbers to the Grand Fleet in August of 1914 (15:17) than it would be at Jutland nearly two years later (16:28). When superior German director fire and armor protection of the dreadnoughts is factored in, the option should grow exceptionally attractive to a "rational" actor.

31. Brodie's circuitous intellectual journey is chronicled in Fred Kaplan, *The Wizards of Armageddon* (New York: Simon & Schuster, 1984).

32. Robert Jervis, *The Illogic of American Nuclear Strategy* (Ithaca: Cornell University Press, 1984), offers a comprehensive exposition of Brodie's dilemma. In terms of arms control policy, the net effects of nuclear parity seem to be mandating significant reductions in nuclear weapons (as evidenced by INF and START).

33. As Kenneth Waltz put it, in *Man, the State and War* (New York: Columbia University Press, 1954), p. 236: "mutual fear of big weapons may produce, instead of peace, a spate of smaller wars."

34. See his "The Renewal of Strategy," in *The Use of Force,* Robert J. Art and Kenneth N. Waltz, eds. (Lanham, MD: University Press of America, 1988).

35. This is the central theme of Robert E. Walters, *Sea Power and the Nuclear Fallacy* (Harmondsworth, Middlesex, England: Penguin Books, Ltd., 1974).

36. From the dawn of the Nuclear Age in 1945, to 1980, 14 interstate wars, all conventional, were fought from start to finish. If most of the rest of the post-Napoleonic period covered by this study is broken down into 35-year periods, it may be seen that the frequency of interstate wars over time has remained quite stable, with 18 fought from 1840–75, 13 from 1875–1910, and 17 from 1910–1945. *Brassey's War Annuals* (London: Pergamon), which include intra-state wars, indicate that, during the 1980s, an average of more than 30 wars were in progress each year. An average of five interstate wars were going on during each year, a figure much higher than that averaged during any decade of the pre-nuclear era (the years 1939–40 with four wars ongoing in each year, have the highest number of contemporaneous interstate wars). This may be an indication that Waltz was right about the " the mutual fear of big weapons" producing, "instead of peace, a spate of smaller wars."

37. This is a formulation which can be based only on counterfactual logic. The point made is that a "rational actor" wouldn't begin a land war just on the basis of material superiority and, if clear evidence of own's one inferior skill were presented (which the Arab League had after the 1948 war), war initiation would not be an actively considered option.

38. This important psychological theory, applicable to the analysis of a state's key decision maker's state of mind, was propounded in Daniel Kahneman and Amos Tversky, "Prospect Theory: an Analysis of Decision Under Risk," *Econometrica,* vol. 47:263–291. Fundamentally, the theory holds that a decision maker tends to be risk averse if he is "sitting on gains," and risk acceptant in efforts to make up for "losses." Thus, uncertainty about "skill," it could be argued, may or may not lead to fewer wars.

39. See Appendix I. Land–sea wars are identified by having a "0" in the "Land" column. The "Sea" column will denote the naval balance. The second line of each war entry denotes the winner, and which side initiated the war.

40. A distinction which Churchill, as First Lord of the Admiralty in 1912, made in a

public speech, and which rankled the Kaiser no end because of the extremely pejorative connotations of the German word *luxus*. Herwig, *'Luxury' Fleet*, p. 77, points out that Churchill's choice of adjective was "a veritable bombshell." The Kaiser's reaction to Churchill was immediately truculent: "My patience as well as that of the German people is at an end" (also from p. 77).

41. Correlli Barnett, *The Swordbearers* (London: Eyre and Spottiswoode, 1963), Chapter 5, reflects the Royal Navy's eagerness for battle, and its sanguine predictions about the outcome. Fisher, the First Sea Lord, wrote of Jellicoe, commander of the Grand Fleet in 1912: "If war comes before 1914 then Jellicoe will be Nelson at the Battle of St. Vincent. If it comes in 1915 he will be Nelson at Trafalgar" (cited on p. 110, from Fisher's correspondence). German novelist Theodor Fontane commented on the Royal Navy's psychological edge: "We do not have a trace of this confidence. . . . We are not mentioned in the Old Testament. The British act as if they had the promise." Admiral Scheer, who commanded the German High Sea Fleet at Jutland, wrote: "The English Fleet had the advantage of looking back on a hundred years of proud tradition which must have given every man a sense of superiority based on the great deeds of the past." Both cited in Herwig, *'Luxury' Fleet*, p. 147.

42. Sergei G. Gorshkov, *The Sea Power of the State* (New York: Pergamon, 1980), offers up his analysis of the best course for Soviet naval development.

43. See Michael MccGwire, "Naval Power and Soviet Global Strategy," *International Security*, vol. 3 (Spring 1979):134–189, for a fuller depiction of the bureaucratic environment, and of Gorshkov's limited (according to the author) successes.

44. The terms are used, respectively, as a means of rating Soviet ability to 1) interdict its enemies' sea lines of communication and 2) achieve positive sea control.

45. Two recent works, which summarize the competing schools of thought and conclude, generally, that the "weak threat" theory is more accurate are: Bruce W. and Susan Watson, *The Soviet Navy: Strengths and Liabilities* (Boulder: Westview Press, 1986); and Bryan Ranft and Geoffrey Till, *The Sea in Soviet Strategy* (Annapolis: Naval Institute Press, 1989). MccGwire, "Naval Power and Soviet Global Strategy," also adheres to the "weak threat" view.

46. Gorshkov, *The Sea Power of the State*, p. 254.

47. Karl Lautenschlager, "The Submarine in Naval Warfare, 1901–2001," *International Security*, vol. 11 (Winter 1986–1987):94–140, p. 94, states that sea control is one of the missions for which submarines are "least capable."

48. See Robert K. Massie, *Peter the Great* (New York: Ballantine Books, 1984), which depicts Peter's unconventional thinking regarding sea control as developing over a period of several decades. His early trip to the Netherlands and later limited conflicts with Tatars and Turks in and around the Black Sea were particularly influential to his thinking.

49. Linton F. Brooks, "Naval Power and National Security: The Case for the Maritime Strategy," *International Security*, vol. 11 (Fall 1986):58–88, argues the case in favor of a maritime strategy, primarily as part of a protracted global conventional conflict. John J. Mearsheimer, "A Strategic Misstep: The Maritime Strategy and Deterrence in Europe," *International Security*, vol. 11 (Fall 1986):3–57, offers the counterargument that the USSR is not very vulnerable to sea power, and that the maritime strategy, as currently elucidated, runs the risk of weakening nuclear crisis stability by threatening Soviet ballistic missile submarine "bastions." Norman Friedman, *The US Maritime Strategy* (London: Jane's, 1988), offers a more recent assessment of this de-

bate, and addresses the major issue of whether or not surface fleets can cope with the threats posed by aircraft and submarines.

Clearly, this study takes issue with Mearsheimer's position on the vulnerability of the FSU to sea power in a conventional war. Mearsheimer's concern regarding nuclear crisis stability is reasonable. However, instead of entirely eschewing submarine operations near the former Soviet bastions, the deployment of a small number of US attack submarines to this area could serve to "pin" hunter-killer subs down in a defensive role. This would severely inhibit their ability to interdict allied sea lines of communication, or to contest more actively for positive sea control.

50. This study should be viewed, therefore, as supporting the argument in favor of "no first use" of nuclear weapons advanced by McGeorge Bundy, George F. Kennan, Robert S. McNamara and Gerard Smith, "Nuclear Weapons and the Atlantic Alliance," *Foreign Affairs,* vol. 60 (Spring 1982):753–768. According to the logic of the dual theory of war, adoption of their proposal would simply consolidate the existing advantages of the Western Alliance. Thus, a response to the concerns of Karl Kaiser, Georg Leber, Alois Mertes and Franz-Josef Schulze, "Nuclear Weapons and the Preservation of Peace," *Foreign Affairs,* vol. 60 (Summer 1982):1157–1171, regarding the weakening of deterrence, would be that, while nuclear threats of first-use are increasingly less credible, a switch to NFU significantly diminishes the likelihood of nuclear conflict while maintaining the West's war-winning advantages intact.

51. In Paul Huth and Bruce Russett, "What Makes Deterrence Work? Cases from 1900 to 1980," *World Politics,* vol. 36 (1984):496–526, and their "Deterrence Failure and Crisis Escalation," *International Studies Quarterly,* vol. 32 (1988):29–46; as well as in Paul Huth, *Extended Deterrence and the Prevention of War* (New Haven: Yale University Press, 1988), it is possible to identify roughly half of all cases of extended deterrence attempted, and a greater percentage of those attempts which failed, with the efforts of maritime powers. The critique offered by Richard Ned Lebow and Janice Gross Stein, "Deterrence: The Elusive Dependent Variable," *World Politics,* vol. 42:336–369, raises serious questions about historical interpretation, but in no way challenges this "maritime phenomenon."

52. Huth and Russett, "Deterrence Failure and Crisis Escalation," p. 38.

53. Reported by Kim Murphy, "Iraq Rejects Warning, Assails Mubarak," *Los Angeles Times,* January 2, 1991, p. A12.

54. In addition to Huth and Russett's findings, one should observe that the onset of almost every global war has witnessed the failure of maritime-based deterrence.

55. See Posen, *The Sources of Military Doctrine,* p. 154 in particular: "Generally, Britain relied on defensive-denial operational capabilities, and the diffuse long-term threat of ultimate imperial mobilization and blockade. It was a ramshackle doctrine, but under the circumstances the best that could be managed. . . ."

56. Huth and Russett, "Deterrence Failure and Crisis Escalation," p. 43, point out that, when cases where defensive treaties exist are controlled for, "the immediate balance of military capabilities matters much less than the nature and strength of the linkages between the defender and the protege." Thus, there may be a way out of the "deterrence dilemma" of the maritime power.

57. See E. H. Carr, *What is History?* (New York: Vintage Books, 1961), p. 10.

Appendix I

Classification of Decisive Interstate Wars, 1815–1980

Key: Outcome = Perspective randomly selected (winner or loser)
　　　　　　　　Dates and winner appear on second line
　　　　　　　　* after winner denotes also initiated
　　Variables = Ratios from perspective of side selected (e.g., "1s" will
　　　　　　　　show winner's perspective)
　　Qualities = "1" for major and/or land
　　　　　　　　"0" for minor and/or land–sea
　Technology = 2 if perspective of superior side chosen
　& Resolve　　1 if neither side is superior
　　　　　　　　0 if opposing side is superior
　　　　 ( ) = Impact of "latecomers"
　　　　 [ ] = Polychotomous coding of sea in minor 1-s wars

Case	Out-come	Skill	Strength	Sea	Major	Land	Tech	Resolve
1. Franco-Sp. 1823, France*	1	1.50	4.00	12.25	0	1	1	1
2. Russo-Turk. 1828–1829, Russia*	1	1.60	3.90	5.13	1	0	1	0
3. Mex.–Amer. 1846–1848, US*	0	1.83	.10	.27	0	0	0	2
4. Aus.–Sard. 1848–1849, Austria–Hungary	1	.64	2.10	1.00	0	0	1	1
5. Schles./Hol. 1848–1849, Germany*	1	1.40	3.40	1.00	0	1	1	0

Case	Out-come	Skill	Strength	Sea	Major	Land	Tech	Resolve
6. Roman Rep.	1	3.50	52.00	11.60	0	1	2	0
1849, France, Austria–Hungary, Two Sicilies*								
7. La Plata	0	.62	.40	1.00	0	1	1	2
1851–1852, Brazil* (defeated Argentina)								
8. Crimean	0	1.64	.32	.12	1	0	1	0
1853–1856, Britain, Italy, France, Turkey (defeated Russia)								
9. Anglo-Persia	1	3.00	97.80	50.00	0	0	2	0
1856–1857, Britain*								
10. Ital. Unif.	0	.80	.55	.25	1	1	1	0
1859, Italy, France (defeated Austria-Hungary)								
11. Span.-Moroc.	1	1.50	5.40	1.00	0	0	2	0
1859–1860, Spain*				[2]				
12. Italo-Roman	1	2.33	2.50	1.00	0	1	1	0
1860, Italy*								
13. Italo-Sic.	0	.67	.39	1.00	0	0	1	2
1860–1861, Italy*				[0]				
14. Franco-Mex.	1	.67	.04	.04	0	0	0	2
1862–1967, Mexico								
15. Ec.-Colombia	1	2.33	5.50	1.00	0	1	1	0
1863, Colombia*								
16. Schles. Hol.	0	.50	.07	1.00	0	1	1	2
1864, Germany*								
17. Lopez War	0	.55	.30	1.00	1	1	1	2
1864–1870, Argentina, Brazil (defeated Paraguay)								
18. Span.-Chile	0	2.33	4.70	1.00	0	0	1	0
1865–1866, Chile, Peru				[1]				
19. 7 Weeks'	1	1.56	1.01	1.00	1	1	1	0
1866, Germany, et al.*								
20. Franco-Prus.	1	2.95	.94	.47	1	1	1	1
1870–1871, Germany et al.								
21. Russo-Turk.	0	.73	.36	.19	1	0	1	2
1877–1878, Russia*								
22. Pacific	0	.27	2.30	1.00	0	0	1	2
1879–1883, Chile* (d. Peru and Bolivia)				[0]				
23. Sino-French	0	.21	1.20	.06	0	0	0	2
1884–1885, France*								
24. Cent. Amer.	0	.25	2.00	1.00	0	1	1	0
1885, El Salvador (defeated Guatemala)								
25. Sino-Japan	0	.50	3.41	.59	0	0	0	2
1894–1895, Japan*								

Case	Out- come	Skill	Strength	Sea	Major	Land	Tech	Resolve
26. Greco-Turk. 1897, Turkey	0	.43	.22	1.00 [0]	0	0	1	0
27. Spanish-US 1898, US*	1	1.00	11.80	6.55	0	0	2	1
28. Boxer Reb. 1900, Japan, Britian, Russia, France, US (defeated China)	0	.50	.75	.02	0	0	0	2
29. Russo-Japan 1904–1905, Japan	1	.53	.45	1.25	1	0	1	1
30. Central Am. 1906, Guatemala* (defeated Honduras and El Salvador)	1	1.50	1.40	1.00	0	1	1	0
31. Central Am. 1907, Nicaragua* (defeated Honduras and El Salvador)	0	.67	6.00	1.00	0	1	1	2
32. Span.-Moroc. 1909–1910, Spain*	1	4.00	14.30	1.00 [2]	0	0	2	0
33. Italo-Turk. 1911–1912, Italy*	0	.43	.61	1.00 [0]	0	0	1	1
34. 1st Balkan 1912–1913, Greece, Serbia, Bulgaria* (defeated Turkey)	0	1.73	2.49	1.00	1	0	1	1
35. 2d Balkan 1913, Turkey, Greece, Serbia Romania (defeated Bulgaria)	1	.42	9.85	1.00	0	0	1	1
36. World War I 1914–1918, Allies	1	.59	1.63 (2.91)	.93 (1.36)	1	0	1	1
37. Russo-Polish 1919–1920, Poland	0	.67	6.35	3.00	1	1	2	0
38. Hungarian 1919, Romania, Czechoslovakia* (defeated Hungary)	0	.83	.20	1.00	0	1	1	0
39. Greco-Turk. 1919–1922, Turkey	1	1.50	1.23	1.00 [2]	1	0	1	2
40. Sino-Soviet 1929, USSR*	1	15.00	2.55	3.33	0	0	2	0
41. Manchurian 1931–1933, Japan* (defeated China)	0	.20	2.49	.07	1	0	0	2
42. Chaco War 1932–1935, Paraguay (defeated Bolivia)	0	.62	2.67	1.00	1	1	2	0
43. Italo-Ethi. 1935–1936, Italy*	1	4.00	8.76	1.00 [2]	0	0	2	0
44. Sino-Japan 1937–1941, Japan*	1	3.00	.64	15.00	1	0	2	0
45. Changkuofeng 1938, Japan* (defeated USSR)	1	2.40	.45	3.25	1	0	1	1

Case	Out-come	Skill	Strength	Sea	Major	Land	Tech	Resolve
46. Nomohan 1939, USSR, Mongolia (defeated Japan)	1	2.50	2.08	.45	1	1	1	2
47. World War II 1939–1945, Allies	1	.49	1.05 (2.38)	2.27 (1.18)	1	0	1	1
48. Russo-Finn. 1939–1940, USSR*	1	.80	78.14	1.80	0	0	2	0
49. Franco-Thai 1940–1941, Thailand	1	.50	3.51	1.00	0	1	0	2
50. Palestine 1948, Israel (defeated Iraq, Syria, Egypt, Jordan)	0	.60	5.83	1.00	0	1	2	0
51. Russo-Hung. 1956, USSR*	0	.33	.03	1.00	0	1	0	2
52. Sinai 1956, Britain, France, Israel* (Egypt)	1	13.04	16.46	1.00 [2]	0	0	2	1
53. Sino-Indian 1962, China*	1	.50	4.81	1.00	0	1	2	0
54. Vietnam War 1965–1973, North Vietnam*	0	1.43	.05	.02	1	0	0	2
55. 2d Kashmir 1965, Pakistan (defeated India)	1	.79	.21	1.00	0	1	1	2
56. Six-Day War 1967, Israel* (defeated Egypt, Jordan, Syria)	1	18.60	.21	1.00	0	1	1	2
57. Attrition 1969–1970, Israel (defeated Egypt)	0	.07	7.00	1.00	0	1	1	0
58. Football War 1969, El Salvador* (defeated Honduras)	1	1.71	1.35	1.00	0	1	1	1
59. Bangladesh 1971, India* (defeated Pakistan)	0	2.67	.25	1.00 [0]	0	0	1	2
60. Yom Kippur 1973, Israel (defeated Iraw, Syria, Jordan, Saudi Arabia, Egypt)	1	4.45	.21	1.00	0	1	1	2
61. Turco-Cyp. 1974, Turkey*	0	2.00	.04	1.00 [0]	0	0	0	2
62. Uganda-Tan. 1978–1979, Tanzania (defeated Uganda and Libya)	0	.50	1.05	1.00	0	1	1	0
63. Sino-Vietnam 1979, Vietnam	1	1.62	.04	1.00	0	1	0	2

Appendix II

Interstate Wars Fought "Overseas," 1815–1980

War	Distance		Relative strength	
	Far	Near	"Fair fight"	Great v. minor power
Crimean	X		X	
Anglo-Persian	X			X
Spain-Morocco		X	X	
Franco-Mexican	X			X
Spain-Chile	X		X	
Sino-French	X			X
Sino-Japanese		X	X*	
Greco-Turkish		X	X	
Spanish-Amer.	X		X*	
Boxer	X			X
Russo-Japan		X**		X
Spain-Morocco		X	X	
Italo-Turk		X		X
World War I	X***		X	
Greco-Turkish		X	X	
Manchurian		X		X
Italo-Ethiopian	X			X
Sino-Japanese		X		X
Changkuofeng		X	X	
Nomohan		X	X	
World War II	X***		X	

War	Distance		Relative strength	
	Far	Near	"Fair fight"	Great v. minor power
Franco-Thai	X		X****	
Sinai	X			X
Vietnam	X			X
Turco-Cypriot		X	X	

*Neither Japan nor the US were great powers yet (Levy).
**Russia already had large land and naval forces in the East.
***Both world wars had distant theaters and Americans overseas.
****France was no longer a great power (1940–1941).

Success rates of those fighting overseas:

Distance	Won	Lost	Rate
Far	9	4	69%
Near	10	2	83%

Controlled for Great versus minor power wars:

Side fighting overseas	Won	Lost	Rate
"Fair fights"	12	4	75%
Great versus minor	7	2	77%

Appendix III

Correlation Matrix of Key Variables

	Win	Skill	COW	Sea power	Technology	Resolve
Win	xxx	.33***	.26**	.23*	.39**	− .21
Skill	.33***	xxx	.06	.97	.29**	− .03
COW	.26**	.06	xxx	.72***	.43**	− .29
Sea	.23*	.07	.72***	xxx	.33**	− .23
Tech	.39**	.29**	.43***	.33**	xxx	− .16
Resolve	− .21	− .03	− .29	− .23	− .16	xxx

Significance levels: *p < .10; **p < .05; ***p < .01.

Note: The COW index of composite capabilities and the Technology variables are good examples that significant bivariate correlation with the dependent variable ("Win") doesn't necessarily persist in multivariate regression.

The potential for disturbance due to multicollinearity between COW and sea power is explored in the text of Chapter 4.

Appendix IV

Interstate Wars in the "Air Power Age"

Wars with one side having air superiority at outset:

War	Superior side	Result for superior side
Russo-Polish	USSR	Loss
Manchurian	Japan	Win
Chaco	Bolivia*	Loss
Italo-Ethiopian	Italy	Win
Sino-Japanese	Japan	Win
Nomohan	Japan	Loss
Russo-Finnish	USSR	Win
Franco-Thai	Vichy France*	Loss
Palestine	Arab Coalition*	Loss
Korean	US/UN	Unclear
Russo-Hungarian	USSR	Win
Sinai	Israel et al.	Win
Vietnam	US	Loss
Six Day	Israel	Win
Attrition	Israel	Win
Yom Kippur	Israel	Win
Sino-Vietnam	China	Loss
Second Gulf	Allies	Win

Opponent had virtually no opposing aircraft.

Overall record for those with air superiority: 10 wins, 7 losses, 1 unclear outcome.

Other wars of the "Air Power Age" in which parity existed at war's outset:

World War I	Sino-Indian
Hungarian	2d Kashmir
Greco-Turkish	Football
Sino-Soviet	Bangladesh
Changkuofeng	Turco-Cypriot
World War II	Uganda-Tanzania

Wars are listed chronlogically from World War I. See Appendix I for dates of wars.

Selected References

Albertini, Luigi. *The Origins of the War of 1914,* 3 vols., trans by I. M. Massey. London: Oxford University Press, 1957.

Alger, John. *The Quest for Victory.* Westport, CT: Greenwood, 1982.

Allison, Graham T. *Essence of Decision.* Boston: Little, Brown, 1971.

Ardrey, Robert. *The Territorial Imperative.* New York: Atheneum, 1966.

Art, Robert J. *The Influence of Foreign Policy on Seapower.* Beverly Hills, CA: Sage, 1973.

Barnett, Correlli. *The Swordbearers.* London: Eyre, 1963.

Barzun, Jacques. *Introduction to Naval History.* New York: Lippincott, 1944.

Ben Zvi, Abraham. *The Illusion of Deterrence.* Boulder, CO: Westview, 1987.

Bennett, Geoffrey. *The Battle of Jutland.* London: Batsford, 1964.

Bergrahn, V. R. *Germany and the Approach of War in 1914.* New York: St. Martin's, 1973.

Bernier, Olivier. *Louis XIV: A Royal Life.* New York: Doubleday, 1987.

Bethmann-Hollweg, Theodor von. *Reflections on the World War.* London: Butterworth, 1920.

Betts, Richard K. *Soldiers, Statesmen, and Cold War Crises.* Cambridge: Harvard University Press, 1977.

Bird, Keith. *German Naval History.* New York: Garland, 1985.

Birnbaum, Karl. *Peace Moves and U-Boat Warfare.* Stockholm: Almqvist and Wiksell, 1958.

Blainey, Geoffrey. *The Causes of War.* New York: Free Press, 1973.

Bond, Brian. *War and Society in Europe 1870–1970.* Leicester: Leicester University Press, 1984.

Boulding, Kenneth. *Conflict and Defense.* New York: Harper, 1962.

———. *Three Faces of Power.* Newbury Pk.: Sage, 1989.

Boxer, Charles. *The Anglo-Dutch Wars.* London: HM Sta. Off., 1974.

Brodie, Bernard. *A Guide to Naval Strategy.* Princeton: Princeton University Press, 1944.

Bueno de Mesquita, Bruce. *The War Trap.* New Haven: Yale University Press, 1981.

Carr, E. H. *What is History?* New York: Vintage, 1961.

Cecil, Lamar. *Wilhelm II: Prince and Emperor.* Chapel Hill, NC: University of North Carolina Press, 1989.

Cipolla, Carlo. *Guns and Sails in the Early Phase of European Expansion.* London: Collins, 1965.

Clausewitz, Carl von. *On War,* ed. and trans. by Michael Howard and Peter Paret. Princeton: Princeton University Press, 1976.

Connaughton, R. M. *The War of the Rising Sun and the Tumbling Bear.* London: Routledge, 1988.

Corbett, Julian. *Drake.* London: Macmillan, 1911.

Craig, Gordon. *The Politics of the Prussian Army 1640–1945.* London: Oxford University Press, 1955.

Cyert, Richard M., and James G. March. *A Behavioral Theory of the Firm.* Englewood Cliffs, NJ: Prentice-Hall, 1963.

Davies, Norman. *White Eagle, Red Star: The Polish-Soviet War, 1919–1920.* New York: St. Martin's, 1972.

Dehio, Ludwig. *The Precarious Balance.* New York: Knopf, 1962.

Delbruck, Hans. *History of the Art of War,* 3 vols. Westport, Connecticut: Greenwood, 1985 ed.

De Seversky, Alexander. *Victory Through Air Power.* New York: Simon and Schuster, 1942.

Doran, Charles F. *The Politics of Assimilation.* Baltimore: The Johns Hopkins University Press, 1971.

Douhet, Giulio. *The Command of the Air.* New York: McCann, 1942.

Dupuy, R. N., and Trevor. *The Encyclopedia of Military History.* New York: Harper & Row, 1970.

Dupuy, Trevor. *Numbers, Predictions and War.* Fairfax: HERO, 1985.

———. *Understanding War.* New York: Paragon, 1987.

Epstein, Joshua. *The Calculus of Conventional War.* Washington, DC: The Brookings Institution, 1985.

Engels, Friedrich. *Anti-Duhring.* New York: International, 1939.

Fay, Sidney B. *The Origins of the World War.* New York: Macmillan, 1928.

Fearon, James D. "Counterfactuals and Hypothesis Testing in Political Science," *World Politics* 43:169–95, 1991.

Fischer, Fritz. *Germany's Aims in the First World War.* New York: Norton, 1961.

Fuller, J. F. C. *Armaments and History.* London: Eyre, 1945.

———. *The Conduct of War, 1789–1961.* New Brunswick, NJ: Rutgers University Press, 1961.

Gemzell, Carl-Axel. *Organization, Conflict and Innovation: A Study of German Naval Strategic Planning, 1888–1940.* Stockholm: Lund, 1973.

George, Alexander L. and Richard Smoke. *Deterrence in American Foreign Policy.* New York: Columbia University Press, 1974.

Gilpin, Robert. *War and Change in World Politics.* Cambridge: Cambridge University Press, 1981.

Glubb, John B. *A Soldier With the Arabs.* London: Hodder, 1956.

Goldstein, Joshua. *Long Cycles.* New Haven: Yale University Press, 1988.

Gorshkov, Sergei. *The Sea Power of the State.* New York: Pergamon, 1980.

Gujarati, Damodar. *Basic Econometrics.* New York: McGraw-Hill, 1978.

Halperin, Morton. *Bureaucratic Politics and Foreign Policy.* Washington, DC: The Brookings Institution, 1974.

Herring, George. *America's Longest War.* New York: Knopf, 1986.

Herwig, Holger H. "Admirals *versus* Generals: The War Aims of the Imperial German Navy," *Central European History* 5:208–33, 1972.

———. *'Luxury' Fleet.* London: Allen & Unwin, 1980.

———. "Miscalculated Risks: The German Declaration of War Against the United States, 1917 and 1941," *Naval War College Review* 39:88–100, 1986.

Howard, Michael. *The Causes of Wars.* Cambridge: Harvard University Press, 1983.

Huntington, Samuel P. *The Common Defense.* New York: Columbia University Press, 1961.

Huth, Paul. *Extended Deterrence and the Prevention of War.* New Haven: Yale University Press, 1988.

Huth, Paul, and Bruce Russett. "What Makes Deterrence Work?" *World Politics* 36:496–526, 1984.

———. "Deterrence Failure and Crisis Escalation," *International Studies Quarterly* 32:29–46, 1988.

Jarausch, Konrad. *The Enigmatic Chancellor.* New Haven: Yale University Press, 1973.

Jenkins, Harold E. *A History of the French Navy.* London: Jane's, 1973.

Jervis, Robert. *Perception and Misperception in International Politics.* Princeton: Princeton University Press, 1976.

———. *The Illogic of American Nuclear Strategy.* Ithaca: Cornell University Press, 1984.

Jones, D. W. *War and Economy in the Age of William III.* New York: Blackwell, 1988.

Kaplan, Fred. *The Wizards of Armageddon.* New York: Simon & Schuster, 1984.

Keegan, John. *The Price of Admiralty.* New York: Viking, 1989.

Kennedy, Paul. "The Development of German Naval Operations Plans Against England," *The English Historical Review* 99:48–76, 1974.

———. *The Rise and Fall of British Naval Mastery.* London: Ashfield, 1976.

———. *The Rise and Fall of the Great Powers.* New York: Random House, 1987.

———. *The Rise of the Anglo-German Antagonism, 1860–1914.* London: Allen and Unwin, 1980.

Keohane, Robert. *After Hegemony.* Princeton: Princeton University Press, 1984.

Krasner, Stephen D. "Are Bureaucracies Important? (Or Allison Wonderland," *Foreign Policy* 7:159–79, 1972.

Lambi, Ivo Nikolai. *The Navy and German Power Politics, 1862–1914.* Boston: Allen & Unwin, 1984.

Lanchester, F. W. *Aircraft in Warfare.* London: Constable, 1916.

Lebow, Richard Ned. *Between Peace and War.* Baltimore: The Johns Hopkins University Press, 1981.

Lebow, Richard Ned, and Janice Gross Stein. "Deterrence: The Elusive Dependent Variable," *World Politics* 42:336–69, 1990.

Levy, Jack S. *War in the Modern Great Power System 1495–1975.* Lexington: University Press of Kentucky, 1983.

Lewis, David. *Counterfactuals.* Cambridge: Cambridge University Press, 1973.

Lippitt, Gordon. *Organizational Renewal.* New York: Appleton-Century-Crofts, 1969.

Lundeberg, Philip K. "The German Naval Critique of the U-Boat Campaign, 1915–1918," *Military Affairs* 27:105–18, 1963.

Luttwak, Edward N. *Strategy.* Cambridge: Harvard University Press, 1987.

Mackinder, Halford. *Britain and the British Seas.* Oxford: Clarendon Press, 1902.

Mahan, Alfred T. *The Influence of Sea Power Upon History, 1660–1783.* Boston: Little, Brown, 1890.

———. *The Influence of Sea Power Upon the French Revolution and Empire,* 2 vols. Boston: Little, Brown, 1894.

Marder, Arthur J. *From the Dreadnought to Scapa Flow,* Vol. II, *The War Years.* London: Oxford University Press, 1965.

Martin, Christopher. *The Russo-Japanese War.* New York: Abelard Schulman, 1967.

Medlicott, W. N. *Bismarck and Modern Germany.* New York: Harper & Row, 1965.

Mitchell, B. R. *European Historical Statistics 1750–1970.* New York: Columbia University Press, 1976.

Modelski, George. *Exploring Long Cycles.* Boulder: Rienner, 1987.

———. *Long Cycles in World Politics.* Seattle: University of Washington Press, 1987.

Modelski, George, and William R. Thompson. *Seapower in Global Politics, 1494–1993.* Seattle: University of Washington Press, 1988.

Morgenthau, Hans. *Politics Among Nations.* New York: Knopf, 1948.

Muller, Admiral G. A. von. *The Kaiser and His Court,* trans. by Walter Goerlitz. New York: Harcourt, Brace & World, Inc., 1964.

Murat, Ines. *Colbert.* Charlottesville: University Press of Virginia, 1984.

Murray, Williamson. *The Change in the European Balance of Power, 1938–1939: The Path to Ruin.* Princeton: Princeton University Press, 1984.

Murray, Williamson, and Allan Millett. *Military Efficiency,* 3 vols. Boston: Unwin, 1989

Organski, A. F. K., and Jacek Kugler. *The War Ledger.* Chicago: University of Chicago Press, 1980.

Posen, Barry. *The Sources of Military Doctrine.* Ithaca: Cornell University Press, 1984.

Quester, George H. *Offense and Defense in the International System.* New York: Wiley, 1977.

Ragin, Charles. *The Comparative Method.* Berkeley: University of California Press, 1987.

Ritter, Gerhard. *The Schlieffen Plan.* New York: Praeger, 1958.

Ropp, Theodore. "Continental Doctrines of Sea Power," in, Edward Mead Earle, ed. *Makers of Modern Strategy,* New York: Atheneum, [1943] 1966.

Rouvroy, Louis de, Duc de Saint-Simon. *Memoirs,* ed. and trans. by Sanche de Gramont. New York: Putnam, 1963.

Sagan, Scott D. "1914 Revisited: Allies, Offense and Instability," *International Security* 11:151–76, 1986.

———. "The Origins of the Pacific War," *Journal of Interdisciplinary History,* Spring 1988, pp. 893–922.

Sapolsky, Harvey M. *The Polaris System Development: Bureaucratic and Programmatic Success in Government.* Cambridge: Harvard University Press, 1972.

Scheer, Reinhard. *Germany's High Sea Fleet in the World War.* New York: Peter Smith, 1935.

Schelling, Thomas. *The Strategy of Conflict.* Cambridge: Harvard University Press, 1960.

Schweizer, Karl W. *England, Prussia, and the Seven Years' War.* New York: Mellen, 1989.

Seabury, Paul, and Angelo Codevilla. *War: Ends and Means.* New York: Basic, 1989.

Simon, Herbert. *Administrative Behavior.* New York: Macmillan, 1948.

———. *Models of Bounded Rationality,* 2 vols. Cambridge: MIT Press, 1982.

Small, Melvin, and J. David Singer. *Resort to Arms.* Beverly Hills, CA: Sage, 1982.

Snyder, Jack. *The Ideology of the Offensive.* Ithaca: Cornell University Press, 1984.

Sofer, Cyril. *Organizations in Theory and Practice.* New York: Basic, 1972.

Sonnino, Paul. *Louis XIV and the Origins of the Dutch War.* Cambridge: Cambridge University Press, 1988.

Steinberg, Jonathan. *Yesterday's Deterrent: Tirpitz and the Birth of the German Battle Fleet.* London: Oxford University Press, 1965.

———. "The Copenhagen Complex," *Journal of Contemporary History* 1:23–46, 1966.

Stoessinger, John. *Why Nations Go to War.* New York: St. Martin's, 1990 (5th edn.).

Symcox, Geoffrey. *The Crisis of French Sea Power.* The Hague: Nijhoff, 1974.

Taylor, A. J. P. *The Origins of the Second World War.* New York: Atheneum, 1961.

Thompson, William R. *On Global War.* Columbia, SC: University of South Carolina Press, 1988.

Till, Geoffrey. *The Sea in Soviet Strategy.* Annapolis: Naval Institute Press, 1989.

Tirpitz, Admiral Alfred von. *Memoirs.* London: Batsford, 1921.

Tuchman, Barbara. *The Guns of August.* New York: Macmillan, 1962.

———. *The Proud Tower.* New York: Macmillan, 1966.

Van Creveld, Herbert. *Technology and War.* New York: Free Press, 1989.

Van Evera, Stephen. "The Cult of the Offensive and the Origins of the First World War," *International Security* 9:58–107, 1984.

Walt, Stephen M. *The Origins of Alliances.* Ithaca: Cornell University Press, 1987.

Walters, Robert E. *Sea Power and the Nuclear Fallacy.* Harmondsworth, Middlesex, England: Penguin, 1974.

Waltz, Kenneth. *Man, the State and War.* New York: Columbia University Press, 1954.

———. *Theory of International Politics.* New York: Random House, 1979.

Weigley, Russell. *The American Way of War.* New York: Macmillan, 1973.

Wilensky, Harold. *Organizational Intelligence.* New York: Basic, 1967.

William II. *My Early Life.* New York: Doran, 1937.

Wilson, James Q. *Bureaucracy.* New York: Basic, 1989.

Wright, Quincy. *A Study of War,* 2 vols. Chicago: University of Chicago Press, 1951.

Ziegler, Gilette. *At the Court of Versailles: Eyewitness Reports from the Reign of Louis XIV.* New York: Dutton, 1966.

Index